ONCE IN A LIFETIME, YOU CAN'T TAKE IT WITH YOU and THE MAN WHO CAME TO DINNER

'Trevor Nunn's production of George S. Kaufman and Moss Hart's 50-year-old American comedy, *Once in a Lifetime*, is a knockout. It's both a hymn to life and a raspberry to Hollywood, and it sends one out of the Aldwych delighting in the rediscovery of a near-forgotten play...a classic comedy that puts a complete society on stage.' (Michael Billington, *Guardian*)

As well as *Once in a Lifetime*, this volume contains two other classic Kaufman and Hart comedies from the thirties. *You Can't Take It With You* presents the uninhibited Sycamore family, oblivious to the problems of the Depression as they happily follow their urge to express themselves in writing, dancing, printing, painting, firework manufacture or whatever else strikes their fancy. *The Man Who Came to Dinner*, based on the career of the larger-than-life theatre critic Alexander Woollcott, recreates in agonising detail the havoc created by a selfish, bad-tempered but inexhaustibly witty radio personality when he is forced to stay with a well-meaning but utterly conventional family in small town Ohio.

Introducing the volume are essays by Hart on Kaufman and by Kaufman on Hart.

The picture on the front cover shows Richard Griffiths as George Lewis, Zoe Wanamaker as May Daniels and Peter McEnery as Jerry Hyland in the 1979 Royal Shakespeare Company production of Once in a Lifetime *directed by Trevor Nunn. The photo is by Donald Cooper. The picture on the back cover shows Moss Hart (standing) and George S. Kaufman.*

THREE PLAYS
BY
KAUFMAN & HART

Once in a Lifetime

You Can't Take It With You

The Man Who Came to Dinner

WITH INTRODUCTORY ESSAYS BY
MOSS HART AND GEORGE S. KAUFMAN

EYRE METHUEN · LONDON

TO

THE MAN

WHO PRODUCED THEM

CONTENTS

MEN AT WORK *by Moss Hart*   ix

FORKED LIGHTNING *by George S. Kaufman*   xix

ONCE IN A LIFETIME   1

YOU CAN'T TAKE IT WITH YOU   117

THE MAN WHO CAME TO DINNER   207

MEN AT WORK

by Moss Hart

THE LADY on my right—the one with the electric smile —was turning toward me, the smile flashing on and off like the new Chesterfield sign. I had the uneasy feeling that I knew what she was going to say. I was right. She proceeded to say it.

"Mr. Hart," she said, "do writers mind being asked questions about their work?"

"Yes—in a word!" I said, as grimly as I knew how, and turned back to my salad.

I could feel the smile coming brilliantly on again; out of the corner of my eye, I caught a glimpse of teeth with Neon lights behind them, and a jeweled hand was laid lightly on my arm, swinging me toward her.

"Now, you're *not* going to finish until you've told me what I want to know," she said, "and bad boys don't get dessert!"

There was a nasty pause, the while I blinked painfully at that glistening expanse of dental art, Model T.

"All right," I thought, "you asked for it, lady!" and turned toward her with a smile of my own, coiled and ready to strike.

So far, the evening had been trying enough, God knows, without this. Warm cocktails, cold food, a long senseless conversation with a visiting English novelist, and now the little horror on my right.

Dinner parties of twenty people, I reflected, are downright uncivilized, anyway, and the hostess, who pins you down with the promise of "Just *us!*" and then surprises you with twenty ill-assorted stuffed shirts, deserves the consequences.

At any rate, I was going to see to it that I was never invited again, and the toothy lady on my right seemed an instrument of darkness admirably suited to my purpose.

"What," I said, "would you like to know?"

The teeth flashed again.

"George Kaufman," she said, "excites me!"

"Physically?" I inquired, politely.

"Really," she trilled, "you writers! I mean, what lies behind those glowering eyes?"

I weighed the matter carefully for a moment.

"That bourne from which no traveler returns," I said, and decided not to go on with it. It wasn't, after all, her fault that the cocktails had been warm and the food dreadful. Met in other surroundings, with a pair of sun glasses to protect one from the brilliance of that smile, she might be innocuous enough. I decided to fulfil my role of the extra man with good grace, and muttered some nonsense about writers being a shy lot.

But no! The lady had saved me the waltz. This time she swung me around by the shoulders and the smile glittered like Radio City on a sunlit November morning.

"What I really want to know," she said, "is, aren't you frightened to *death* of him? You've written all those plays together and I don't see *how* you do it. Truly, Mr. Hart, aren't you scared of George Kaufman? Just a little teentsy-weentsy bit? 'Fess up, now!"

I suppose, at least I have thought since, that it was the phrase, " 'Fess up, now," that made me behave so badly. For I proceeded to behave very badly indeed, and I am not, as a rule, a rude person. I can, on occasion, summon up a passive resistance that will see me through even the dullest of dinners. But at the combination of "teentsy-weentsy" and " 'Fess up now," something snapped inside.

Dream Girl either heard the snap—it seemed to me quite audible—or was aware of it physically, for she turned on the teeth again and said: "Am I boring you, Mr. Hart?"

This time I didn't hesitate. "Frankly, yes," I said. "You are boring the living b'jesus out of me!"

The smile froze on her lips.

Now, I have, like most avid readers of detective stories, read a good deal about smiles freezing on lips, without ever quite believing the phrase, but I actually proceeded to see it carried out before my eyes. It is quite true—smiles can freeze. The mechanism is a very definite one. The lips twist grotesquely; the teeth, I could swear, grow two shades darker; the mouth clicks shut and draws the lips into a thin line of open fury. I watched, fascinated.

There followed, then, a little silence of the rugged grandeur variety and, wrapping her dignity about her like an imperial Roman toga, the lady proceeded to give me her back for the rest of the dinner, a back which I promptly christened Little America, so glacial was its aspect.

Afterward, mellowed by some excellent brandy, I experienced an acute sense of guilt. It seemed to me, as the brandy chortled through my digestive tract, that I had been ill mannered and a boor. I decided to apologize, but when I came upon the lady in the drawing room later, she would have none of me.

The teeth flashed with a new brilliance; the smile glittered handsomely. But the mood had changed; that first fine careless rapture had gone.

"There is no need," she said sweetly, "for you to apologize, Mr. Hart. One either has good manners, or one hasn't, don't you think?"

And once more I was given a bird's-eye view of Little America.

Well, she was right, I am afraid, and this is being written as a gesture of atonement and humility. Should her glistening eye happen to stray over these pages, she will find here such random thoughts as I have been able to gather on the working method of Mr. Kaufman and I hope, if she cannot find it in her heart to forgive me, she will at least find her unfortunate question answered.

For, if the truth must be told, she was right, in more ways than one. Perhaps, subconsciously, I resented the question because of its very truth. The plain fact is George Kaufman *did* frighten me to death originally. He frightens everyone, I suppose. I know now, of course, that underneath that beetling brow and behind that acidulous manner of speech there lies, to coin a new phrase, a heart of purest marshmallow.

And this I must admit—it took two plays, a number of rides on a carrousel, and what is tenderly known as an English summer for me to find it out. Our original contact was for me a decidedly frightening one, and our later meetings were not helped greatly by the fact that I was prone to stare for long periods at Mr. Kaufman, inarticulate and with what I can only describe now as a generally cow-like expression about the eyes. For I came upon George Kaufman very much as a boy of ten would come upon Dick Merriwell, or the captain of the winning eleven.

I was, at our first meeting, coming face to face with my hero, and that makes it just about as difficult for the hero as for anybody else. I think he suspected as much, for he snarled a great deal, his manner was brusque and wintry, and I left the office elated at having met him but conscious that I had undergone a baptism of fire.

The occasion of our meeting was his decision to participate in the rewriting of *Once in a Lifetime*, and for days before that I had swung breathless between prayers that he would decide to collaborate and an unholy excitement at the prospect of an interview, whether he decided to participate or not.

He was, to me, already a legendary figure. As a high-school boy, I had been entranced by *Dulcy* and *To the Ladies*; I had made my long-suffering family take the *Morning World* instead of the *American* so that I might follow his all-too-few-and-far-between contributions to F. P. A.'s column, while the Sunday drama section of the *Times,* of which he was then editor, became a weekly religious ritual. By the time I had seen *Merton of the Movies* and *Beggar on Horseback*, I had developed one all-consuming ambition—to write plays in the Kaufman tradition.

I may say that it was while I sat in the gallery of the Broadhurst Theatre, drinking in a performance of *June Moon* that the idea of *Once in a Lifetime* struck me—if that is the word one uses for those creative occasions. As a matter of fact, I started the first act that night on my return from the theatre and three weeks later saw the play finished. I dimly realized that what it lacked in technique it perhaps made up in freshness of approach, and while I was not altogether unhopeful of its ultimate sale, I truly believe that it was basically written for the sole purpose of procuring an interview with George Kaufman. That he would like it well enough to collaborate, I don't believe ever crossed my mind. In some childlike fashion I considered it as a letter of introduction that might serve in some way to procure that precious interview. At best, I had fond hopes of some obscure position as second stage manager with a play of his, if it aroused his interest sufficiently.

When I received word that he had read the play, and not only liked it but definitely wanted to collaborate on the revisions, I suppose my excitement was a little unearthly, so that I entered the office for that first meeting wide-eyed with hero worship and drunk with my own perfume.

It was only later that I discovered he shied at the slightest display of emotion as most men flee from smallpox.

and when I recall that my performance that afternoon was mildly reminiscent of Lillian Gish in *The White Sister*, I can understand a little better the sharpness of his tone and the brevity of the interview. I left the office, however, mad with power, for I had not only met George S. Kaufman, but we were to start work the very next day. I recall also that my father and mother were not a little startled, on my return, to find me talking in strange, clipped accents, addressing my bewildered brother as "Mr. H.," and my shocked aunt as "The Old Lady from Dubuque." I was, of course, already talking like George Kaufman, and for some two months after that my dismayed friends and family suffered from the curious combination of what they knew to be a rank sentimentalist talking in terms of a rabid Algonquinite. It was a difficult time, I imagine, for that particular section of Brooklyn known as Flatbush.

At any rate, I reported for work the next morning, stupidly innocent and blissfully eager, and there began what I now fondly call "The Days of the Terror." Our working day consisted of ten o'clock in the morning until exhausted—somewhere, perhaps, around one or two o'clock the next morning—with perhaps fifteen minutes out for such meals as Mr. Kaufman considered necessary to keep alive. Since he cared nothing for food, I found myself, at the end of the day, not only exhausted but starved as well.

Also, to add to my growing alarm, work proceeded at what I considered a maddeningly slow pace. Two hours would be spent sometimes in shaping one short sentence into a mosaic-like correctness. A whole day would pass in merely discussing an exit. If I had had visions of an early production, I was to learn the fitness of that time-worn phrase, "Plays are not written, but rewritten." And the rewriting process under the guidance of the eagle-eyed Mr. Kaufman slowly formulated itself in my mind

as a combination of the Spanish Inquisition and the blood-
iest portions of the First World War.

I was to discover, also, that a series of personal idiosyn-
crasies on the part of Mr. Kaufman were as much a part
of the actual working day as sitting at the typewriter, and
I came to watch for them much as one watches a steadily
falling barometer on a rough day at sea.

I was to learn, for instance, that a slow and careful picking of lint from the carpet was invariably the forerunner
of the emergence of a good line. I was to learn that Mr.
Kaufman's lanky form stretched full-length on the floor
for long periods at a time meant trouble. And I came to
know that what Mr. Kaufman needed much more than
fresh air and food was the immediate necessity to remove
his shoes and to pace madly before he could even think
of working. Shoelaces drove him crazy and so, I discovered much later on, did my cigar smoking; but since he
never complained I puffed contentedly on, not quite real-
izing that a major portion of his pacing was a frantic
effort to elude the blue clouds of smoke with which I
filled the room. Moreover, since the room we worked in
didn't provide enough pacing space for two, I was the one
who sat stiffly for long hours in an overstuffed chair while
I watched Mr. Kaufman perform gymnastics that would
make *The Man on the Flying Trapeze* turn green with
envy.

With "Curtain" finally typed—we had begun in December and it was now June—I heaved a breathless sigh
of relief, but the relief was short lived. Rehearsals, to
which I had looked forward with such eagerness, were a
trifle marred by the fact that what had seemed so right
at the typewriter seemed suddenly so wrong on the stage.
And it became the regulation thing, as rehearsals proceeded, to sit up most of the night rewriting and to appear at rehearsals fresh and bright at ten o'clock the next
morning.

The dress rehearsal I remember only as an unpleasant nightmare. The train ride to Atlantic City I remember not at all, and the opening I have been living down quietly ever since. I am, I suppose, notorious for the way I behave on the opening night of any play of mine, and this first play was no exception. The fact that I am unable to retain food of any kind for at least three days before an opening is unpleasant enough, but the horrible fact that I am compelled to spend most of the opening night in the men's room of the theatre, unable to witness the performance at all, has always been the sore spot in my career as a writer. I emerged long enough, however, to catch fleeting glimpses of Mr. Kaufman on the stage. He was, you may remember, Lawrence Vail, the playwright, in *Once in a Lifetime,* and the greenish pallor of his face sent me scurrying back to my retreat as fast as I could go.

It was not an auspicious opening. Mr. Kaufman had told me—I may say that I still called him Mr. Kaufman in those days—that his experience with Sam Harris had taught him that if Sam Harris liked a play, he remained for the full week of its tryout in Atlantic City. If he didn't like the play, he said nothing but quietly slipped out of town the next morning. I waited then, not so much for the reviews in the Atlantic City papers, but to see if Mr. Harris still remained in town. He didn't. I learned, to my horror, that he had not even waited until the next morning. He had left at eleven-thirty that night, leaving only a message in our box which said, "It needs work, boys," which sentence I have since had engraved as the largest understatement since the spring of 1910.

We played out the week in Atlantic City, and another week at Brighton Beach. There was obviously so much work to be done, the play was so unwieldy, so cumbersome, so filled with actors, scenery and costumes, that the only possible thing to do was to close it and get back to a typewriter as fast as we could. That was the tenth of

July. There followed, then, the longest, hottest, most exhausting summer I have spent or ever hope to spend. Mr.
Kaufman, in the face of disaster, seemed suddenly to come
to life. If I had thought that our working sessions were
tough before, it seemed to me now that I had wandered
into a concentration camp, and an eraser took on all the
semblance of a rubber truncheon. This time, Mr. Kaufman forgot entirely about food. He paced two rooms
instead of one. There were days at a time when we never
left the house. And I remember reflecting bitterly that if
this were what the theatre was like, I had sooner be a
good insurance agent. Because, in my dim-witted way, I
began to realize that this was but the beginning. And I
was right.

For the second production, rehearsals took on a new
ghastliness. I was depressed by the fact that Mrs. Kaufman, for whose critical judgment I had come to have an
enormous respect, liked the new third act not at all and
by the time the Philadelphia opening rolled around, a
numbness had crept into my bones which I thought nothing, not even the biggest hit in the world, would assuage.

There was a large contingent of New Yorkers who came
down for the opening, and I remember my panic when I
saw them leave in the middle of the third act. It meant
only one thing to me: dire failure. I didn't realize that they
had to leave, whether they liked it or not, to catch the
midnight back to New York, and since we had only
reached the middle of the third act by midnight, it will
be noted by even the least theatrically wise person that
our play was a shade too long.

And then came the dawn. Only we never saw the dawn,
nor the day, nor the night either. For in the next six days
I never left my room at the hotel. Mr. Kaufman had to
leave because he was acting in the play, but his schedule,
and I still cannot realize how he managed to do it, ran
something like this: he returned from the theatre at eleven-

thirty. We worked steadily through the night until ten o'clock the next morning. He would then leave to put the new stuff into rehearsal and rehearse until two. Then, while the actors learned the new lines for the evening's performance, he would return to my room at the hotel and work until eight-thirty; then back to the theatre for the performance; then back to my room again to work all night until ten o'clock the next morning.

I may add, resentfully, that he seemed to blossom through all this; that his eyes sparkled with an unwonted brightness; that his hand holding a pencil was like a surgeon's hand holding a scalpel. I may also add that one three o'clock in the morning, strolling out for a breath of fresh air, which I insisted upon, we came upon a children's carrousel in some little public playground, and it was there I discovered the marshmallow heart. Instinctively, we both made for the carrousel, and for half an hour, in the ghostly light of a Philadelphia dawn, we swung madly around on it. Whether, by this time, I was growing less frightened of him, as the dear lady suggested, I do not know; but his essential kindliness, his great good humor, the curious kind of nobility which he possesses more than any other man I know, had given me a fondness for him that enveloped my original timidity. And I found by the closing night in Philadelphia that while he still remained my hero, he was a hero I could talk to comfortably.

The night before the New York opening, the night of the final dress rehearsal at the Music Box, he unbent sufficiently to smile and say, "Don't worry too much. It's been swell anyway. And let's do another one." So that I didn't care particularly whether the play went well the next night or not. It had been pretty fine, at that. And as you can see by this book, we married and had several beautiful children.

FORKED LIGHTNING

By George S. Kaufman

Some years ago, during a visit to London, Moss Hart found that the nightly round of top hat, Savoy Grill and Quaglione's was beginning to wear him down. There had been about a week of it, uninterrupted, and a good night's sleep was indicated. So at nine o'clock of a dismally foggy night he put aside all temptation, pulled the shades down in his hotel room and settled himself for at least twelve good hours of slumber.

Sure enough, his watch said nine-thirty when he awoke. A bit of fog was still coming through the window cracks, but Moss was enormously refreshed. He bounced out of bed with high vigor, bathed, shaved, and phoned down for toast, eggs, coffee and marmalade. By the time he had stowed this away he was fairly bursting with vitality. Nothing like a good night's sleep!

He would like the morning papers, he told the phone operator. "Yes, sir!" Up they came, and for twenty eager minutes Moss buried himself in the news. And then presently he came across an item that had a vaguely familiar ring. Hadn't he read that yesterday? Yes, he had. And here was another such item. And another. Then he pulled himself together and looked at the date line. It was yesterday's newspaper.

Back on the telephone, he demanded to know how they could do such a thing. "But you must be mistaken, sir—those are this morning's newspapers." "But I tell you they aren't." "But if you'll look at the date, sir—"

Moss looked, and a horrible foreboding took possession of him. "What time is it?" he asked the operator. "Ten o'clock, sir." "Ten o'clock when?" "Ten o'clock Tuesday evening, sir."

The mystery was solved, of course. Moss had slept exactly half an hour.

Now, I don't for a minute say that this could not happen to anybody but Moss, but it is a little bit remarkable that so many similar incidents have managed to crowd themselves into his life. Nothing happens to Moss in the simple and ordinary terms in which it happens to the average person. The most normal of human experiences is crowded with drama where Moss is concerned.

Nothing, for example, could be more within the simple range of human activity than a visit to the dentist. We have all gone through it, lingered for our unpleasant hour, and gone on our way. But not Moss. When Moss went to the dentist it was at once discovered that a couple of teeth were growing out of his knee, or his elbow, or something. The dentist called in another dentist, and he brought along two more. It seemed it would require quite a course of treatment.

And it did. For something like three months Moss went to the dentist. But he didn't go the way you or I would. Oh, no! Moss would get there at eleven o'clock in the morning, and he would be there until four or five in the afternoon. Then, one epochal day, he arrived at eleven in the morning and stayed until nine o'clock that evening! This was so whimsical a procedure, even for Moss, that he felt I would not possibly believe him. So he brought along an affidavit from the dentists—there were three or four, and they worked on him in relays—testifying to its truth.

There were weeks, then, that Moss could not keep a dinner engagement because he had to be at the dentists'. This was a new reason for breaking dinner dates, and his friends were somewhat perplexed. But he was only build-ing up to the grand climax. On the final day of treatment Moss arrived at the dentists' at ten o'clock in the morning and left at two o'clock the following morning! There were no affidavits this time, because he knew I wouldn't even believe the affidavits. But it was true.

Nor was that all. This was followed by a complete nervous breakdown on the part of the dentists, although Moss felt fine. And as a complete you-can't-top-this finish to the whole business, the dentists gave Moss a beautiful present when it was all finished, and Moss reciprocated by buying them cuff links!

Now, is that going to the dentist or isn't it?

Forked Lightning, I called him. Only I am not sure that it plays around his head. I think his head plays around the lightning, deliberately.

And that is one of the reasons, if you ask me, why he is a good playwright. The prodigality that marks the sim-plest moments of his life is matched by the prodigality of his mind. Ideas pour forth, and the simplest things of life are highlighted and made interesting. His is an instinctive sense of drama, on and off. Life, like the plays, cuts itself neatly into acts, with climaxes, second-act curtains, and interesting minor characters.

There are times, I think, when he is not completely sure whether the curtain is up or down. There was, for ex-ample, that moment when he decided to drive North in-stead of South. He woke to a day that promised no partic-ular activity of interest—that same trip down to the office to see what was going on. He decided, suddenly, that he would not drive down to the office at all—he would drive in the other direction.

Drama took the wheel of the car at this point, and at the end of about an hour Moss found himself far up in the city, and just around the corner from the school he

had attended as a boy. He would drive around and look
at it. He remembered the day the school had opened—
there had been a terrific ceremony, and they had all pa-
raded from the old building to the new. The principal had
headed the procession. Professor Cartwright. Twenty-five
years ago, almost. Was he still there, he wondered?

And then, since the story had to have a second act,
Moss got out of the car and went in. There was a door
marked PRINCIPAL, and he knocked on it. A voice said
"Come in!" and there was a little man back of a desk—a
man who might very well have been Professor Cartwright, and who, in the manner of good dramatic construction, was indeed he.

"Professor Cartwright?" asked Moss, eagerly.

"What do you want?" The professor's tone was uncom-
promising.

"Is this Professor Cartwright?"

"What do you want?"

"My name is—Moss Hart." Moss waited hopefully for
the minor sensation which this revelation was supposed
to bring about, but nothing happened. "I—uh—I used to
go to school here when I was a boy. My name is—Moss
Hart."

"Well, what do you want?"

"Why—nothing. I just thought I'd—my name is Moss
Hart." Still with a shade of hope. "I just happened to be
near by, and thought I'd—uh—you know."

"Is that all?"

"Well, is it all right if I just go through the school—
look around?"

"All right. Here's a pass."

Moss went up a flight of stairs, and there was Room
No. 5. He had sat in that room for many hours, dutifully
trying to learn things that would be of no help in the
theatre.

A stern-looking woman opened the door. This time drama had sprung one of its surprises—it was not his old teacher.

"My name is—Moss Hart." A little bit of hope still sticking.

"Oh, yes. You're the father of one of the boys, aren't you?"

"No, no. I write—plays. Plays. I used to go to this school, so—"

"Oh, come right in. . . . Boys, this is—what is the name?"

"Moss Hart."

"Yes. He used to go to school here. Sit right down, Mr. Hart."

So for two hours Moss went back to school, and very dull he found it. But there was a curtain coming, of a sort. When it was all over the teacher pulled a manuscript out of her desk drawer.

"Did you say you wrote plays, Mr. Hart? I just happen to have written a play myself. . . ."

I think, on the way out, that Moss opened the door of the principal's room just a crack. Instinctively he felt the need of a finish. Professor Cartwright might be lying dead on the floor, a knife of peculiar design plunged into his heart. But the professor was still sitting at his desk. He looked up just for a second. "What do you want?" he said.

Forked Lightning. Only Moss could have planted thirty-five hundred new trees on his farm in Bucks County, and only Moss, in the midst of plenty, could have failed to find water at the end of three months and the digging of something like seventeen wells. Only Moss could have bought a hundred pigs to give his caretaker enough interest in the place to persuade him to stay on. Only Moss and his family, after *Once in a Lifetime*, could have moved out of their Sheepshead Bay house overnight, leaving every piece of furniture, every shred of clothes and every kitchen utensil right where it was. Only Moss could have written a show that called for four revolving stages, double the number that had ever been used before.

Forked Lightning.

But it makes for awfully good shows.

ONCE IN A LIFETIME

Once in a Lifetime was produced by Sam H. Harris at the Music Box Theatre, New York, on Wednesday night, September 24th, 1930, with the following cast:

GEORGE LEWIS	HUGH O'CONNELL
MARY DANIELS	JEAN DIXON
JERRY HYLAND	GRANT MILLS
THE PORTER	OSCAR POLK
HELEN HOBART	SPRING BYINGTON
SUSAN WALKER	SALLY PHIPPS
CIGARETTE GIRL	CLARA WARING
COAT CHECK GIRL	OTIS SCHAEFER
PHYLLIS FONTAINE	JANET CURRIE
MISS FONTAINE'S MAID	MARIE FERGUSON
MISS FONTAINE'S CHAUFFEUR	CHARLES MACK
FLORABEL LEIGH	EUGENIE FRONTAI
MISS LEIGH'S MAID	DOROTHY TALBOT
MISS LEIGH'S CHAUFFEUR	EDWARD LOUD
BELLBOY	PAYSON CRANE
MRS. WALKER	FRANCES E. BRANDT
ERNEST	MARC LEOBELL
HERMAN GLOGAUER	CHARLES HALTON
MISS LEIGHTON	LEONA MARICLE
LAWRENCE VAIL	GEORGE S. KAUFMAN
WEISSKOPF	LOUIS CRUGER
METERSTEIN	WILLIAM MCFADDEN
FIRST PAGE	STANLEY FITZPATRICK
SECOND PAGE	EDWIN MILLS
THREE SCENARIO WRITERS—KEMPTON RACE, GEORGE CASSEL-BURY AND BURTON MALLORY	
RUDOLPH KAMMERLING	WALTER DREHER

3

FIRST ELECTRICIAN	JACK WILLIAMS
SECOND ELECTRICIAN	JOHN O. HEWITT
A VOICE PUPIL	JANE BUCHANAN
MR. FLICK	HAROLD GRAU
MISS CHASEN	VIRGINIA HAWKINS
FIRST CAMERAMAN	IRVING MORROW
THE BISHOP	GRANVILLE BATES
THE SIXTH BRIDESMAID	FRANCES THRESS
SCRIPT GIRL	GEORGIA MACKINNON
GEORGE'S SECRETARY	ROBERT RYDER

Staged by GEORGE S. KAUFMAN

SCENES

ACT ONE

Scene I.   A room in the West Forties, New York.
Scene II. A Pullman Car.
Scene III. The Gold Room of the Hotel Stilton, Los Angeles.

ACT TWO

Reception Room of the Glogauer Studio

ACT THREE

Scene I.   On the set.
Scene II. The Pullman Car.
Scene III. The Reception Room.

ACT ONE

SCENE I

(*A room in the West Forties, New York City. It is a replica of the countless other furnshed rooms in the district — cheerless and utterly uninviting. There is a bed, a washstand, an easy chair, two faded pictures on the walls. A pretty dismal place, all in all—yet* GEORGE LEWIS, *seated in the easy chair, seems completely content.* GEORGE *is about twenty-eight, a clean-cut, nice-looking young fellow, with the most disarmingly naïve countenance it is possible to imagine. Completely without guile. He is the sort of person insurance men and book agents instinctively head for, and in the case of* GEORGE, *it might be noted, usually succeed in selling. Withal, there is a quiet sincerity about* GEORGE *and a certain youthful ardor and genuineness that make him a decidedly likeable person.*

He is sunk deep down in the easy chair, at the moment, immersed to the exclusion of all else in that Bible of show business, VARIETY. *He has a large plate of Indian nuts on the arm of the easy chair, and these he proceeds to crack and eat with a methodical thoroughness, stopping only to turn a page of the paper or to brush some of the shells off his trousers. It is a picture of a man thoroughly content and blissfully happy in the moment. There is a sharp knock at the door.* GEORGE *murmurs a "Come in" and* MAY DANIELS *enters. She is quite a person, this* MAY DANIELS. *It is evident from the moment*

*she enters the room. There is a sharp, biting incisiveness
about everything she says and does—a quick mind, and
a hearty, earthy sense of humor. Tall and slender, she
carries herself with the conscious ease and grace of a
person who has always been thoroughly sure of herself,
and her blonde good looks are a bit clouded just now
by a tired line between the eyes and a discouraged
droop at the corners of the mouth. With one glance she
takes in* GEORGE, VARIETY, *and the Indian nuts—then
sits dejectedly on the edge of the bed)*

MAY. Jerry not back yet, huh?

GEORGE. No.

MAY. Anything new since this afternoon? You haven't
heard anything, have you?

GEORGE. No. Are you going to stay and talk, May? I'm
reading.

MAY. What time's Jerry coming back, do you know?

GEORGE. He went to a show.

MAY. It's wonderful how you two take it. You off to ball
games every day, Jerry going to shows! What about the
old vaudeville act? Are we gonna get some bookings or
aren't we?

GEORGE. I don't know anything about it, May. I'm reading.

MAY. Still "Variety?"

GEORGE. Uh-huh.

MAY. One of these days you'll pick up a paper that's written in English, and you'll have to send out for an inter-
preter.

GEORGE. What do you mean, May? "Variety" is in English.

MAY. All right.

GEORGE. It has news of the show world from different
countries, but it's all in English.

MAY (*willing to call the whole thing off*). I said all right,
George.

GEORGE. Want some Indian nuts?

MAY. No, thanks. (*He cracks a nut—and a good sturdy crack it is.* MAY *surveys him*) Don't your teeth ever bother you?

GEORGE. No. Why?

MAY. I dunno—after all those damn things you've eaten. Do you realize, George, that you've left a trail of Indian nuts clean across the United States? If you ever commit a crime they could go right *to* you.

GEORGE (*going back to his reading*). Aw!

MAY. You've thrown them shells under radiators in every dollar-and-a-half hotel from here to Seattle. I can visualize hundreds of chambermaids, the country over, coming in the morning you check out and murmuring a blessing on your head. Don't you ever have bad dreams, George, with that on your mind?

GEORGE. Listen, May, are you gonna keep talking till Jerry gets here?

MAY (*nervously*). What's Jerry up to, George? Is he going to land us something or isn't he? How much longer are we going to lay around here?

GEORGE. Don't ask me—ask Jerry.

MAY. I'm gonna—and we'll have a showdown tonight. The Automat don't spell home to me.

GEORGE (*just a literal boy*). We don't live there.

MAY. We do everything but sleep there, and we'd be doing that if they could get beds into them slots.

GEORGE. You oughta have patience, May. We've only been here four weeks.

MAY. George, listen. Dumb as you are, you ought to be able to get this: the bank-book says there's just one hundred and twenty-eight dollars left. One hundred and twenty-eight dollars. Get that?

GEORGE. Sure.

MAY. Well, how long do you think three people can live on that, with Jerry going to opening nights and you taking in the world series?

GEORGE. Something'll turn up. It always does. (*And for good luck he cracks another nut*)

MAY. Well, I'm glad you like those goddam things—you're certainly a lucky fellow. Because the way things are going you may have to live on 'em in another week.

GEORGE. Go on, May—nobody could live on Indian nuts. There isn't enough to 'em. Look—that's all they are. (*He cracks another; exhibits the contents*)

MAY. All right, George. (*A moment's restless pacing*) Well, I suppose it's another week of hanging around offices, and another series of those nickel-plated dinners. I'm so sick of the whole business I could yell.

GEORGE. You're just blue, May.

MAY. I wouldn't wonder. Living alone in that hall bedroom—without even the crack of an Indian nut to cheer me up. . . . Well! I wanted to do it, and here I am. I guess it's better than selling ninety-cent perfume to the feminine population of Connellsville, Pennsylvania, but there's times when I wish I was back there.

GEORGE (*brightly*). Maybe we'll play there some day.

MAY (*that's all she needs yet*). It wouldn't surprise me.

GEORGE. I wonder if we'll ever play Medallion—I haven't been back for four years.

MAY. Has it got an Automat?

GEORGE. I don't think so.

MAY. We'll never play it.

GEORGE. Jerry played it once—that's where he discovered me. He played the theatre I was working in—I was an usher.

MAY. Yah, I remember. Too bad that was pre-Roxy, George—you'd have had a career.

GEORGE. If I'd have stayed I might have been a lieutenant. One of the boys I started with is a major.

MAY. Do you think they'll ever have conscription for ushers?

GEORGE. Then Jerry came along and offered me this job. He said I was just right for it.

MAY. He had a good eye. As far as I'm concerned you're best dead pan feeder in all show business.

GEORGE. Don't the audiences like me, too?

MAY. No one ever gave birth in the aisle, George, but you're all right.

GEORGE. I love doing it, too. The longer we play the act the more I like it.

MAY (suddenly looking at him). George, you and Jerry have been bunking together for four years. Isn't Jerry a swell guy?

GEORGE. He's been a wonderful friend to me.

MAY. I wouldn't tell this to him, George, but I'll never forget what I owe Jerry Hyland. (Quickly) And don't you go telling him, either.

GEORGE. I won't tell him. How much do you owe him?

MAY (nearly ready to give up). George, please stop eating those things—they're going to your head. I don't mean I owe him any money. But he's never made me feel that we were anything but good friends, or that I'd have to feel anyways else to keep the job.

GEORGE (not to be outdone). He never made me feel anything, either.

MAY. Well, that's just dandy.

GEORGE. Shall I tell you something, May?

MAY. I wish you would.

GEORGE. I think Jerry likes you.

MAY. All right, George.

GEORGE. No—I mean he really likes you—a whole lot.

MAY. O.K., George. The question is: What do we do about bookings? Are we going to crash the big time or aren't we?

GEORGE. We were doing all right on the small time. We could be working right along—you know what the Booking Office told us.

MAY. And you know where the Booking Office books us.
Bellows Falls, Vermont.

GEORGE. I liked it there.

MAY. What?

GEORGE. We had a good dinner there. With jello.

MAY. Look, George. Don't you want to do anything else
all your life but knock about all over the map as a
small-time vaudeville actor?

GEORGE. No.

MAY. You don't?

GEORGE. No.

MAY. Well, I guess that settles that, doesn't it? You might
as well go ahead and read.

GEORGE. No, I feel like talking now.

MAY. I feel like reading now.

(*At which the door is flung rather violently open and*
JERRY HYLAND *enters the room.* JERRY HYLAND *is your
idea of the complete bond salesman. Looking like one
of those slick Men's Clothing Advertisements in "Vanity
Fair," he completes the illusion by talking as if he had
just stepped out of the picture. It is almost impossible
not to like* JERRY *immediately, and, if his talent for
salesmanship has been submerged by that for second-
rate acting, he makes up for it by being the first to tell
you what a bum actor he really is and outlining a proj-
ect to merge Ford and General Motors.* JERRY *is in the
early thirties, and the major part of his late twenties
have been spent in concocting one scheme or another
to get them out of Vaudeville and into the Big Money.
Just at the moment he is laboring under the stress of
some tremendous piece of news, and it is a moment or
two before he can find the breath to tell them*)

MAY. Well, here we are! When do we play the Palace?

GEORGE. Hello, Jerry!

MAY. Or did you settle for the last half in Bridgeport?

JERRY. May, it's here!

MAY. You got bookings?

GEORGE. Is it the Palace?

JERRY. Never mind about that! I've got some news for you! I saw history made tonight!

MAY. What are you talking about?

GEORGE. You saw what?

JERRY. I've just been to the opening of Al Jolson's talking picture, "The Jazz Singer."

MAY. Well, what of it?

JERRY. And I'm telling you it's the greatest thing in the world!

MAY. There've been good pictures before, Jerry—

JERRY. I'm not talking about the picture! I mean the Vitaphone!

MAY. The what?

JERRY. The Vitaphone—the talkies!

GEORGE. They talk.

MAY. Oh, that!

JERRY. That! You ought to hear them cheering, May! Everybody went nuts! I tell you, May, it's going to revolutionize the entire industry. It's something so big I bet even the Vitaphone people don't know what they've got yet. You've got to hear it, May, to realize what it means. Why, in six months from now—

MAY. Come out of it, Jerry! What are *you* getting so het up about? It's no money in *your* pocket, even if it *is* good!

GEORGE. No!

JERRY (*pretty calmly, for him*). No? (*He takes in the pair of them*) Well, we're leaving for Los Angeles in the morning.

MAY. What did you say?

JERRY. We're leaving for Los Angeles in the morning.

GEORGE (*all he wants are the facts*). What time?

MAY. Are you out of your mind?

JERRY. Don't you understand, May? For the next six

months they won't know which way to turn! All the old standbys are going to find themselves out in the cold, and somebody with brains and sense enough to use them is going to get into the big dough! The movies are back where they were when the De Milles and the Laskys first saw what they were going to amount to! Can't you see what it would mean to get in *now*?

MAY. What do you mean get in, Jerry? What would *we* do there—act, or what?

JERRY. No, no! Acting is small potatoes from now on! You can't tell what we'll do—direct, give orders, tell 'em how to do things! There's no limit to where we can go!

MAY (*vaguely groping*). Yah, but what do we know about—

JERRY. Good Lord, May! We've been doing nothing but playing the act in all the small-time houses in the country. Suppose we *do* cut loose and go out there? What have we got to lose?

GEORGE. A hundred and twenty-eight dollars.

MAY. Shut up, George! I don't know, Jerry—

JERRY. We gotta get out there, May! Before this Broadway bunch climbs on the bandwagon. There's going to be a gold rush, May. There's going to be a trek out to Hollywood that'll make the 49'ers look sick.

MAY. Y'mean thar's gold in them hills, Jerry?

JERRY. Gold and a black marble swimming pool, with the Jap chauffeur waiting outside the iron-grilled gate—all that and more, May, if we can work it right and get in *now*! They're panic-stricken out there! They'll fall on the neck of the first guy that seems to know what it's all about! And that's why we gotta get there quick!

MAY. Yah, but give me time to think, Jerry. (*A hand to her head*) Suppose we don't catch on right away—how are we going to live? You heard what the boy wonder said—a hundred and twenty-eight dollars.

JERRY (*exploding the bombshell*). I've got five hundred more!

MAY. What!

JERRY. I've got five hundred more! Right here!

MAY. Where'd you get it?

JERRY. Now don't yell, May! I sold the act!

MAY. You did what?

JERRY. I sold the act! I took one look at that picture and sold the act outright to Eddie Garvey and the Sherman Sisters for five hundred cash! Now don't get sore, May! It was the only thing to do!

MAY. (*slowly*). No, I'm not getting sore, Jerry, but—

GEORGE (*coming to life*). You sold the act to the Sherman Sisters?

JERRY. My God, if people once took a mule and a covered wagon, just because they heard of some mud that looked yellow, and endured hardships and went all the way across the country with their families—fought Indians, even—think what it'll mean, May, if we win out! No more traveling all over the country—living in one place instead of—

MAY (*catching some of his excitement*). Okay, Jerry— I'm with you! You had some helluva nerve, but count me in!

JERRY. Good for you! How about you, George?

GEORGE. What?

JERRY. Are you willing to take a chance with us—leave all this behind and cut loose for Hollywood?

GEORGE. Well, but look—if you sold the act—

JERRY. Sure I sold the act! We're going out and try this new game! Now what do you say?

MAY. Come on, George!

JERRY. It's the chance of a lifetime!

GEORGE. But what'll we do there?

JERRY. We can talk that over on the train! The important thing is to get out there and to get there fast!

GEORGE. But if you've sold the act—

(JERRY *gives up;* MAY *leaps into the breach. They are working in relays now*)

MAY (*as to a child of ten*). George, listen. We're giving up the act. We're not going to do the act any more. Don't you understand that?

GEORGE. Yah, but he sold the act—

(*It seems that they sold the act*)

MAY. I *understand* that he sold the act. Look, George. There is a new invention called talking pictures. In these pictures the actors will not only be seen, but will also talk. For the first time in the history of pictures they will use their voices. (*And in that moment a notion comes to her. Slowly she turns to* JERRY) I've got an idea.

JERRY. What?

MAY. I think I know what we're going to do out there.

JERRY. Well?

MAY. Most of these bozoes haven't ever talked on a stage! They've never spoken lines before!

JERRY. They gotta learn, that's all!

MAY. You bet they do! And who's going to teach them? We'll open a school of elocution and voice culture!

JERRY. What?

MAY. We'll open a school, Jerry—teach 'em how to talk! They're sure to fall for it, because they'll be scared stiff! We'll have them coming to us instead of our going to them!

JERRY. Yah, but—but *us* with a school, May! We don't know anything about it!

MAY. Maybe *you* don't, but *I* went to one once, and it's easy!

JERRY. But what do you have to do? Can I learn it?

MAY. Sure! Anyhow, I'll do all that!

GEORGE (*five minutes behind, as usual*). What are you going to do?

MAY. I tell you it's a natural, Jerry!

JERRY (*quieting both of them*). Shut up a minute, will you? Let me think! Maybe you got hold of something! A school of elocution—it might not be a bad idea.

GEORGE (*getting right down to the root of it*). What's elocution?

MAY. It's a swell idea! And if I know actors, Jerry, they'll come running! Why, between you and I and the lamppost here— (*She takes in* GEORGE, *and it's really the best notice he's had from her in some time*) —it's the best idea anybody ever had! How soon we gonna leave?

JERRY. Tomorrow! I want you to see the picture first!

MAY. O.K.! Twenty-five of that five hundred goes for books on elocution first thing in the morning! I'll learn this racket or know the reason why!

GEORGE. But what'll *I* do? I don't know anything about elocution!

MAY. George, you don't know anything about anything, and if what they say about the movies is true, you'll go far! (*Swinging to* JERRY) So help me, Jerry, it'll work out like a charm—you watch if it doesn't! It's coming back to me already—I remember Lesson No. 1.

JERRY. Well, if you're sure you can get away with it, May—

MAY. It's a cinch! Just watch! Come here, George!

GEORGE. What?

MAY. Say "California, here I come."

GEORGE. Huh?

MAY. Don't argue—say it!

GEORGE. "California, here I come."

MAY. Now, then—stomach in, chest out! Wait a minute —maybe it's the other way around! No, that's right— stomach in, chest out! Now say it again!

GEORGE (*better this time*). "California, here I come."

MAY (*working him up to a pitch*). Now this time with feeling! You are about to start on a great adventure—

the covered wagon is slowly moving across the plains
to a marble swimming pool!

JERRY. Come on, George—give it everything!

GEORGE (*with feeling plus*). "California, here I come.

JERRY. Yay!

MAY. It works, Jerry—it works!

JERRY. And if it works on George it'll work on anybody!

MAY. California, here we come!

Curtain

SCENE II

(*The corner of a Pullman car, on a train Los Angeles
bound. The regulation Pullman, with* MAY, JERRY, *and*
GEORGE *slumped down in their seats in various attitudes.*
JERRY *is in the middle of his hundredth cross-word
puzzle,* GEORGE *is busy with* VARIETY *and the inevitable
Indian nuts, while* MAY *gazes straight ahead, a troubled
expression in her eyes. There is a silence, broken only
by the cracking of the shells*)

MAY. This dust is about an inch thick on me. (*There is a
pause, and, as usual in any pause,* GEORGE *cracks an Indian nut*) George!

GEORGE. Yeah?

MAY. Do those things come without shells on them?

GEORGE. I don't think so. Why?

MAY. A few more days of hearing you crack them and
I'll go bugs.

GEORGE. I didn't know they were bothering you, May.

MAY. I was keeping it secret. (*Opens the book on her lap.
Reads with venom*) "To teachers of the culture of the
human voice—"

JERRY (*busy over his puzzle*). What's a four-letter word for actor?

MAY (*she knows that one*). Dope. (*Reading again*) "We strongly urge the use of abdominal breathing as a fundamental principle in elocutionary training. This is a very simple operation and the following methods may be used."

(*There enters, pillow in hand, a negro* PORTER)

PORTER. You ready to have your berth made up?

MAY. No!

PORTER. Yes, ma'am.

MAY. All you people know is make up berths. The minute it gets dark you want to make up berths.

PORTER. Lots of times folks wants 'em made up.

MAY. Where are we now—pretty near out of this desert?

PORTER. No'm, I guess we're still in it. Pretty dusty, all right.

MAY. It is, huh?

PORTER. Yes, ma'am, it's dusty, all right. Dust all over. See here? (*He shows her*)

MAY. Thanks.

PORTER (*blandly wiping the dust off on the pillow*). You welcome. Anything else you want?

MAY. No, that's all, thank you. I just wanted to know if it was dusty.

PORTER. Yes, ma'am, it is.

MAY. I'm ever so much obliged.

PORTER. I guess this your first trip out, ain't it, ma'am?

MAY. How did you know?

PORTER. 'Count of your noticing the dust that way. I've taken out lots of folks—I mean that was going out for the moving pictures, like you folks—and they always notices the dust.

MAY. They do, huh?

PORTER. Yes, ma'am. But coming back they don't generally

care so much. (*And having planted this sweet thought he departs*)

MAY. Did you hear that? Coming back they don't generally care so much.

JERRY. Oh, come out of it, May! If we don't put up a front like a million dollars, we're lost!

MAY. You know how much of a bankroll we've got, Jerry, and how long it's going to last. And this elocution idea —how do we know it's going to work?

JERRY. It's just around the corner, if we keep our nerve! Think what it'll mean, May, if we put it over!

MAY. Well, I mustn't go out there this way—it's aging me. But my God, wouldn't you think the railroad would put a couple of mountains in here somewhere? I'm so sick of looking at wheat and corn— (*A nut cracks*) —and those nuts cracking are beginning to sound like cannons going off.

GEORGE. Why, May—

MAY. Oh—go ahead and crack two at a time and see if I care. I'm going out to the ladies' smoker—maybe I'll hear a good dirty story.

(*She goes. In the distance the train whistle is heard*)

JERRY. George!

GEORGE (*deep in* VARIETY). Uh-huh.

JERRY. You and I have got to pull May out of this. Y'understand?

GEORGE. Sure.

JERRY. We've got to keep her spirits up—keep telling her we're going to get away with it.

GEORGE. All right.

JERRY. If she starts anything with you, come right back at her. We can't fail. We're pioneers in a new field. The talkies are the thing of the future and there's going to be no stopping them. Got that?

GEORGE (*glibly*). The legitimate stage had better look to its laurels.

JERRY (*somewhat bowled over*). What?

GEORGE. The legitimate stage had better look to its laurels. It's in "Variety."

JERRY. Sure! That's the idea.

GEORGE. Here is a medium that combines the wide scope of the motion picture with the finer qualities of the stage proper. It's an interview with Mr. Katzenstein.

JERRY. Let me see it.

GEORGE (*wound up*). It affords opportunities for enter· tainment—

JERRY. All right, all right.

(MAY *returns*)

MAY. Say, what do you think?

GEORGE. What?

MAY. I just saw somebody I know—anyhow, I *used* to know her.

JERRY. Who is it?

MAY. This may mean something, Jerry—maybe the luck's changing.

JERRY. It's Gloria Swanson and she wants to take lessons.

MAY. Gloria Swanson nothing! It's Helen Hobart!

GEORGE. Helen Hobart! I read her stuff.

MAY. Sure you do, and a million like you. America's foremost movie critic.

GEORGE. And she's on this train?

JERRY. How well do you know her?

MAY. We used to troupe together. I knew her well enough to tell her she was a rotten actress.

JERRY. What'll we do? Can we get her in here?

MAY. We've got nothing to lose.

JERRY. Ring the bell, George!

GEORGE (*pressing the buzzer*). Helen Hobart!

JERRY. Say, if she ever sponsored us we'd have all Hollywood begging to get in. She's a powerful important lady, and don't you forget it.

MAY. I don't know whether she'll remember me or not—

I didn't dare stop and say hello. The way I feel today I'd break down and cry if anybody ritzed me.

JERRY (*as the* PORTER *appears*). There's a woman named Miss Helen Hobart in the next car—

MAY. Talking to a young girl. You page her and tell her Miss May Daniels would like to see her.

PORTER. Yes, ma'am.

MAY. And come right back and tell me what she says. (*The* PORTER *goes*) I'd like to talk to the old battleship again, if only to see her strut her stuff. She's the original iron horse, all right.

JERRY. How long is it since you knew her?

MAY. Plenty. Now listen. If you ever let her know we're just a small-time vaudeville act you'll get the prettiest freeze-out you ever saw. Unless she thinks you're somebody she won't even notice you.

JERRY. Well, what'll we tell her? Let's get together on a story!

MAY. Leave it to me. This is my party.

GEORGE. Don't make up any lies about me.

JERRY. Say, if we could ever get her interested! Her stuff is syndicated all over the country.

GEORGE. It's in two hundred and three newspapers. I was just reading it. (*He produces the paper*)

MAY. Yah. It's an awful thought, Jerry, but there must be thousands of guys like George reading that stuff every day.

GEORGE. But it's good.

MAY. And thinking it's good, too. (*She takes the paper from* GEORGE) Get this, Jerry. "Hollywood Happenings, by Helen Hobart. Well, movie fans, Wednesday night was just a furore of excitement—the Gold Room at the Stilton just buzzed with the news. But your Helen has managed to get it to you first of all. What do you think? Tina Fair is having her swimming pool done over in egg-shell blue." How do you like that?

GEORGE. Nice color.

JERRY. They've *all* got swimming pools!

MAY. And if I know Helen she lives and acts just like this
column of hers. Did I hear that door? I did. (*She has
taken a quick peep*) Here she comes!

(*Making quite an entrance of it,* HELEN HOBART *comes in.*
HELEN *is an important figure in The Fourth Largest
Industry, and she looks and acts pretty much like an
important figure in The Fourth Largest Industry. She
positively glitters. Jewels stud her person from the smart
diamond arrow in her hat to the buckles of her shoes,
and her entire ensemble is the Hollywood idea of next
year's style à la Metro-Goldwyn*)

HELEN. My dear! How perfectly lovely! How nice to think
of your being on this train!

MAY. Helen, you look marvelous!

HELEN. Thank you dear, you haven't changed at all.

MAY. Really? I expected living abroad would change me
somewhat.

HELEN. What?

MAY. But let me introduce you to my business manager,
Mr. Jerome Hyland—

HELEN. How do you do?

MAY. And my technical advisor, Doctor Lewis.

HELEN. How do you do, Doctor?

(JERRY *murmurs an acknowledgment, but* GEORGE *is too
stunned to speak*)

MAY. Please sit down, Helen, and chat a while.

HELEN. Thanks, I will. There's some little girl back in my
car who discovered I was Helen Hobart, and she simply
won't let me be. That's why I was so glad to get away.
She's been reading my column, and she just can't believe I'm human like herself—(*A modest little laugh*)
—thinks I'm some sort of goddess. If you *knew* how
much of that sort of thing I get!

MAY (*innocently*). You're doing some sort of newspaper work, aren't you?

HELEN (*amazed*). My dear—didn't you *know*?

MAY. Don't tell me you're a film actress?

HELEN (*with measured definiteness—from a great height*). I write the most widely syndicated column in the United States. Anybody who reads the newspapers— but where on earth have you *been*, my dear, that you haven't heard about *me*?

MAY. I've been living in England for the last eight years, Helen. That's probably why I didn't know. But go on and tell me. I'm frightfully interested.

HELEN. Well—! (*She settles herself—after all, this is quite a chance*) If you don't *know*, my dear, I can't quite tell you *all*! But I think I can say in all modesty that I am one of the most important figures in the industry. You know, it was I who gave America Gary Cooper and Rex the Wonder Horse. Yes, I've done very well for myself. You know I always *could* write, May, but I never expected to be *the* Helen Hobart! Oh, I can't tell you *everything*, one-two-three, but movie-goers all over the country take my word as law. Of course I earn a perfectly fabulous salary—but I'm hardly allowed to *buy anything*—I'm simply *deluged* with gifts. At Christmas, my dear—well, you'll hardly believe it, but just before I came East they presented me with a home in Beverly Hills!

MAY (*in spite of herself*). No kidding!

HELEN. They said I deserved it—that I simply *lived* in the studios. I always take an interest in new pictures in production, you know, and suggest things to them— and they said that I ought to have a home I could go to and get away from the studios for a while. Wasn't that marvelous?

MAY. Marvelous!

HELEN. I call it Parwarmet. I have a penchant for titles.

MAY. You call it *what*?

HELEN. Parwarmet. You see, I always call my gifts after the people who give them to me—rather a nice thought, you know. And I didn't want to offend anybody in this case, so I called it after the three of them—Paramount, Warner, Metro-Goldwyn—the first syllable of each. Parwarmet.

GEORGE. Won't Fox be sore?

HELEN. Oh, no, Doctor. Because the Fox Studios gave me a wonderful kennel, and I have twelve magnificent dogs, all named after Fox executives. But listen to me rattling on and not asking a word about *you*! Tell me what you've been doing. And what in the world took you abroad for eight years? The last I heard of you—

MAY (*quickly*). Yes, I know. Well, of course, I never expected to stay in the theatre—that is, not as an actress. I always felt that I was better equipped to teach.

HELEN. Teach?

MAY. Voice culture. I began with a few private pupils, and then when I was abroad Lady Tree persuaded me to take her on for a while, and from that I drifted into opening a school, and it's been very successful. Of course I accept only the very best people. Mr. Hyland and Dr. Lewis are both associated with me, as I told you—

HELEN. And now you're going to open a school in Hollywood!

MAY. What? Why, no—we hadn't expected—

JERRY. Hollywood? We hadn't thought about it.

HELEN. *Wait* till I tell you! Of course you don't know, but something is happening at the present time that is simply going to revolutionize the entire industry. They've finally perfected *talking pictures*!

MAY. No!

HELEN. Yes! And you can't imagine what it's going to

mean! But here's the point! Every actor and actress in
the industry will have to learn to talk, understand? And
if *we* were to open the first school—my dear!

MAY. But Helen, we couldn't *think* of such a thing!

JERRY. Oh, no, Miss Hobart!

GEORGE. Sure! That's why we—

(JERRY *silences him*)

HELEN. I simply won't take no for an answer!

MAY. But what about our school in London?

JERRY. We've got a good deal of money tied up in London,
Miss Hobart.

HELEN. May—America needs you. You're still, I hope, a
loyal American?

MAY. Oh, yes, yes. But—

HELEN. Then it's settled. This is Fate, May—our meeting
—and in the industry Fate is the only thing we bow to.

MAY. But—

HELEN. Now please—not another word! Oh, but this is
marvelous—right at this time! Of course it'll take a certain amount of money to get started, but I know just
the man we'll take it to—Herman Glogauer! You know
—the Glogauer Studios!

MAY. Well, I'm not sure—

JERRY. Oh, yes, of course!

GEORGE. Yah!

HELEN. I'll send him a telegram right away, and ask for
an appointment.

JERRY. That's a good idea! George!

(GEORGE *presses the buzzer*)

MAY. Is he important?

HELEN. Oh, my dear!

JERRY. *Is* he important?

GEORGE. You bet!

HELEN. One of the biggest! And he's the man who first
turned down the Vitaphone!

MAY. He did?

HELEN. So he buys *everything* now! Why, he just signed
that famous playwright—you know, May—that Arme-
nian who writes all those wonderful plays and things.

MAY. Noel Coward.

HELEN. That's right! Of course you people can't realize,
but a school of voice culture, opening up at this time—
well! I should say my half interest alone would bring
me in I just don't know how much! (*It seems that*
HELEN *is declaring herself in*) Because there's absolutely no limit to where the talkies are going—just no
limit! Tell me, Doctor—

(GEORGE *fails to respond*)

Doctor

(GEORGE, *spurred on by* JERRY, *pays attention*)
What do you think of this marvelous development in
the motion pictures? Just what is your opinion?

MAY (*trying to save the day*). Well, the Doctor hasn't
had much time

JERRY. He looks after the scientific end.

GEORGE (*coming right through with it*). I think the legitimate stage had better look to its laurels.

HELEN. My words exactly! Just what I've been saying in
my column!

GEORGE (*blossoming*). It combines the wide scope of the
motion picture with the finer qualities of the stage
proper.

HELEN. That's *very* true. May, you've got a great brain
here. (*To* GEORGE *again*) I *do* want to talk to you some-
time, Doctor. I want to discuss voice and body control
with you.

GEORGE. It affords opportunities for entertainment—

(*There arrives, at this point,* MISS SUSAN WALKER. *The first
glimpse of* SUSAN *makes it obvious that she and* GEORGE
have been "made for each other." SUSAN WALKER, *to
give you the idea immediately, is the female counter-
part of* GEORGE, *very young, very pretty, very charm-*

ing, and, as you must have guessed by this time, very dumb. She has a number of cute little mannerisms of the sort that intrigue the stronger sex, and a complete and unshakeable belief in her powers as an actress. She flutters about a good deal, and her anxiety not to lose her contact with HELEN *makes her positively twitter)*

SUSAN (*who is not at all bashful*). Oh, hello, Miss Hobart! You said you were coming back, and I waited—

HELEN. Yes, dear, but this is very important. I can't talk to you now.

SUSAN. When *can* you talk to me?

HELEN. I'm sure I don't know. Later.

SUSAN. I only want to ask you some questions.

HELEN. I understand, but I'm busy, dear.

SUSAN. Because you could be of such help to me.

HELEN. *Yes*, dear.

GEORGE (*who has been showing a growing interest*). Wouldn't you like to sit down?

SUSAN. Oh, thank you. I—

HELEN (*compelled to introduce her*). This is little Miss—

SUSAN. Susan Walker.

HELEN. Susan Walker. She's the little girl I was telling you about.

GEORGE (*to* SUSAN). Are you going to act in the pictures?

HELEN. She wants to—yes. Tell me, Doctor—

SUSAN. I'm going to try to, if I can get started. I don't know very much about it.

HELEN. She doesn't know very much about it.

GEORGE. You could go to our school! May!

SUSAN. What?

HELEN. Yes, yes, of course. Now run along, dear, and read the Book of the Month or something. We're very busy.

SUSAN. Well, but you *will* let me talk to you later, won't you?

HELEN. Yes, of course, dear.

SUSAN. Good-bye. (*Her glance sweeps the others; rests timidly on* GEORGE *for a second*)

GEORGE. Are you right in the next car?

SUSAN. No, I'm in Number 20—with my mother.

HELEN. She's with her mother.

GEORGE. I'll take you back, if you want.

MAY. Yes, you do that, George. That'll be fine.

SUSAN. Oh, thank you very much.

HELEN. You won't stay long, will you Doctor? Because I want to hear more of your ideas. I can see that you've given it thought.

GEORGE (*piloting* SUSAN *out*). No, I'll be right—that is, unless— (*He takes refuge in turning to* SUSAN) —what's your mother's name? Mrs. Walker?

(*They go*)

HELEN. What a man! He must have been enormous in England!

MAY. Very big! Wasn't he?

JERRY. Yes, indeed!

HELEN. May, *do* you think we can keep him in America?

MAY. Jerry, can we keep him in America?

JERRY. I think we can keep him in America.

MAY. I guess we can keep him in America—

HELEN. Marvelous! How much would it cost, May, to start things going?

JERRY. Fifty thousand!

MAY. A hundred thousand!

HELEN. Oh, that's more like it. Now we get to Hollywood Tuesday! On Wednesday everybody gathers at the Stilton—

(*The falling curtain cuts them off*)

SCENE III

(*The gold room of the Hotel Stilton, in Los Angeles. Early de Mille. Gold-encrusted walls, heavy diamond-cut* chandelier, gold brocade hangings and simply impossible settees and chairs. There is an air of such complete phoneyness about the room that an innocent observer, unused to the ways of Hollywood, rather expects a director suddenly to appear from behind a door and yell: "All right, boys! Take it away!"

This particular room, for all its gaudiness, is little more than a passage to the room where Hollywood really congregates—so you can imagine what THAT is like. The evening's function is approaching its height, and through the room, as the curtain rises, there pass various gorgeous couples—one woman more magnificently dressed than another, all swathed in ermine and so hung with orchids that it's sometimes a little difficult to see the girl. The women, of course, are all stunningly beautiful. They are babbling of this and that phase of Hollywood life as they cross the room—"This new thing, dialogue"—"Why didn't you introduce me to him—I just stood there like a fool"—"It wasn't the right time—I'll take you to him when they're ready to cast the picture." Through it all an unseen orchestra is grinding out "Sonny Boy," and it keeps right on playing "Sonny Boy" all evening. Because it seems there was a man named Jolson.

Weaving through the guests is a CIGARETTE GIRL—but not just an ordinary cigarette girl. Like every other girl in Hollywood, she is beautiful enough to take your breath away. Moreover, she looks like Greta Garbo, and knows it. Hers is not a mere invitation to buy her wares: on the contrary, her "Cigars! Cigarettes!" is charged with emotion. You never can tell, of course, when a director is going to come along.

The COAT CHECK GIRL, certainly the most beautiful girl in the world, buttonholes the CIGARETTE GIRL as the crowd thins out)

COAT CHECK GIRL. Say, I got a tip for you, Kate.

CIGARETTE GIRL. Yah?

COAT CHECK GIRL. I was out to Universal today—I heard they was going to do a shipwreck picture.

CIGARETTE GIRL. Not enough sound. They're making it a college picture—glee clubs.

COAT CHECK GIRL. That was this morning. It's French Revolution now.

CIGARETTE GIRL. Yah? There ought to be something in that for me.

COAT CHECK GIRL. Sure! There's a call out for prostitutes for Wednesday.

CIGARETTE GIRL. Say, I'm going out there! Remember that prostitute I did for Paramount?

COAT CHECK GIRL. Yah, but that was silent. This is for talking prostitutes.

(*She drops into a respectful silence as a great procession enters the room. It is headed by* PHYLLIS FONTAINE *and* FLORABEL LEIGH, *two of filmdom's brightest and most gorgeous lights—or at least they were until yesterday, when Sound hit the industry. They are dressed to the hilt and beyond it—ermines, orchids, jewels. Behind each of them walks a* MAID, *and the* MAIDS *are hardly less beautiful than their mistresses. Next come a pair of* CHAUFFEURS—*tall, handsome men, who were clearly cut out to be great lovers, and who will be just as soon as the right director comes along. Each of the* CHAUFFEURS *leads a Russian wolfhound—smartly jacketed animals who are doing their respective bits to celebrate the fame of their mistresses. For on one jacket is lettered: "Phyllis Fontaine in 'Diamond Dust and Rouge,'" and on the other: "Florabel Leigh in 'Naked Souls.'" All in all, it is an imposing procession. Led by its haughty stars, it advances and prepares for the Grand Entrance The maids remove their mistresses' ermine coats: perform those last little powdering rites*)

MISS LEIGH'S CHAUFFEUR. Is the staircase clear?

COAT CHECK GIRL. Yes, it is.

MISS LEIGH'S CHAUFFEUR. The staircase is clear.

MISS LEIGH'S MAID. The staircase is clear, Miss Leigh.

MISS FONTAINE'S MAID. The staircase is clear, Miss Fontaine.

MISS LEIGH'S MAID (*signalling to a* CHAUFFEUR). Boris, please.

(*One of the great dogs is passed over to his mistress*)

MISS FONTAINE'S MAID (*repeating the operation*). Katrina, please.

(*Dogs on leash, they are posed for their moment of triumph. As they sweep out of the room you hear their voices for the first time. May they be charitably described as Pretty Bad?*)

FLORABEL (*from the depths of her bower of orchids*). If they put us at that back table I'm going to raise an awful stink.

PHYLLIS. Yes, God damn it, they ought to know by this time. . . .

(*They are gone. There is a moment's relaxation on the part of the Other Half*)

A CHAUFFEUR. You girls working this week?

CIGARETTE GIRL. No, we ain't.

THE OTHER CHAUFFEUR. Universal's doing a college picture.

(*A* BELLBOY *bounds in*)

BELLBOY. Say, I hear you boys are all set out at Universal! French Revolution picture.

CHAUFFEUR. No, they changed it. It's a college picture.

BELLBOY. It's Revolution again—they just changed it back, down in the Men's Room.

CIGARETTE GIRL. Oh, that's good!

BELLBOY. Yah, on account of the sound. They're going to be playing the guillotine all through. (*He strums an imaginary banjo*)

MAID. That means I'm out of it. I don't know one note from another.

CHAUFFEUR. You can't tell. Let's see what it is in the morning.

(*The* MAIDS *and* CHAUFFEURS *are gone*)

BELLBOY. What do you think happened about five minutes ago? I was down in the Men's Room, singing, and Mr. Katzenstein came in.

COAT CHECK GIRL. That's a break!

CIGARETTE GIRL. Did he hear you?

BELLBOY. You bet he heard me! Said I had a great voice and told me to come and see him! What do you think of that?

COAT CHECK GIRL. Gosh, I wish he'd come into the ladies' room.

(*They go*)

(*There runs on, in great excitement,* MISS SUSAN WALKER. *She is followed by her mother*)

SUSAN. Mother! Come on! Hurry up!

MRS. WALKER. Yes, dear.

SUSAN. This is wonderful here! Look! (*Peers into the next room*) There's where they're all going to eat!

MRS. WALKER. Yes, dear. Don't over-excite yourself.

SUSAN. But mother, imagine! Practically every big star in Hollywood will be here.

MRS. WALKER. Yes, I know, dear.

SUSAN. This is where they come every Wednesday. They're all over the place now. Look! Can you recognize any one?

MRS. WALKER (*peering*). Isn't that John Gilbert?

SUSAN. Where? Where?

MRS. WALKER. Over there! Right near that post!

SUSAN. Mother! That's a waiter!

MRS. WALKER. Well, I'm sure I don't know how one is to tell. Every man we see looks more and more like John Gilbert.

SUSAN. Well, we'll see some of the real ones tonight, mother. Dr. Lewis said we're sure to see everyone.

MRS. WALKER. If there's so many people trying to be picture actors, I'm afraid they'll never give *you* a chance.

SUSAN. Oh, but it's different now—

(*And right now* JOHN GILBERT *himself enters the room. Anyhow it looks like him. It is a careful, measured entrance—obviously designed to impress. With a good deal of deliberation he slowly turns his head, revealing the profile of an Apollo.* SUSAN *and her mother are terrifically impressed. At this moment a new couple enter the room—a dashingly handsome couple, of course*)

THE MAN (*chatting as he enters*). I just saw her downstairs. Wouldn't you think, after the preview of that last picture, that she'd stay home and hide?

THE GIRL. They've no shame, some of them.

THE MAN (*sighting the handsome stranger*). Oh, Ernest!

ERNEST (*for that is indeed his name*). Yes, Mr. Weisskopf?

THE MAN. I'm expecting some guests—two gentlemen and a lady. Will you see that they're brought to my table?

ERNEST (*bowing much too low for John Gilbert*). Yes, sir. Very good, sir.

(*The couple continue their stroll as* SUSAN *and her mother relax in disappointment*)

THE GIRL. Who was that man that came over to Diane's table—must have been one of her new ones, eh?

THE MAN. Must have been.

THE GIRL. I give him about three weeks.

(*They go. The late John Gilbert addresses* SUSAN *and* MRS. WALKER)

ERNEST. Anything I can do for you, Madam?

MRS. WALKER. Why, no, I guess not.

SUSAN. Have any of the stars arrived yet?

ERNEST. Very few, Miss. It's only nine-thirty. There are one or two cowboy stars here, but I don't suppose you'd be interested in them.

SUSAN. Oh, no.

MRS. WALKER. I don't like Westerns very much.

ERNEST. Of course no one of any consequence gets here before ten. You get a smattering of First National and Pathé about nine-thirty, but you don't get United Artists until ten-fifteen.

SUSAN. But they'll all *be* here, won't they?

ERNEST. Oh, yes. Everyone who is of any importance in the industry comes here every Wednesday night.

MRS. WALKER. My, you must find it interesting!

ERNEST. Yes, you get *life* out here. In fact, I get most of the ideas for my scenarios right here in the hotel.

SUSAN. Scenarios? Mother, he's a scenario writer!

MRS. WALKER. Really?

ERNEST (*modestly*). I dabble a bit, that's all.

SUSAN. Have you had any produced? Who was in them?

ERNEST. Well, Paramount is dickering for something of mine right now.

MRS. WALKER. It is?

SUSAN. How proud you must feel!

ERNEST. Well, of course, one never knows.

MRS. WALKER. But to have Paramount dickering!

SUSAN. Who is the story for? I hope it's Greta Garbo.

ERNEST. Well, Miss Garbo's all right, but— (*He breaks off, apparently sighting someone in the next room. The women excitedly follow his gaze*)

SUSAN. Who is it?

ERNEST. I *think*—yes, it is! It's Buddy Rogers!

SUSAN. It is?

MRS. WALKER. Really? Where?

ERNEST. You're very lucky, ladies! Only nine-forty-five and you've got Buddy Rogers!

(*The women rush off, gurgling in their excitement. As* ERNEST *follows them another couple crosses the room, talking as they go*)

THE MAN. So I said to Katzenstein, "Why don't we buy it?

It's the biggest thing in New York to-day—'Strange In-
terlude.' And look at the name you get! Eugene O'Neill!"

THE GIRL. Well, did he write the music too?

THE MAN. No, he just did the libretto. But if we can get
him out here I've got a great guy to team him up with.
He's a little Jewish fellow—

(*They are gone. But already another couple is present*)

THE MAN. What's the use of your meeting him? The part
isn't your type. The girl is eighteen years old and a
virgin.

THE GIRL. Well, I look eighteen under lights, and I can talk
like a virgin.

(*They too depart. On their heels enters* GEORGE—*rather a
bewildered* GEORGE, *a good deal impressed by everything that is going on around him. His eyes take in the
room. The* CIGARETTE GIRL *glides on; finding someone
present, she at once drops into character*)

CIGARETTE GIRL (*in the well-known Garbo manner*). Will
—you—have—some—cigarettes?

GEORGE (*scared*). Why—no. No.

CIGARETTE GIRL (*and from her tone you gather that* GEORGE
is really the father of her child). Very well. I'm—sorry—
I—intruded. (*She goes.* GEORGE *weighs his decision for
a moment, then decides that he had better get out of
there. Before he can do so, however,* SUSAN *rushes in*)

SUSAN. Hello, George. Isn't it exciting? Seeing all the stars
and everything!

GEORGE. I should say so!

SUSAN. I left mother at the staircase, watching them all
walk down. Hollywood is even better than I dreamed
it would be! Aren't you crazy about it?

GEORGE. It's wonderful, all right. It kinda reminds me of
the first time I went to the circus—only there's no ele-
phants.

SUSAN. I can hardly wait till I become a star—when I can

do the things they do, and have myself pointed out to tourists.

GEORGE. I'll tell you something, Susan, if you promise not to breathe it. Who do you think we're going to meet here tonight?

SUSAN. Who?

GEORGE. Herman Glogauer, one of the biggest motion-picture producers in the country.

SUSAN. Really? Oh, George, will you tell him about me—see if he'll give me a part?

GEORCE. Sure. That's what I'm meeting him for.

SUSAN. Oh, George!

(MRS. WALKER *enters in excitement*)

MRS. WALKER. Susan, I just saw—

SUSAN. Mother, what do you think? Dr. Lewis is meeting Herman Glogauer here tonight and he's going to tell him all about me!

MRS. WALKER. Well, isn't that fine? A big man like that coming here to talk about Susan!

SUSAN. Where's he going to be? Right here? Will you introduce me to him?

MRS. WALKER. You just leave it to Dr. Lewis, dear.

GEORGE. I think you'd be just great in talkies—the way you recite and everything. I told May all about those poems you recited. Especially that one—what was it?

MRS. WALKER. "Boots"? By Rudyard Kipling?

GEORGE. Yes, that's it.

SUSAN (*to a pedal accompaniment*). "Boots, boots, boots, boots, movin' up and down again—Five, seven, nine, eleven, four and twenty miles today—"

GEORGE (*trying to stop her*). Yeah, yeah, that's the one. She told me she sort of felt Susan recited "Boots" from the minute she laid eyes on her. Does she do that one about "It Takes a Heap of Loving to—"

SUSAN. "To Make a House a Home"? Oh, yes.

MRS. WALKER. That's one of her best.

GEORGE. Miss Daniels said you probably did. She felt a lot more things about you, too. I guess she's pretty interested.

MRS. WALKER. Would she want to give her an audition?

GEORGE. I don't think she'll have to. I told her how Susan made me feel—when that man in the poem goes crazy how I felt sort of weak myself—and she said she wouldn't want to take a chance.

MRS. WALKER. You've been wonderful to us, Doctor. I'd just trust Susan anywhere, anywhere with you—I told her today I thought you were the most harmless motion-picture man in the business.

GEORGE. Say, I'm going to try to live up to that.

(MAY *comes in. She's followed by* JERRY)

MAY. Good evening! What's going on here?

MRS. WALKER. Hello, Miss Daniels. Mr. Hyland.

GEORGE. Oh, May! Susan does know that poem, about living in a house or something.

MAY. Sure she does. She knows "Ring Out, Wild Bells," too, don't you, Susan?

MRS. WALKER. That was one of her first ones.

MAY (*to* JERRY). That's five you owe me.

JERRY. O.K.

MRS. WALKER. Well, come on, Susan. We'll get on out. We know you're going to meet Mr. Glogauer.

MAY. Oh, did George tell you we're going to meet Mr. Glogauer?

SUSAN. Oh, yes.

JERRY. Isn't that fine?

GEORGE. I just mentioned it.

MRS. WALKER. I think it's just wonderful, what Dr. Lewis has accomplished.

MAY. How's that?

MRS. WALKER. Just wonderful!

SUSAN. Good-bye.

GEORGE. Good-bye.

MAY. Take care of yourselves. (SUSAN *and* MRS. WALKER *go*) Jerry!

JERRY. Huh?

MAY (*a look at* GEORGE). Would there be some way of making him silent as well as dumb?

GEORGE. I didn't hurt anything.

JERRY (*peering into the next room*). Well, kid, here it is! Hollywood! And was I right? Did you hear 'em downstairs? Scared stiff!

MAY. Not nearly as scared as I am.

JERRY. All we got to do is play our cards right! This is the time and place! Chance to make a million or lose a million!

MAY. Which do you think we ought to do?

JERRY. If things go right for us, May, it won't be long now. And we'll do it in style, too.

GEORGE. What do you mean, Jerry—that you and May are going to get married? Are you, May?

MAY. Look, George, we've got all kinds of things on our mind. You'll be the first to know.

JERRY. Yes, sir, it's all up to how we click with Glogauer—and we'll click with him, too!

GEORGE. He's pretty lucky we came out here.

MAY (*in measured tones*). George, when Mr. Glogauer gets here and you're introduced to him, just say, "Hello." See? In a pinch, "Hello, Mr. Glogauer." Then from that time on—nothing.

GEORGE. But suppose I have a good idea?

MAY. That's when I sing "Aida."

JERRY. Say, Glogauer ought to be getting here. Where's Helen?

MAY. Down talking terms with a couple of hundred movie stars. I was out at Parwarmet to-day. Only twenty-two rooms—just a shack, really.

JERRY. *That* part's all right. She's been damned nice to us.

MAY. Sure. For fifty per cent of the gross she'd be damned nice to Mae West.

(*Outside the door you hear a little crescendo of voices. It is topped by* HELEN HOBART, *bidding her public be patient. She will talk to them all later, the dears. She enters, on the crest of the wave*)

HELEN. My dear, *everyone* is here tonight! And such excitement! Nobody knows where they're at! (*There are greetings from the three, which* HELEN, *in her excitement, rides right over*) And of course, wherever you turn all you hear is Sound! Sound! One has to be very careful whom one insults these days—they may be the very ones to survive!

MAY. Things are pretty well topsy-turvy, aren't they?

HELEN. I should say so! What do you think I just heard? You know that tremendous spectacle the Schlepkin Brothers are putting on—"The Old Testament." Well, Mr. Schlepkin—I mean the oldest of the twelve brothers—the real brains of the business—he used to have the cloak-room privilege in all the West Coast theatres—he just told me that they've stopped work on the picture and they're scrapping the whole thing. They're not going to make anything but talkies from now on!

JERRY. Big people, the Schlepkins. I'd like to meet them.

MAY. Are they all here tonight?

HELEN. Oh, all twelve of them. That shows you what they think of the talkies—it's the first time in years that they've all been in Hollywood at the same time. They generally keep two with their mother—she lives in Brooklyn and they fly back and forth. Such a lovely thought! Why, their aeroplane bill alone is ten thousand dollars a month.

(*The* BELLBOY *enters, followed by two uniformed policemen*)

HELEN. Oh, Mr. Glogauer must be coming now. Is that for Mr. Glogauer?

BELLBOY. Yes, Miss Hobart. His car just drew up.

(*They march out*)

HELEN. They always give him an escort, so he can get through the lobby. If he says "yes" to our little proposition we can turn this into a celebration.

MAY. It's marvelous you were able to get him to come.

JERRY. Yes, indeed.

HELEN. Oh, they'll all come running now. Even the big ones. Besides, Glogauer is scared stiff. He's the man who first turned down the Vitaphone—I told you.

MAY. Oh, yes.

HELEN. Anyhow, that's the story. Of course, he's never admitted it, and no one's ever dared mention it to him.

JERRY. I wouldn't think so.

GEORGE (*ever literal*). What did he turn it down for?

HELEN. He just didn't know, Doctor, what it was going to amount to. He didn't have enough vision. (*As a young girl enters, pleading*) No, dear, not now. Later on, maybe. (*She waves the girl out*) Someone wanted to meet the Doctor.

GEORGE. What?

HELEN. Oh, I lost no time, Doctor, in telling them about you. Isn't it marvelous, May—

(*From outside the door comes a rising tide of voices, presently mounting into a roar. Fighting its way into the room comes a streaming and screaming mob, which the* BELLBOY *and the* POLICEMEN *are trying to hold in check. You hear "Mr. Glogauer!" . . . "Mr. Glogauer!" . . . "Mr. Glogauer, can I have just a minute?" And then the voice of* GLOGAUER—"No, no, no! See me at my office! Write me a letter!" The attendants beat back the mob;* GLOGAUER *finally disentangles himself*)

GLOGAUER. I can't see anyone now! Close the doors! Let's have a little peace here!

(*With no little difficulty the* BELLBOY *and the two* POLICEMEN *get the doors closed.* HERMAN GLOGAUER, *who now stands brushing himself off, emerges as a nervous little man who probably has a bad stomach. You can't go through that kind of thing every day without it's having some effect)*

HELEN (*as the noise subsides*). Well, here's the great man himself—and on time, too! Mr. Glogauer, this is Miss Daniels, Mr. Hyland, and Dr. Lewis.

GLOGAUER. How are you?

BELLBOY (*who has been biding his time*). Mr. Glogauer, are you in the market for a great trio?

GLOGAUER. What? (*For answer the* BELLBOY *and the* PO-LICEMEN *burst loudly into* "*Pale hands I love!*") No, no, no! Go away! Go away!

(*They go*)

MAY. What's all that about?

GLOGAUER. These people!

HELEN. You see, they all know Mr. Glogauer, and they try to show him they can act.

GLOGAUER. It's terrible! Terrible! Everywhere I go, they act at me! Everyone acts at me! If I only go to have my shoes shined, I look down and someone is having a love scene with my pants.

HELEN. That's the penalty of being so big a man.

GLOGAUER. All over the hotel they come at me. Ordinarily I would say, "Let's go out to my house," where we got some peace. But Mrs. Glogauer is having new fountains put in the entrance hall.

HELEN. It's the most gorgeous house, May. You remember —we saw it from the train.

MAY. Oh, yes. With the illuminated dome.

HELEN. And the turrets.

GLOGAUER. In gold leaf.

HELEN. But the *inside,* May! I want you to see his bath-room!

MAY. I can hardly wait.

HELEN. It's the show place of Hollywood! But they can see it some other time—can't they, Mr. Glogauer?

GLOGAUER. Any Wednesday. There is a guide there from two to five. I tell you what you do. Phone my secretary —I send my car for you.

MAY. Why, that'll be wonderful.

HELEN. Yes, and what a car it is! It's a Rolls Royce!

MAY. You don't say?

GEORGE. What year?

(*It is, to say the least, an awkward moment*)

JERRY (*coming to the rescue*). Well, Mr. Glogauer, we understand that you're in the midst of quite a revolution out here.

HELEN. I should say he is!

GLOGAUER. Is it a revolution? And who have we got to thank for it? The Schlepkin Brothers. What did they have to go and make pictures talk for? Things were going along fine. You couldn't stop making money—even if you turned out a *good* picture you made money.

JERRY. There is no doubt about it—the entire motion picture is on the verge of a new era.

HELEN. Mr. Glogauer, I tell you the talkies are here to stay.

GEORGE (*who knows a cue when he hears one*). The legitimate stage had better—

MAY. All right, George.

GLOGAUER. Sure, sure! It's colossal! A fellow sings a couple of songs at 'em and everybody goes crazy! Those lucky bums!

HELEN. He means the Schlepkin Brothers.

GLOGAUER. Four times already they were on their last legs and every time they got new ones. Everything comes to those Schlepkin Brothers! This fellow Lou Jackson— sings these mammies or whatever it is—he comes all the way across the country and goes right to the Schlepkin Brothers.

(*The* BELLBOY *enters*)

BELLBOY. I beg your pardon, Mr. Glogauer?

GLOGAUER. Yes, yes? What is it?

BELLBOY. The twelve Schlepkin Brothers would like to talk to you. They're downstairs.

GLOGAUER. Tell 'em later on. I come down later.

BELLBOY. Yes, sir. (*Goes*)

GLOGAUER. Schlepkin Brothers! I know what they want! They're sitting on top of the world now—with their Lou Jackson—so they try to gobble up everybody! All my life they been trying to get me! Way back in the fur business already, when I had nickelodeons and they only had pennylodeons. Always wanting to merge, merge! And because there's twelve of them they want odds yet!

JERRY. But you can teach your own people to talk! Why not let us take them in hand and give them back to you perfect in the use of the English language?

HELEN. I told you about their school in London—Lady Tree!

MAY. It's entirely a matter of correct breathing, Mr. Glogauer. Abdominal respiration is the keynote of elocutionary training.

JERRY. We'll not only teach your people to talk, Mr. Glogauer, but we'll have them talking as well as you do.

GLOGAUER. Well, I don't ask miracles.

(*Again the* BELLBOY *enters*)

BELLBOY. Mr. Glogauer!

GLOGAUER. Well? Well? What now?

BELLBOY. The Schlepkin Brothers are flying to Brooklyn in half an hour. They say they've got to see you right away.

GLOGAUER. Tell 'em in a minute. And tell Phyllis Fontaine and Florabel Leigh I want to see 'em up here right away. (*To the others*) Two of my biggest stars. (*To the* BELLBOY) Tell 'em to come up alone—without any of the Schlepkin Brothers.

BELLBOY. Yes, sir. (*Goes*)

GEORGE. Excuse me—I'll be right back. (*He dashes out*)

GLOGAUER. Phyllis Fontaine—$7500 a week she draws down. And in the old days she was worth it! Every time she undressed in a picture it was sure-fire!

HELEN. The most beautiful legs in America!

GLOGAUER. But you can't hear 'em! That's just the trouble. They're beautiful girls, but unspeakable. You know what I do now? The biggest stage actress in America I am bringing out—from New York. Ten thousand a week I'm paying her! What's her name, anyhow?

HELEN. Dorothy Dodd.

GLOGAUER. That's it! All day I was trying to remember.

(PHYLLIS *and* FLORABEL *return*)

PHYLLIS AND FLORABEL (*in those awful voices*). Hello, Hermie!

GLOGAUER. Ah, here we are, girls! This is the ladies I was telling you about. Phyllis Fontaine and Florabel Leigh.

HELEN. Hello, darlings!

FLORABEL. Hello, Helen!

GLOGAUER. Listen, girls—this is Miss Daniels and Mr. Hyland—voice specialists from England.

PHYLLIS. Voice specialists!

FLORABEL. Whaddye know?

GLOGAUER. Well, here they are, Miss Daniels. This is what I'm up against.

MAY. I'd like to listen to their breathing, if I may, Mr. Clogauer.

HELEN. You know, it's all a question of breathing.

JERRY. That's the whole story!

MAY. May I ask if you ladies have ever breathed rhythmically?

PHYLLIS. What?

FLORABEL. Why, not that I know of.

MAY. You see, rhythmic breathing is the basis of all tonal quality.

JERRY. It's the keynote.

MAY. If you are able to breathe rhythmically then there is every reason to believe that you will be able to talk correctly.

HELEN. That's right!

GLOGAUER. Well—what about it? (*To the girls*) Can you do it?

MAY (*as the girls look blank*). If you'll permit me, I think I can tell you.

GLOGAUER (*impressed*). Sure, sure.

(*There is a momentous silence as* MAY *goes to* PHYLLIS *and puts her head to her chest*)

MAY. Will you please breathe? (*She listens a moment; then raises her head. They expect some word; the suspense is terrific*)

GLOGAUER. Well?

HELEN. Sssh!

(MAY *passes on to* FLORABEL)

MAY. Please breathe. (*She repeats the operation.* GLOGAUER *is on edge*)

GLOGAUER (*when it is over*). Well? How about it? (MAY *nods, sagely*)

GLOGAUER. We got something?

MAY (*quietly*). Absolutely.

HELEN. Isn't that wonderful?

PHYLLIS. We can do it?

GLOGAUER. Keep still, girls! We got something, huh? We ain't licked yet? What's next? What do they do now?

MAY. For the present they should just keep breathing.

GLOGAUER. Hear that, girls? Wait around—don't go home. Now I tell you how we handle this! I give you rooms right in the studio and as fast as you turn 'em out we put 'em right to work! We got to work fast, remember?

JERRY. Right!

MAY. Right!

GLOGAUER. You teach these people to talk and it's worth all the money in the world!

JERRY. We'll teach 'em.

GLOGAUER. You people came just at the right time! We'll show 'em—with their Lou Jackson! This is a life saver! To hell with the Schlepkin Brothers!

(GEORGE, *breathless, runs back into the room, dragging* SUSAN *after him. You begin to understand what he went out for*)

GEORGE (*indicating* GLOGAUER). There he is, Susan! Right there!

SUSAN (*rushing right up to him and starting in*). "Boots," by Rudyard Kipling.

GLOGAUER. What?

SUSAN (*making the most of her opportunity*). "Boots, boots, boots, boots—"

GLOGAUER. What? What? I don't want any boots!

SUSAN. "Marchin' up and down again . . ."

(*The* BELLBOY *again returns*)

BELLBOY. The Schlepkin Brothers!

(*As* SUSAN *continues her recitation the* SCHLEPKIN BROTH-ERS *march in. And when the* SCHLEPKIN BROTHERS *march in they march in. There are twelve of them—all shapes and sizes. Two abreast, they head for* GLOGAUER)

MOE SCHLEPKIN (*at the head of the line*). Listen, Herman, we're flying back to New York tonight—

GLOGAUER. No, sir! I wouldn't merge! I got something better! I wouldn't merge!

SUSAN. "Five, seven, nine, eleven, four and twenty miles today . . ."

The curtain is down

ACT TWO

(*The scene is the reception room at the Glogauer studio,
and it may be briefly described as the God-damnedest
room you ever saw. Ultra-modernistic in its décor, the
room is meant to impress visitors, and it seldom falls
short of its purpose. The walls are draped in heavy grey
plush, the lighting fixtures are fantastic, and the furniture is nobody's business. It is the sort of room that could
happen only as the reception room of a motion picture
studio. In addition to a semi-circle of chairs, designed
for those who are hopefully waiting, the furniture in-
cludes one desk—modernistic as hell, but a desk. It belongs to the reception secretary, who is seated there at
the moment, languidly examining this paper and that.
She is pretty much like the furniture. She wears a flowing black evening gown, although it is morning, fondles
a long string of pearls, and behaves very much like
Elinor Glyn*)

(*Also present is* LAWRENCE VAIL—*a nervous young man
who is waiting, none too comfortably, in one of the
modernistic chairs. He wears the hunted look of a man
who has been waiting for days and days, and is still
waiting*)

(*Things are buzzing—the telephone is ringing; an office girl is crossing the room with papers*)

MISS LEIGHTON (*for that is the name of the Reception Secretary*). Miss Leighton at this end. (*She is answering
the 'phone, it might be explained*)

OFFICE GIRL (*putting papers on desk*). Requisition Department! (*She goes*)

MISS LEIGHTON. Requisition right!

(*Two men, named* METERSTEIN *and* WEISSKOPF, *cross the room*)

WEISSKOPF. But the important thing is your retakes.

METERSTEIN. That's it—your retakes.

WEISSKOPF. You take your retakes, and if they aren't good you've got no picture.

METERSTEIN. Oh, it's the retakes.

WEISSKOPF. Yeh, it's the retakes, all right.

(*They are gone*)

MISS LEIGHTON (*on 'phone through all this*). I shall have to consult the option department . . . Oh, no, all options are taken care of by the option department . . . That would be Mr. Fleming of the option department . . . Correct! (*Hangs up*)

(*There is quiet for a second. Then a* Page *enters, wearing a simply incredible uniform—all gold braid and tassels. He carries an illuminated sign, on which is lettered:* MR. GLOGAUER IS ON NUMBER FOUR. *He shows the sign to* MISS LEIGHTON, *who acknowledges it with a little nod, then to* VAIL, *whose nod is a shade more vicious. A nasty fellow, this* VAIL. *As the* PAGE *goes the telephone rings again*)

MISS LEIGHTON. Miss Leighton at this end . . . Who . . . Oh, yes. Yes, he knows you're waiting . . How many days? . . . Well, I'm afraid you'll just have to wait . . . What? . . . Oh, no, you couldn't possibly see Mr. Glogauer . . . No, I can't make an appointment for you. Mr. Weisskopf makes all Mr. Glogauer's appointments. . . . Oh, no, you can't see Mr. Weisskopf . . . You can only see Mr. Weisskopf through Mr. Meterstein . . . Oh no, no one *ever* sees Mr. Meterstein. (*She hangs up*)

(*Another* PAGE *enters with a sign reading:* MR. WEISSKOPF IS ON NUMBER EIGHT. *Clicks his heels in military fashion;* VAIL *must again nod a response*)

(*A third* PAGE *enters, with some papers, which he gives to* MISS LEIGHTON)

PAGE. Waiting to see Miss Daniels.

MISS LEIGHTON. Miss Daniels is still busy with the ten
o'clock class. Take them into Number Six. I will be there
in three minutes.

PAGE. Number Six in three minutes. Yes, Miss Leighton.
(*He goes*)

(*A couple of men come in*—SULLIVAN *and* MOULTON, *their
names are*)

SULLIVAN. Get it? She makes believe she's falling for this
rich bozo—to save her sister, do you see?—*and the show
goes on!* Plenty of spots for numbers in the revue scenes
—are they ready for us, sister?

MISS LEIGHTON. Waiting for you, Mr. Sullivan. Number
Ten.

SULLIVAN (*hardly stopping*). And the kid sister thinks she's
double-crossing her. Of course she sees her kissing this
fellow—

(*Another man comes on. The name, if it matters, is* OLIVER
FULTON)

FULTON. Hello, boys.

SULLIVAN. Hello, Ollie—you're just in time. They're waiting
to hear it.

FULTON. O.K.

SULLIVAN. Wait till I tell you the new twist. She makes believe she's falling for the rich guy—for her sister's sake,
get it?

FULTON. And the show goes on! For God's sake, Art, I told
you that at lunch yesterday.

SULLIVAN. Did you?

FULTON. I don't mind your stealing from Fox or Metro—
that's legitimate—but if we steal our own stuff we'll
never know where we are.

(*They go. The 'phone again*)

MISS LEIGHTON. Miss Leighton at this end . . . No, Miss
Daniels is still with the ten o'clock class . . . Oh, no,

the lisp and nasal throat toners are at one . . . Didn't
you receive the notification? . . . I'll have Miss Daniels'
secretary send you one. . . . You're welcome. (*Another*
PAGE. *Another sign*) (MISS LEIGHTON *finally notices* VAIL)
I beg your pardon, but I forget whom you're waiting to
see.

VAIL. I don't wonder.

MISS LEIGHTON. I beg your pardon?

VAIL. I am waiting to see Mr. Clogauer.

MISS LEIGHTON. Mr. Glogauer is on Number Nine.

VAIL. Napoleon just informed me.

MISS LEIGHTON. How's that?

VAIL. I said Lord Nelson just came in here with a sign.

MISS LEIGHTON. Have you an appointment with Mr. Glogauer?

VAIL. Yes, ma'am—direct. Right through Mr. Meterstein to
Mr. Weisskopf to Mr. Glogauer.

MISS LEIGHTON. If you'll give me your name I'll tell Mr.
Weisskopf.

VAIL. My name is Lawrence Vail. I gave it to you yesterday, and the day before that, and the day—I would like
to see Mr. Glogauer.

MISS LEIGHTON. I'll tell Mr. Weisskopf.

VAIL. I'm ever so much obliged.

MISS LEIGHTON (*as the 'phone rings again*). Miss Leighton
at this end . . . Yes . . . Yes . . . Very well—holding
the line for thirty seconds.

(*A* PAGE *enters with a sign reading:* MR. WEISSKOPF IS ON
NUMBER SIX. *Shows it*)

VAIL. Thank you so much.

FIRST PAGE. You're welcome, sir.

VAIL. Wait a minute. Now I'll give you a piece of news. I'm
going to the Men's Room and if anybody wants me I'll
be in Number Three. (*He goes. So does the* PAGE)

MISS LEIGHTON (*continuing into telephone*). Miss Leighton at this end. . . . You will receive yesterday's equipment slips in seven minutes. Kindly have Mr. Weisskopf O.K. them. Thank you. (*Hangs up*)

(PHYLLIS *and* FLORABEL *come in*)

PHYLLIS (*as she enters*). . . . by the seashore. She sells seashells by the seashore.

FLORABEL. Sixty simple supple sirens, slick and smiling, svelte and suave.

PHYLLIS. Ain't it wonderful, Miss Leighton? We can talk now.

MISS LEIGHTON. Really?

FLORABEL. Yes, and a damn sight better than most of them.

MISS LEIGHTON. I think your progression has been just marvelous. I can't see why they keep bringing people from New York.

FLORABEL. Yeh—people from the "legitimate" stage, whatever that is.

PHYLLIS. Yes, Miss Leighton, we've been wondering about that. What the hell *is* the legitimate stage, anyway?

MISS LEIGHTON. It's what Al Jolson used to be on before he got famous in pictures. He worked for some real estate people—the Shuberts.

FLORABEL. Do you know what someone told me at a party the other day? They said John Barrymore used to be on the legitimate stage.

PHYLLIS. I heard the same thing and I didn't believe it.

MISS LEIGHTON. My, you'd never know it from his acting, would you?

FLORABEL. And that ain't all. I heard that since *he's* made good some sister of his is trying to get out here.

MISS LEIGHTON. Yes, Elsie Barrymore. . . . It must have been kind of interesting, the legitimate stage. Of course, it was before my time, but my grandfather used to go to it. He was in the Civil War, too.

PHYLLIS. The Civil War—didn't D. W. Griffith make that?

(MAY *enters*)

MAY. Got a cigarette, Miss Leighton?

MISS LEIGHTON. Right here, Miss Daniels.

PHYLLIS. Oh, Miss Daniels! I got the seashells.

FLORABEL. And I got the supple sirens.

MAY. Well, that's fine. But I won't be happy till you get the rigor mortis.

PHYLLIS. Oh, that'll be wonderful!

FLORABEL. I can hardly wait!

(*They go*)

MISS LEIGHTON. There are some people outside for the ten o'clock class, Miss Daniels. Are you ready for them? They're the stomach muscles and abdominal breathing people.

MAY. You heard the girls' voices just now, Miss Leighton.

MISS LEIGHTON. Yes, Miss Daniels.

MAY. How did they sound to you?

MISS LEIGHTON. Oh, wonderful, Miss Daniels.

MAY. You didn't hear anything about their tests, did you? Whether Mr. Glogauer has seen 'em yet?

MISS LEIGHTON. No, I haven't. But I'm sure they'll be all right.

MAY. Thanks.

MISS LEIGHTON. Miss Daniels, I know you're very busy, but sometime I'd like you to hear me in a little poem I've prepared. "Boots" by Rudyard Kipling.

MAY (*smiling weakly*). Fine. I've never heard "Boots."

MISS LEIGHTON. I've been having some trouble with the sibilant sounds, but my vowels are open all right.

MAY. Any fever?

(*A* PAGE *enters*)

PAGE. Miss Leighton, please!

MISS LEIGHTON. Excuse me. (*Her eyes sweep the message*) Oh, dear! Some of the nasal throat toners are out there with the abdominal breathers. What shall I do about it?

MAY. Tell 'em to pick out two good ones and drown the rest.

MISS LEIGHTON. How's that?

MAY. Oh, send 'em in. I'll make one job of it.

MISS LEIGHTON. Yes, ma'am. (*To* PAGE) Understand?

(*The* PAGE *goes*)

(JERRY *comes briskly in*)

JERRY. Say, May! (*His watch*) You've got a class waiting, haven't you?

MAY. I know.

JERRY. Oh, Miss Leighton—Mr. Glogauer busy? I want see him.

MISS LEIGHTON. Afraid he is, Mr. Hyland.

JERRY. Tell him I've got some figures on the school—just take a minute.

MISS LEIGHTON. I'll tell him. But he has conference after conference all morning. In fact, at 11:57 two of his conferences overlap. I'm so ashamed. (*Goes*)

JERRY. Well, the old school is working on high, isn't it?

MAY. Jerry, are you busy for lunch?

JERRY. Afraid I am, May. Booked up pretty solid for the next two days.

MAY. Oh, I see.

JERRY. Kinda hard finding time for everything.

MAY. Isn't it, though?

JERRY. This school's a pretty big thing. You don't realize, just with the classes. But the business end keeps a fellow tied down.

MAY. Of course, Jerry. I suppose you're busy tonight?

JERRY (*nods*). Party up at Jack Young's.

MAY. Ah, yes. Still I—I would like to have a little chat with you—sometime.

JERRY. Why? Anything special?

MAY. We haven't really had a talk for—of course, I kinda expected to see you last night—

JERRY. Oh, yes. Sorry about that, May, but I knew you'd understand. Got to trot with the right people out here.

I'm meeting everybody, May. I was sorry I had to break
that date with you, but—

MAY. Oh, that's all right about the date, Jerry. I wouldn't
bother you, but I do think it's kind of important.

JERRY. Why? What's happened?

MAY. Oh, nothing's happened, but—Glogauer was supposed to hear those tests last night, wasn't he?

JERRY. Sure—you mean Leigh and Fontaine?

MAY. Well, what about them? We haven't heard anything
yet.

JERRY. How do you mean—you're not nervous, are you?
He just hasn't got round to it.

MAY. He was pretty anxious to get 'em—calling up all
afternoon.

JERRY. Say! He's probably heard 'em already and buying
up stories—that's more like it! Stop worrying, May! We
haven't got a thing in the world to worry about. We're
sitting pretty. (*Goes*)

(MAY *stands looking after him a moment. She is worrying,
just the same.* GEORGE *appears, brightly. He carries a
single book*)

GEORGE. May!

MAY. What is it?

GEORGE. Is it stomach in and chest out or stomach out and
chest in or the other way around?

MAY. Huh?

GEORGE. I've got the class all in there with their chests out
and now I don't know what to do about it.

MAY. George, are you fooling with that class again?

GEORGE. I was just talking to them till you got ready.

MAY. Look, George. You know that big comfortable chair
over in the corner of my office?

GEORGE. You mean the blue one?

MAY. That's right. Will you go and just sit in that, until
about February?

GEORGE. Huh?

MAY. You know, I'm only one lesson ahead of that class myself. That's all we need yet—your fine Italian hand.

GEORGE. My what?

MAY. That's all right.

GEORGE. May!

MAY. Yes?

GEORGE. Susan's doing all right in the school, isn't she?

MAY. Sure—great.

GEORGE. She's got a new poem that would be fine for a voice test.

MAY. All right, George.

GEORGE. "Yes, I'm a tramp—what of it? Folks say we ain't no good—"

MAY. Yes, George!

GEORGE. "Once I was strong and handsome—"

MAY. George, will you go on in there?

GEORGE. She does it wonderful, May. Susan's a wonderful girl, don't you think?

MAY. Yes, George.

GEORGE. She's the kind of girl I've always been looking for. And she says *I* am, too.

MAY. George, it isn't serious between you two, is it?

GEORGE. Well, Susan says she won't get married until she's carved out her career.

MAY. Oh, that's all right, then.

GEORGE. She likes me—*that* part of it's all right—but she says look at Eleanora Duse—her career almost ruined by love. Suppose I turned out to be another D'Annunzio?

MAY. She's certainly careful, that girl.

GEORGE. May, now that the school's a success, what about you?

MAY. What?

GEORGE. What about you and Jerry?

MAY. Jerry's a busy man these days, George. We've de
cided to wait.

GEORGE. Oh!

MAY. Just the minute there's any news, I'll let you know.

GEORGE. Thanks, May.

MAY. Before *you* tell *me*.

GEORGE. It was a wonderful idea of Jerry's—coming out
here. I guess you must be pretty proud of him.

MAY (*nods*). I'm working on a laurel wreath for Jerry,
evenings.

GEORGE. I won't say anything about it—it'll be a surprise.

MAY. Look, George. Even when Susan has carved out her
career—and I want to be there for the carving—you
just do a good deal of figuring before you get married.
And you come to me before you take any steps. Understand?

GEORGE. Why? I love Susan, May.

MAY. I understand, but of course all kinds of things can
happen. You never can tell.

GEORGE. Can happen to Susan, you mean?

MAY. I'll tell you what might happen to Susan. She's going
to be reciting "Boots" some day, and a whole crowd of
people is going to start moving toward her.

GEORGE. With contracts?

MAY. Well, contracts and—

(*A* PAGE *enters*)

PAGE. There's a lady asking for Miss Susan Walker.

MRS. WALKER (*entering on the heels of the* PAGE). Oh,
Miss Daniels, can Susan get away for a little while?
Hello, Doctor! You won't mind if Susan goes away for a
little while, will you?

MAY. No, no.

GEORGE. Is anything the matter?

MRS. WALKER. It's nothing to worry about—Susan's father
is going to call us up—long distance. Down at the hotel

in ten minutes—that really leaves us nine minutes. He
sent a telegram and says he wants to talk to us.

GEORGE. Well, I'll get Susan. Will it be all right if I went
along with you, while you telephoned?

MRS. WALKER. Why, I'd love to.

GEORGE. You don't care, do you, May?

MAY. No, indeed.

GEORGE (*calling*). Susan! (*He hurries off*)

MAY (*about to withdraw*). I'm awfully sorry, but—

MRS. WALKER. Oh, Miss Daniels! Please don't go! I wonder
if I could talk to you about Susan? I mean about how
she's getting along in the school?

MAY (*hooked*). Of course.

MRS. WALKER. I've been kind of worried about her lately.
You do think she's doing all right?

MAY. Oh, sure. I—ah—I think she's got Garbo licked a
dozen ways.

MRS. WALKER. Really, Miss Daniels? What at?

MAY. Oh, pretty near everything. Crocheting—

MRS. WALKER. Oh, I'm so happy to hear you say that, because her father gets so impatient. I've tried to explain
to him that it isn't so easy out here, even if you're the
kind of an actress Susan is.

MAY. It's even harder if you're the kind of an actress Susan
is.

MRS. WALKER. Of course. Then last week I wrote and told
him what you said about her—you know—that you
thought Technicolor would help? And he said for me
to say to you—that you are doing the most courageous
work out here since the earthquake. I couldn't understand what he was driving at.

MAY. Thanks. Just tell Mr. Walker that I'm doing the best
I can, and that the Red Cross is helping me.

MRS. WALKER. Oh, yes, it's a wonderful organization—
(GEORGE *and* SUSAN *run in*)

SUSAN. Mother, what does father want?

GEORGE. We've got six minutes!

MRS. WALKER. I don't know, dear. My, we've got to hurry. Six minutes. We mustn't keep Mr. Walker waiting.

GEORGE. What kind of a man is he, Mrs. Walker? Do you know him very well?

(*They are gone.* MAY *alone is left. Back comes* VAIL—*a nod to* MAY, *who returns it in kind. Immediately* VAIL *sinks into his chair again*)

MAY (*surveying him*). Isn't there some disease you get from sitting?

VAIL. If there is, I've got it.

MAY. What do you do about your meals—have them sent in?

VAIL. What's the record for these chairs—do you happen to know?

MAY. I'm not sure—I think it was a man named Wentworth. He sat right through Coolidge's administration.

(*A* GIRL *peeps in through one of the doors*)

GIRL. Oh, Miss Daniels, we're waiting for you.

MAY. What?

GIRL. We're still breathing in here.

MAY (*rolling up a sleeve*). Yah? Well, I'll put a stop to that. (*She goes*)

(VAIL *is alone. He rises; goes to the table and inspects a magazine. He gives it up for another, which he also glances idly through. Takes it back to his seat, drops it onto the chair and sits on it*)

(MISS LEIGHTON *enters. Sees* VAIL. *It is as though she had never seen him before*)

MISS LEIGHTON. Yes?

VAIL. Don't you remember me, Princess? I'm the Marathon chair warmer.

MISS LEIGHTON. What is the name, please?

VAIL. Lawrence Vail. I am waiting to see Mr. Glogauer.

MISS LEIGHTON. Oh, yes. I gave him your name, but he doesn't seem to remember you. What was it about, please?

VAIL. It's about a pain in a strictly localized section.

MISS LEIGHTON. How's that?

(RUDOLPH KAMMERLING, *a German director, enters. He is in a mood*)

KAMMERLING. Where is Mr. Glogauer, Miss Leighton? Get hold of him for me right away.

MISS LEIGHTON. He's on Number Eight, Mr. Kammerling.

KAMMERLING. I just come from Number Eight—he is not there.

MISS LEIGHTON. Then he must be in conference with the exploitation people, Mr. Kammerling.

KAMMERLING. Maybe he is just through. Try his office.

MISS LEIGHTON. I've just come by there. He isn't in his office.

KAMMERLING. Gott in Himmel, he must be *some* place. Try number eight again.

MISS LEIGHTON. Yes, sir.

KAMMERLING (*pacing nervously up and down*). For two cents I would go back to Germany and Ufa!

MISS LEIGHTON (*at 'phone*). Number Eight! Mr. Kammerling calling Mr. Glogauer! Imperative!

KAMMERLING. America! Reinhardt begged me not to come! On his knees in the Schauspielhaus he begged me!

MISS LEIGHTON. Hello? Mr. Glogauer not there? Just a moment. . . . He isn't there, Mr. Kammerling. Any message?

KAMMERLING (*beside himself—shouting*). Yes! Tell them I take the next boat back to Germany! Wait! Who is it on the phone?

MISS LEIGHTON. Mr. Weisskopf.

KAMMERLING. Give it to me! (*Takes the phone;* MISS LEIGHTON *leaves*) Hello! This is Kammerling . . . How much publicity is there sent out on Dorothy Dodd?

. . . What? . . . We are lost! . . . Why? I tell you why? Because I have just seen her and she is impossible! I will not ruin my American career! . . . (*Hangs up*) What a country! Oh, to be in Russia with Eisenstein! (*He storms out*)

(TWO ELECTRICIANS *enter. They carry work kits, and they're tough specimens*)

1ST ELECTRICIAN. You take all this studio equipment—they don't know what they're getting when they buy this stuff.

2ND ELECTRICIAN. They certainly pick up a lot of junk.

1ST ELECTRICIAN. Look at that base plug—torn half way out of the socket. Socket all wrenched out of shape, too. Haven't got a new one in your bag, have you?

2ND ELECTRICIAN. Don't think so. Wait a minute. (*He looks through his tools, whistling as he does so*) No. Nothing doing.

1ST ELECTRICIAN. No use till we get one— it's all torn out. (*The other man, while packing up his tools, shakes his head. Still whistling*) Say, what is that? (*The* 2ND ELECTRICIAN *whistles a bit further—interrogatively, as if to inquire if he was referring to the melody*) Yah—is it yours? (*Still whistling, the other man nods*) Start it again. (*He does so; whistles a phrase*) I think I got the lyric. (*He improvises to the other man's whistling*)

"By a babbling brook at twilight.
Once there sat a loving twain —"

2ND ELECTRICIAN. That's great!

1ST ELECTRICIAN (*Hotly*). And this one doesn't go to Paramount, after the way they treated us.

(*They go, whistling and singing*)

(MISS LEIGHTON *enters; notices* VAIL. *As usual, she never saw him before*)

MISS LEIGHTON. Yes?

VAIL (*ready to commit murder*). Say it ain't true, Duchess —say you remember?

MISS LEIGHTON. Oh, yes. An appointment, wasn't it?

VAIL. That's it—an appointment. I got it through a specu-
lator. Listen, maybe this will help. I work here. I have
an office—a room with my name on the door. It's a big
room, see? In that long hall where the authors work?
The people that write. Authors! It's a room—a room
with my name in gold letters on the door.

MISS LEIGHTON (*visibly frightened by all this*). What was
the name again?

VAIL. Lawrence Vail.

MISS LEIGHTON. Oh, you're Lawrence *Vail*. Well, I'll tell
Mr. Weisskopf—

VAIL (*stopping her*). No, no! Nothing would come of it.
Just let the whole thing drop. Life will go on. Only tell
me something—they make talking pictures here, is that
right?

MISS LEIGHTON. What?

VAIL. This is a picture studio? They make pictures here
—pictures that talk? They do *some*thing here, don't
they?

MISS LEIGHTON (*edging away*). I'll tell Mr. Weisskopf—

VAIL. Don't be afraid of me, little girl. I'll not harm you.
It's just that I've been in that room—my office—the
place with my name on the door—for months and
months—nobody ever noticed me—alone in there—the
strain of it—it's been too much. And so I came out. I
don't expect to see Mr. Glogauer any more—I just want
to go in and wander around. Because tomorrow I'm
going home, and I want to tell them I saw 'em made.
Who knows—maybe I'll run into Mr. Glogauer—I'd
love to know what God looks like before I die. (*He
goes*)

MISS LEIGHTON. Yes—yes—I'll tell Mr. Weisskopf. (*Sinks
into her chair*)

(HELEN HOBART *bustles in*)

HELEN. Good morning, Miss Leighton!

MISS LEIGHTON (*weakly*). Good morning.

HELEN. My dear, what *is* the matter? You're shaking.

MISS LEIGHTON. There was a drunken man in here just now.

HELEN. You poor child. Well, they'll soon be weeded out —Will Hays is working as fast as he can.

MISS LEIGHTON. Yes, I know.

HELEN. Dorothy Dodd get here, Miss Leighton?

MISS LEIGHTON. Yes, she got in this morning.

HELEN. I do want to meet her. You know, more people have told me I look like her. . . . Tell me, Miss Leighton. My paper wants me to try to find— (*Delving into bag*)—what *is* his name? He works here.. (*Finds slip of paper*) Lawrence Vail.

MISS LEIGHTON. Lawrence Vail? No, I don't think I ever heard of him. Is he a director?

HELEN. No, no, he's a playwright. From New York. He's supposed to have come out here a long time ago and nothing's been heard of him. He seems to have just disappeared.

MISS LEIGHTON. Why, isn't that terrible? Have you tried Paramount?

HELEN. No, he's not at Paramount. They've lost six playwrights of their own in the past month. Once they get out of their rooms nobody knows what becomes of them. You'd think they'd lock the doors, wouldn't you?

MISS LEIGHTON (*going to her desk and taking a stack of cards from a drawer*). Yes—that's what we do. (*Looking through cards*) Lawrence Vail. I'm sure he isn't one of our playwrights, because if he was I'd be sure to— (*Finds the card*)—well, isn't that strange? He *is* one of our playwrights. (*Reads*) "Lawrence Vail."

HELEN (*looking over her shoulder*). That's the man.

MISS LEIGHTON (*eyes on card*). Yes—he came out here on Oct. 18. "From New York City." He was one of a shipment of sixteen playwrights.

HELEN (*reading*). "Dark hair, brown eyes—"

(MAY *returns*)

MAY. Oh, hello, Helen.

HELEN (*with no warmth whatever*). May, dear.

MISS LEIGHTON. Suppose I look in the playwrights' room. Maybe he's there.

HELEN. Oh, thanks, Miss Leighton. Shall I come along with you?

MISS LEIGHTON. No, if he's there I'll find him. Though I hate to go into the playwrights' room. It always scares me—those padded walls, and the bars over the windows. (*She goes*)

HELEN (*plainly anxious to slide out*). My, nearly twelve o'clock! I'd no idea!

MAY. Oh, must you go? You're quite a stranger these days.

HELEN. Yes—the mad, mad pace of Hollywood! I have two luncheons to go to—the Timken Ball Bearing people are having a convention here and it's also the fifth anniversary of Golden Bear cookies.

MAY. Well, if you have just a minute—

HELEN. The cookie people are so prompt—

MAY. I just wondered how you thought everything was going, Helen.

HELEN. Oh, wonderful, wonderful! You know, my column is being translated into Spanish now—they'll be reading it way over in Rome.

MAY. Yes, that's fine. But what I was going to ask you was —have you heard anything about the school lately?— how everybody thinks it's going?

HELEN (*evasively*). Well, of course you'd know more than I do about that—after all, it's *your* enterprise. Naturally I'd be the last person to—

MAY. Then you *have* heard something, haven't you, Helen? Who from—Glogauer?

HELEN. Why, of course not, May—whatever gave you such an idea? Of course you never can tell about things out here—sometimes something will just happen to catch on, and then again—*well!*

(*The final "Well!" is a sort of grand dismissal of the subject, coupled with relief at having got that far. She is on the verge of departure*)

MAY (*with quiet dignity*). Thanks, Helen. I'm very grateful.

HELEN. Well, I—ah— (*Turning to her*) I don't imagine you've made any plans?

MAY. Not yet.

HELEN. After all, I suppose you've got all of your friends in England—it's only natural that—

MAY. Oh, yes. All of them.

HELEN. Well, I may be coming over in the spring—and if I do we must get together.

MAY. By all means.

HELEN. Well! (*She beams on her*) Bon voyage! (*She goes. MAY stands looking after her. A gentleman named MR. FLICK, carrying various strange boxes, looms in the doorway*)

FLICK. Pardon me, but can you tell me where I am?

MAY. What?

FLICK. I'm looking for the office of— (*Takes out paper*) —Miss May Daniels.

MAY. Huh?

FLICK (*reading*). Miss May Daniels, Mr. Jerome Hyland, Dr. George Lewis.

MAY. I'm Miss Daniels. What do you want?

FLICK. Oh, I don't want you. I just want to know where your office is.

MAY (*a gesture*). Right through there.

FLICK. Thanks. (*Starts*)

MAY. You won't find anybody in there.

FLICK. Oh, that's all right. I've only got to do some work on the door.

MAY. Oh! On the door?

FLICK. I just gotta take the names off.

MAY. You mean Daniels, Hyland and Lewis are coming off the door?

FLICK. That's right.

MAY. So that's your business, is it—taking names off doors?

FLICK. Well, I put 'em on too. I do more door work than anybody else in Hollywood. Out at Fox the other day I went right through the studio—every door. Why, some of the people didn't even know they were out till they saw me taking their names off.

MAY. Must have been a nice surprise.

FLICK. Yes, sometimes they leave their office and go out to lunch and by the time they get back it says Chief Engineer.

MAY. We aren't even out to lunch.

FLICK. Well, if you'll excuse me—

MAY. Yes, you've got your work to do. Well, it's been very nice to have met you.

FLICK. Much obliged.

MAY. You're sure you know where it is? Right at the end of the corridor—see?

FLICK. Oh, yes. Miss May Daniels, Mr. Jerome Hyland— (*He is gone*)

(MAY *stands at the door a moment. A few office workers come in and go again—things are pretty busy. And then* JERRY. *Brisk, businesslike, whistling gayly*)

MAY (*quietly*). Jerry.

JERRY. Huh?

MAY. Have you got a minute?

JERRY. Gosh, May—afraid I haven't.

MAY. Yes, you have.

JERRY. I've got to see Weisskopf right away.

MAY. No, you don't.

JERRY. What?

MAY. You don't have to see Weisskopf.

JERRY. Yah, but I do.

MAY. No, you don't.

JERRY. What are you talking about?

MAY (*very lightly*). Did you ever hear the story of the three bears?

JERRY. Huh!

MAY. There was the Papa Bear, and the Mama Bear, and the Camembert. They came out to Hollywood to start a voice school—remember! A couple of them were engaged to be married or something—that's right, they were engaged—whatever happened to that?

JERRY. Wha-at?

MAY. Well, anyway, they *did* start a voice school—what do you think of that? They started a voice school, and had a big office, and everything was lovely. And then suddenly they came to work one morning, and where their office had been there was a beautiful fountain instead. And the Mama Bear said to the Papa Bear, What the hell do you know about that?

JERRY. May, stop clowning! What is it?

MAY. And this came as a great big surprise to the Papa Bear, because *he* thought that everything that glittered just *had* to be gold.

JERRY. Say, if you're going to talk in circles—

MAY. All right—I'll stop talking in circles. We're washed up Jerry.

JERRY. What are you talking about?

MAY. I said we're washed up. Through, finished, and out!

JERRY. What do you mean we're out? Why—who said we were out?

MAY. I knew it myself when we didn't hear about those tests—I felt it. And then ten minutes ago Helen Hobart walked in here.

JERRY. What did she say?

MAY. She handed the school right back to us—it seems she had nothing to do with it. That tells the story!

JERRY. That doesn't mean anything! You can't tell from what she says!

MAY. Oh, you can't, eh? Then I'll show you something that does mean something, and see if you can answer this one! (*She starts for the door through which* MR. FLICK *has vanished. The arrival of* GEORGE *stops her*)

GEORGE. May! May, something terrible has happened!

MAY. I know it!

GEORGE. You can't! It's Mr. Walker! Susan has to go back home—they're leaving tomorrow!

JERRY. May, what were you starting to tell me?

GEORGE. Did you hear what I said, May? Susan has got to go back home!

JERRY. Shut up, George! (*To* MAY) What were you going to tell me?

MAY (*breaking in*). For God's sake, stop a minute! George, we've got more important things!

GEORGE. There couldn't be more important things!

JERRY. Oh, for the love of—

MAY. Well, there are! We're fired, George—we haven't got jobs any more!

GEORGE. What?

JERRY. How do you know, May? How do you know we're fired?

MAY. I'll show you how I know! (*She goes to the door and opens it. In a trance, they follow her and look off*)

JERRY (*in a hushed tone*). Gosh!

GEORGE. You mean the window washer?

JERRY (*stunned*). Why—why, I was talking to Glogauer only yesterday—

MAY. Well, there you are, Jerry. So you see it's true.

GEORGE. You mean—you mean there isn't any school any more?

MAY. That's the idea, George.

GEORGE. But—but—why? Then—what about Susan?

MAY. Oh, let up on Susan! Besides, I thought you said she was going home.

GEORGE. Yah, but if we could get her a job right away!

(MR. FLICK *returns with scraper and tool-kit in hand. Crosses cheerfully, with a nod to all*)

MAY. Well, that was quick work.

FLICK. Oh, it don't take long. You see, I never use permanent paint on those doors.

(*A pause after his departure*)

MAY. Well, I suppose we might as well get our things together. (*She looks at the disconsolate figure of* JERRY) Don't take it so hard, Jerry. We've been up against it before.

JERRY. But everything was so—I don't know which way to turn, May. It's kind of knocked me all of a heap.

MAY. Don't let it lick you, Jerry—we'll pull out of it some way. We always have.

JERRY. Yah, but—not this. A thing like this sort of—what are we going to do?

MAY. What do you say we go to Hollywood? I hear they're panic-stricken out there. They'll fall on the necks of the first people—

(*They go*)

(GEORGE *is alone. The two studio men,* METERSTEIN *and* WEISSKOPF, *come in with their interminable chatter*)

WEISSKOPF. But the important thing is your retakes.

METERSTEIN. That's it—your retakes.

WEISSKOPF. You take your retakes and if they aren't good you've got no picture.

METERSTEIN. Oh, it's the retakes.

WEISSKOPF. Yah, it's the retakes, all right.

(*They go*)

(SUSAN *comes in. Pretty low*)

GEORGE (*eagerly*). Susan! Anything happen? After I left?

SUSAN (*forlornly*). I just came back to get my books and things. (*In his arms*) Oh, George!

GEORGE. Susan, you can't go back like this—it isn't fair!
Why, you were just made for the talkies—you and I
both! Did you tell your father we were waiting for
Technicolor?

SUSAN. He just said stop being a God-damn fool and come
on home.

GEORGE. But giving up with your career only half carved!

SUSAN. He wants mother home, too. He says eating all his
meals in restaurants that it's ruining his stomach.

GEORGE. But you've got your own life to live—you can't
give up your career on account of your father's stomach!

SUSAN. It's no use, George. You don't know father. Why,
when the first talking picture came to Columbus he
stood up and talked right back to it.

GEORGE. I guess your father's a pretty hard man to get
on with.

SUSAN. Oh, you don't know, George. It's going to be terrible, going back to Columbus, after all this.

GEORGE. I'm not going to let you go back, Susan. Something's got to be done about it.

SUSAN. But it's so hopeless, George. (*She leaves him*)

(GEORGE *stands a moment, puzzled.* MISS LEIGHTON *enters,
still carrying the* LAWRENCE VAIL *card*)

GEORGE. Could you find Mr. Glogauer for me?

MISS LEIGHTON. Sorry, Doctor—I'm terribly worried. I'm
looking for a playwright, and there's a drunken man
following me all around. (*As she goes* LAWRENCE VAIL
immediately enters. Goes to chair for his coat. GEORGE
*watches him as he brings his magazine back to the
table*)

GEORGE. Excuse me, but have you seen Mr. Glogauer?
(VAIL, *his eyes on* GEORGE, *drops the magazine onto the
table*) I've been trying to find him, but nobody knows
where he is.

VAIL. You one of the chosen people?

GEORGE. What?

VAIL. Do you work here?

GEORGE. Oh! I thought you meant was I—yah. I'm Dr. Lewis.

VAIL. Oh, yes. About Mr. Glogauer. Tell me something —it won't go any further. Have you ever seen Mr. Glogauer?

GEORGE. Oh, yes. Lots of times.

VAIL. Is that so? Actually seen him, huh? I suppose you've been here a good many years.

GEORGE (shakes his head). No. Only about six weeks.

VAIL. Only six weeks. I wouldn't have thought it possible.

GEORGE. Do you work here too?

VAIL. Yes. Yes. You see, Doctor, I'm supposed to be a playwright. Probably it doesn't mean anything to you, but my name is Lawrence Vail. (GEORGE's face is a complete blank) It doesn't mean anything to you, does it?

GEORGE. No.

VAIL. No, I wouldn't have thought so.

GEORGE. Well, is that what you're doing here—writing plays?

VAIL. Not so far I'm not.

GEORGE. Well then, what are you doing?

VAIL (sadly). Don't ask me that. I don't know. I don't know anything about it. I didn't want to come out to this God-forsaken country. I have a beautiful apartment in New York—and friends. But they hounded me, and belabored me, and hammered at me, till you would have thought if I didn't get out here by the fifteenth of October every camera in Hollywood would stop clicking.

GEORGE. You don't say?

VAIL. And so I came. In a moment of weakness I came. That was six months ago. I have an office, and a secretary, and I draw my check every week, but so far no one has taken the slightest notice of me. I haven't received an assignment, I haven't met anybody outside

of the girl in the auditor's office who hands me my
check, and in short, Dr. Lewis, I haven't done a single
thing.

GEORGE. Why do you suppose they were so anxious to have
you come out, then?

VAIL. Who knows? Why do you suppose they have these
pages dressed the way they are, and those signs, and
that woman at the desk, or this room, or a thousand
other things?

GEORGE. Don't you like it out here?

VAIL. Dr. Lewis, I think Hollywood and this darling industry of yours is the most God-awful thing I've ever
run into. Everybody behaving in the most fantastic
fashion—nobody acting like a human being. I'm
brought out here, like a hundred others, paid a fat
salary—nobody notices me. Not that I might be any
good—it's just an indication. Thousands of dollars
thrown away every day. Why do they do that, do you
know?

GEORGE. No, sir.

VAIL. There you are. Plenty of good minds have come out
here. Why aren't they used? Why must everything be
dressed up in this God-damn hokum—waiting in a room
like this, and having those morons thrust a placard
under your nose every minute? Why is that?

GEORGE. I don't know.

VAIL. Me neither. The whole business is in the hands of
incompetents, that's all. But I don't have to stay here,
and I'm not going to. I've tried to see Mr. Glogauer—
God knows I've tried to see him. But it can't be done.
So just tell him for me that he can take his contract and
put it where it will do the most good. I'm going home,
and thank you very much for listening to me.

GEORGE. There's a lot in what you say, Mr. Vail. I've been
having a good deal of trouble myself.

VAIL. You bet there's a lot in what I say. Only somebody ought to tell it to Glogauer.

GEORGE. That's right. Well, look—why don't you make an appointment with Mr. Glogauer and tell him?

(*It is too much for* VAIL. *He goes*)

(GEORGE *is alone. He thinks it over, then decides that action of some sort has to be taken. He goes to the telephone*)

GEORGE. Hello . . . This is Dr. Lewis . . . Dr. Lewis . . . Well, I work here. That is, I—ah—I've got to get in touch with Mr. Glogauer.

(CLOGAUER *and* KAMMERLING *enter, in the middle of a hot argument.* GEORGE, *of course, hangs up the receiver immediately*)

GLOGAUER. What can I do about it now? Miss Leighton! Where is Miss Leighton? You know just how we are fixed! What can I do about it at a time like this? You know just who we've got available—what do you want me to do about it?

GEORGE. Mr. Glogauer, could I talk to you for a minute?

KAMMERLING. There is no use of going on! Dorothy Dodd will not do! I will go back to Germany and Ufa before I shoot a foot!

GLOGAUER (*into the 'phone*). Get Miss Leighton for me —right away.

GEORGE. Mr. Glogauer—

GLOGAUER. Do you realize that I brought that woman from New York, took her out of a show, and she's on a play-or-pay contract for the next three months? Besides, she's got a big legit name! Take her out, he says!

(GEORGE, *a little bowled over by the momentum of all this, is between the two fires*)

KAMMERLING. But I will not have my work ruined! She will be terrible—she is not the type!

GLOGAUER. Then go to work on her! What are you a director for?

KAMMERLING. No, no—she is a good actress, but it is the wrong part. The part is a country girl—a girl from the country!

GLOGAUER. Don't I know that?

KAMMERLING. But Dorothy Dodd is not a country girl! She is a woman—a woman who has lived with a dozen men—and looks it! Can I make her over? I am just a director—not God!

GLOGAUER. But if it was explained to her! How long would it take to explain a country girl?

KAMMERLING. But everyone knows about her—it's been in the newspapers—every time they break a door down they find *her*!

GLOGAUER. But what am I to do at a time like this?

KAMMERLING. Get somebody else! Somebody that looks it!

GEORGE. Mr. Glogauer—

KAMMERLING. My work would go for nothing! My work would be ruined!

GLOGAUER. Let me get this straight—you mean she *positively* won't do?

KAMMERLING. *Positively.*

GLOGAUER. Well, if it's positively I suppose there's nothing for it.

KAMMERLING. Ah!

GLOGAUER. We got to get somebody then, and quick!

KAMMERLING. Now you're again the artist! Somebody like Janet Gaynor—she would be fine! Maybe Fox would lend her to you!

GEORGE (*weakly*). I know who could do it.

GLOGAUER. Maybe Warners would lend me John Barrymore! Don't talk foolish Kammerling! I went over our list of people with you and you know just who we've got available.

GEORGE (*stronger this time*). I know somebody could do it.

GLOGAUER. I can't do a magician act—take somebody out of my pocket! You know just who we got!

GEORGE (*making himself heard*). But I know exactly the person!

GLOGAUER. You what?

GEORGE (*excited*). I know an actress who would fit the part perfectly.

KAMMERLING. Who?

GLOGAUER. What's her name? Who is she?

GEORGE. Her name is Susan Walker.

KAMMERLING. Who?

GLOGAUER. I never heard of her. What's she done?

GEORGE. She hasn't done anything.

GLOGAUER. Hasn't done anything! Taking up our time with a girl—we must have a name! Don't you understand? We must have a name!

GEORGE. Why?

GLOGAUER. What's that?

GEORGE. Why must you have a name?

GLOGAUER. Why must we have—go away, go away! Why must we have a name? I spend three hundred thousand dollars on a picture and he asks me—because Susan Walker as a name wouldn't draw flies—that's why! Not flies!

GEORGE. But she could play the part.

GLOGAUER. So what? Who would come to see her? Why do you argue on such a foolish subject? Everybody knows you can't do a picture without a name. What are you talking about?

GEORGE (*his big moment*). Mr. Glogauer, there's something you ought to know.

GLOGAUER. What?

GEORGE. This darling industry of yours is the most God-awful thing I've ever run into.

GLOGAUER. Huh! (*Stares at him*)

GEORGE. Why don't people act human, anyhow? Why are you so fantastic? Why do you go and bring all these people out here, whoever they are, and give them all

this money, and then you don't do anything about it.
Thousands of dollars—right under your nose. Why is
that?

GLOGAUER. Huh?

GEORGE. Can you tell me why in the world you can't make
pictures without having the stars playing parts they
don't fit, just because she's got a good name or something? How about a girl that hasn't got a good name?
And how about all these signs, and this room, and that
girl, and everything? And everything else? It's the most
God-awful—all kinds of people have come out here—
why don't you do something about it? Why don't you
do something about a person like Miss Walker, and give
her a chance? Why, she'd be wonderful. The whole
business is in the hands of incompetents, that's what's
the trouble! Afraid to give anybody a chance! And you
turned the Vitaphone down! (GLOGAUER *gives him a
startled look*) Yes, you did! They're all afraid to tell it
to you! That's what's the matter with this business. It's
in the hands of—you turned the Vitaphone down!

GLOGAUER (*stunned; slowly thinking it over*). By God, he's
right!

GEORGE (*not expecting this*). Huh?

GLOGAUER. He's right! And to stand up there and tell me
that—that's colossal!

GEORGE. You mean what I said?

GLOGAUER. That's what we need in this business—a man
who can come into it, and when he sees mistakes being
made, talk out about them. Yes, sir—it's colossal.

GEORGE (*if it's as easy as that*). Why, it's the most God-
awful thing—

KAMMERLING. Who is this man? Where did he come from?

GLOGAUER. Yes, who are you? Didn't I sign you up or
something?

GEORGE. I'm Dr. Lewis.

GLOGAUER. Who?

GEORGE. You know—the school.

GLOGAUER. You are with the school? But that school isn't any good.

GEORGE (*moved to an accidental assertiveness*). It *is* good!

GLOGAUER. Is it?

GEORGE (*with sudden realization that an emphatic manner can carry the day*). Why, of course it is. You people go around here turning things down—doing this and that—

GLOGAUER (*to* KAMMERLING). He's right! Look—I pretty near fired him! I did fire him.

GEORGE. You see? And here's Susan Walker—just made for the talkies.

GLOGAUER. Say, who is this girl?

KAMMERLING. Where is she?

GLOGAUER. Tell us about her.

GEORGE. Well—Mr. Kammerling knows her—I introduced her.

GLOGAUER. She's here in Hollywood?

GEORGE. Oh, sure! She just went—

KAMMERLING. I remember! She might be able to do it! She is dumb enough.

GEORGE. Shall I bring her in?

GLOGAUER. Yes, yes—let's see her!

GEORGE. She's right out here. (*Rushing out*)

GLOGAUER. Fine, fine! There is a big man, Kammerling! I can tell! Suddenly it comes out—that's the way it always is!

KAMMERLING. In Germany, too!

GLOGAUER. Turned the Vitaphone down—no one ever dared say that to me! I got to hang on to this fellow —take options.

(MISS LEIGHTON *enters*)

MISS LEIGHTON. Did you send for me, Mr. Glogauer?

GLOGAUER. Yes! Where's my coffee? I want my coffee!

MISS LEIGHTON. Yes, Mr. Glogauer—where will you have it?

GLOGAUER. Where will I have it? Where *am* I! Answer me that! Where am I?

MISS LEIGHTON. Why—right here, Mr. Glogauer.

GLOGAUER. All right—then that's where I want my coffee!

MISS LEIGHTON. Yes, sir.

GLOGAUER. And tell Meterstein I want him—right away! And Miss Chasen, with her notebook.

MISS LEIGHTON. Yes, sir. (*Goes*)

GLOGAUER. Now I show you how we handle this! We'll have her and a name too! We'll create a name for her! I've done it before and I do it again!

KAMMERLING. If only she looks like it—

GEORGE (*rushes in with* SUSAN). Here she is, Mr. Glogauer —here she is!

GLOGAUER. Yes! Yes! She can do it! He's right!

KAMMERLING. Ya, ya! Wunderbar!

GEORGE. Of course I'm right.

KAMMERLING. Say "I love you."

SUSAN. "I love you."

KAMMERLING. Ya! Sie kann es thun!

GLOGAUER. That's wonderful!

GEORGE. Sure it is!

GLOGAUER. No time to talk salary now, Miss Walker—but you don't have to worry!

SUSAN. Oh, George!

GEORGE. Susan!

KAMMERLING (*to* SUSAN). "I hate you!"

SUSAN. "I hate you!"

KAMMERLING. Ya, ya!

(MISS CHASEN *enters*)

MISS CHASEN. Yes, Mr. Glogauer?

GLOGAUER. Ah, Miss Chasen! Where's Meterstein? I want Meterstein!

(METERSTEIN *rushes in*)

METERSTEIN. Here I am, Mr. Glogauer!

GLOGAUER. Listen to this, Meterstein! Miss Chasen, take this down! Tell the office to drop everything they're doing and concentrate on this! Drop everything, no matter what it is!

MISS CHASEN (*over her notes*). Drop everything.

GLOGAUER. Wire the New York office that Susan Walker, a new English actress we've just signed, will arrive in New York next week— (*A quick aside to* GEORGE) I want her to go to New York first!

GEORGE. Yes, sir.

SUSAN. Does he mean me?

KAMMERLING. Yes, yes!

GLOGAUER. Have them arrange a reception at the Savoy-Plaza—get her pictures in every paper! Tell them I want her photographed with Mayor Walker!

METERSTEIN. Mayor Walker.

GLOGAUER. I want everybody in the studio to get busy on this right away! Everybody! And get hold of Davis for me right away!

MISS CHASEN. Get Davis!

METERSTEIN (*calling out the door*). Get Davis!

VOICE IN THE DISTANCE. Get Davis!

VOICE STILL FURTHER AWAY. Get Davis!

GLOGAUER. Get hold of Photoplay and Motion Picture Magazine and the trade papers—I want them all! Send for Helen Hobart and tell her I want to see her personally! And I want Baker to handle this—not Davis! Don't get Davis!

METERSTEIN. Don't get Davis!

VOICE IN THE DISTANCE. Don't get Davis!

VOICE STILL FURTHER AWAY. Don't get Davis!

GLOGAUER. I want national publicity on this—outdoor advertising, twenty-four sheets. everything! Meterstein,

arrange a conference for me with the whole publicity
department this afternoon! That's all!

METERSTEIN. Yes, sir. (*Goes*)

SUSAN. Oh, George! What'll father say now?

GLOGAUER. Miss Chasen, shoot those wires right off!

MISS CHASEN. Yes, sir.

GLOGAUER. I'll be in my office in ten minutes, and no appointments for me for the rest of the day! That clear?

MISS CHASEN. Yes, sir. (*Goes*)

GLOGAUER. Now then, Doctor, tear up your old contract!

GEORGE. I haven't got one!

GLOGAUER. You are in charge of this whole thing—understand? What you say goes!

GEORGE. Yes, sir.

SUSAN. George, does this mean—

GLOGAUER. When I have faith in a man the sky's the limit!
You know what I do with you, Doctor? I make you
supervisor in full charge—over all productions of the
Glogauer Studio!

SUSAN. George—!

GEORGE (*very matter-of-factly*). All right.

(MAY *and* JERRY *enter*—JERRY *carrying a brief case,* MAY
with her hat on, both obviously ready to leave)

GEORGE. May! Jerry! What do you think! I've just been
made supervisor!

SUSAN. Yes!

JERRY. Huh!

MAY. What!

GEORGE. I told him about the Vitaphone!

MAY. You did what?

GLOGAUER. The one man! (*To* GEORGE) Tomorrow morning you get your office—with a full staff!

GEORGE (*to* MAY *and* JERRY). Hear that?

GLOGAUER. That's the way we do things out here—no time
wasted on thinking! I give you all the people you need
—anybody you want! All you got to do is say so!

GEORGE. I know who I want, Mr. Glogauer!

GLOGAUER. Already he knows—see, Kammerling?

KAMMERLING. Wonderful!

GLOGAUER. All right! Name 'em—name 'em!

GEORGE. I want Miss Daniels and Mr. Hyland!

JERRY. What is this?

GLOGAUER. What? Those people? (*A deprecatory wave of the hand*) You don't want them! They're fired!

GEORGE. Mr. Glogauer, I know who I want!

GLOGAUER. But you could have Weisskopf, Meterstein—

GEORGE. No, sir. I have to have Miss Daniels and Mr. Hyland or I can't do anything. And if I can't have them— (*In a very small voice*) —I walk right out.

SUSAN. George, you mustn't!

MAY. California, here we go!

(*But it doesn't seem to be true.* GLOGAUER *fairly throws his arms around* GEORGE, *pleading with him to stay*)

GLOGAUER. No! No! . . . Miss Daniels! Mr. Hyland!

MISS LEIGHTON (*entering, followed by two* PAGES *bearing an enormous silver coffee service*). Here you are, Mr. Glogauer. (*The* PHONE *rings*) Miss Leighton at this end—

The curtain is down

ACT THREE

SCENE I

(A set on the GLOGAUER lot. The curtain rises on a scene
of tremendous but rather vague activity. Set against a
background of church wall and stained-glass windows,
are pews, altar, wedding bell, and all the other para-
phernalia that go to make up the filming of a movie
wedding. In and out of this, all talking, all shouting,
all rushing, weave cameramen, assistant directors, electricians, routine studio workers, and actors. In this particular instance the players are costumed to represent
bridesmaids and ushers, and above a hammering and
sawing and shouting, bits of: "Hey, WEBER—we're taking the truck shot with your camera!" "Use your soft
lights for the altar shots, BUTCH" are heard from the
cameramen, etc., and snatches of: "Where are you going, LILY?" "Oh, I don't know—get a soda." "You just
had one." "Say, I hear Paramount sent a call out."
"What for?" "Dunno—just heard they had a call out,"
come from the bridesmaids and ushers. Sitting a little
apart from the rest of the actors is a gentleman dressed
in the gorgeous robes of a BISHOP, peacefully snoozing
away until it is time to play his part.
It is the last day of shooting on SUSAN WALKER's picture,
"Gingham and Orchids," and all these incredible goings-
on are nothing more than the usual "getting set" of
camera and lights, the usual yelling and the usual standing about, the inevitable waiting that is part and parcel
of the whole business of taking pictures.

A PAGE BOY, *in the regular studio page uniform, enters, calling for* MR. METERSTEIN. *He arouses, for the first time, the* BISHOP.)

BISHOP (*who is a shade less spiritual than you might expect*). Oh, boy! Can you go out and get me a copy of "Racing Form"?

PAGE. I'll try.

LIGHT MAN. Hey, Spike!

BISHOP. Yeh?

LIGHT MAN. What are you playing?

BISHOP. I've got one in the fourth at Caliente, looks good. Princess Fanny.

LIGHT MAN. Whose?

BISHOP. Princess Fanny.

(*A wandering* BRIDESMAID *strolls on*)

BRIDESMAID. Where the hell's the Bishop? Oh, there you are.

BISHOP. What's up?

BRIDESMAID. Send me up a case of gin, will you—same as last time.

BISHOP. O.K.

(*In the distance a voice is heard: "Oh,* BUTCH! *When we get through here we go over on twenty-eight." And hammering and sawing. Endless hammering and sawing*)

BISHOP (*seating himself in a pew*). You know, these pews are damned comfortable. I should have gone to church long ago.

A BRIDESMAID. Good night.

BISHOP. There's nothing like a good Simmons pew.

ELECTRICIAN. Hey, Mixer! Mixer!

MIXER (*in the distance*). What do you want?

ELECTRICIAN. How are we on sound?

MIXER. O.K.

(MRS. WALKER *bustles on, carrying* SUSAN'S *bridal bouquet*)

MRS. WALKER (*to the* BRIDESMAIDS). Well, I've just had the most exciting news! Susan's father is coming on for the wedding. Isn't that just too lovely?

A BRIDESMAID. I'm all choked up inside.

MRS. WALKER. He wasn't coming at first—it looked as if he'd have to go to Bermuda with the Elks. You know, the Elks are in Bermuda.

BRIDESMAID (*to another* BRIDESMAID). The Elks are in Bermuda.

THE OTHER BRIDESMAID (*telling still another*). The Elks are in Bermuda.

NEXT BRIDESMAID (*singing it*). The Elks are in Bermuda.

FINAL BRIDESMAID (*singing, of course*). The farmer's in the dell.

BISHOP. There's a horse named Elk's Tooth running at Tia Juana. I think just on a hunch I'll—

(MISS CHASEN *hurries on*)

MISS CHASEN. Is Dr. Lewis on the set?

(*They tell her he isn't*)

MRS. WALKER. He's at the architect's.

MISS CHASEN. Well, Mr. Glogauer wants to know the minute he gets here. Will you have somebody let me know? (*She goes.* KAMMERLING *comes on—a great show of activity. The actors leap to their feet. The script girl enters; various actors stroll back onto the set*)

KAMMERLING. Good morning, everybody! Good morning! Is Dr. Lewis here yet?

MRS. WALKER. He's at the architect's. I'll get Susan for you. *She dashes off*)

KAMMERLING. Now listen, everybody! We take first the scene on the church steps—

(*Along comes* JERRY—*so busy*)

JERRY. Well, we're on the home stretch, eh?

KAMMERLING. That is right. We do first the retake on the steps.

(SUSAN *enters in full bridal regalia*)

SUSAN. Oh. Mr. Kammerling, I'm ready to be shot!

KAMMERLING. Fine! We take the scene on the church steps.

SUSAN. The what?

KAMMERLING. The scene on the church steps.

SUSAN. But I don't think I know that scene.

JERRY. Didn't May rehearse you in that this morning?

SUSAN. No—she didn't.

KAMMERLING. Miss Daniels! Where is Miss Daniels!

VOICE OFF. Miss Daniels on the set!

KAMMERLING. She knew we were going to take it. (*Calling*) Miss Daniels!

SUSAN. Jerry, did mother tell you—we just had a telegram from father?

JERRY. No. What's up?

THAT BRIDESMAID. He's joined the Elks.

(MAY *arrives*)

MAY. Does there seem to be some trouble?

JERRY. May, what about the church steps? Susan says you didn't rehearse her.

MAY. Susan, I know your memory isn't very good, but I want you to think way back to—Oh, pretty near five minutes ago. We were sitting in your dressing room —remember?—and we rehearsed that scene?

SUSAN. But that isn't the scene he means.

MAY (*to* KAMMERLING). Outside the church, is that right?

KAMMERLING. Yes, yes!

SUSAN. Outside the church—Oh, yes, we did *that*! You said the church steps.

KAMMERLING. That's right! That's right!

MAY. Susan—we feel that it's time you were told this. Outside the church and the church steps are really the same scene.

SUSAN. Are they?

MAY. Yes. In practically all churches now they put the steps on the outside.

SUSAN. Oh, I see.

KAMMERLING. Then are we ready?

MAY. I doubt it. Do you remember the scene as we just rehearsed it, Susan? You remember that you ascend four steps—then turn and wave to the crowd—

SUSAN. Oh, yes—Now I remember! (*She waves her hand —a violent gesture*)

MAY. No, no—you do not launch a battleship. You see, they'd have to get a lot of water for that.

KAMMERLING. Is it then settled what you are doing?

SUSAN. Well, I think I understand. . . . The steps are outside the church. . . .

A BRIDESMAID. Lily, want to make a date tonight? Those exhibitors are in town again.

LILY. Who?

BRIDESMAID. Those two exhibitors.

LILY. Oh, Mr. Hyland, do you want us tonight?

JERRY. Can't tell till later.

LILY. Well, I've got a chance to go out with an exhibitionist.

(*The crowd is all gone by this time.* MAY *and* JERRY *are alone*)

JERRY. May, I just came from Glogauer and he's tickled pink.

MAY. He must look lovely.

JERRY. Picture finished right on schedule, advancing the opening date—it's the first time it ever happened!

MAY. Yah.

JERRY. You don't seem very excited about it! Picture opening in three days—and it's going to be a knockout too!

MAY (*who has heard all this before*). Now, Jerry.

JERRY. Well, it is, and I don't care what you think.

MAY. But Jerry, use a little common sense. You've seen
the rushes. What's the use of kidding yourself?

JERRY. All right. Everybody's wrong but you.

MAY. I can't help what I see, Jerry. The lighting, for example. Those big scenes where you can't see anything
—everybody in shadow—what about those?

JERRY. That's only a few scenes. You know that—George
forgot to tell them to turn the lights on, and they
thought he meant it that way. Nobody'll notice it.

MAY. All right. But I caught something new yesterday.
That knocking that goes on—did you get that?

JERRY. Well, we're trying to find out about that. The sound
engineers are working on it.

MAY. Don't you know what that was?

JERRY. No. What?

MAY. That was George cracking his God-damn Indian nuts.

JERRY. Is that what it was?

MAY. I suppose nobody's going to notice that, either.

(*There is a great hubbub outside—cries of* "DR. LEWIS *is
coming!*" "*Here comes the* DOCTOR!" *And presently he
does come—preceded by a pair of pages bearing a silver
coffee service and the inevitable box of Indian nuts,
and followed by his secretary and a stream of actors.
There come along, too, the three scenario writers—
pressing for his attention*)

GEORGE. Good morning! Good morning! Good morning!
(*He sights* SUSAN) Good morning, darling. Well, Kammerling? What have I done this morning?

KAMMERLING. We have taken the retake on the church
steps.

GEORGE. Well, what have I got to decide?

KAMMERLING. There is only the last scene—the wedding
ceremony.

JERRY. Right on schedule.

GEORGE. There's just the one scene left to take?

KAMMERLING. That is all.

GEORGE (*a snap of the fingers; the decision has been reached*). We'll take that scene.

KAMMERLING. Everybody on the set, please! Everybody on the set!

GEORGE. I'll decide everything else at two o'clock.

SECRETARY. Yes, sir.

MAY (*coming to* GEORGE). Dr. Lewis, I met you in New York. I'm Miss Daniels.

GEORGE. Hello, May.

KAMMERLING. Are we then ready? Ready, Dr. Lewis?

ONE OF THE SCENARIO WRITERS. Dr. Lewis, we left a scenario in your office—

SECRETARY. No answers on scenarios until two o'clock.

GEORGE. That's right.

WRITER. But it's five weeks now.

GEORGE. All right. We'll take the scene from wherever we left off.

KAMMERLING. We will take the end of the wedding ceremony, where we left off! Places, please! We are going to take the end of the wedding ceremony. Everybody in their places.

(*The wedding party takes its place at the altar*)

KAMMERLING (*to the* BISHOP). Oh, Mr. Jackson, have you got this straight?

GEORGE (*sternly*). Get this straight, Mr. Jackson.

BISHOP. What?

GEORGE (*to* KAMMERLING). Yes—what?

KAMMERLING. About the ceremony. You understand that when she says "I do," you release the pigeons.

BISHOP. Oh, sure.

KAMMERLING. They are in that little cottage up there. When Miss Walker says "I do," you pull that ribbon and the pigeons will fly out.

BISHOP. They ain't gonna fly down on me again, are they?

KAMMERLING. No, no, they have been rehearsed.

GEORGE. Those pigeons know what to do. They were with Cecil DeMille for two years.

BISHOP. Oh, that's where I met 'em.

GEORGE. Oh! I forgot! There aren't any pigeons.

KAMMERLING. What?

GEORGE. Well, they had to stay up in there so long, and I felt kinda sorry for them, so I had them sent back to the man.

KAMMERLING. Well, what shall we do?

GEORGE. I know! Let's not have any. That's what we'll do —we won't use them.

KAMMERLING. Very well, Doctor.

MAY. He certainly meets emergencies.

SUSAN. Oh, George! Is that all I say during the entire ceremony—just "I do"?

GEORGE. Is that all she says, May?

MAY. That's all. That's the part she knows, too.

SUSAN. But that's so short.

GEORGE. Yes!

MAY. Maybe she could perform the ceremony, then she could do all the talking.

GEORGE. But that wouldn't fit the scenario—

(*In the distance comes the cry that signals the approach of the great. "*MR. GLOGAUER *is coming!" "*MR. GLOGAUER *is coming!" He arrives all bustle and importance. He is followed by one page who carries a portable desk and a telephone, by a second page who brings a small folding chair, and by the ubiquitous* MISS CHASEN *and her notebook. Immediately the* PAGE *puts together the desk and plugs in the telephone;* MISS CHASEN *settles herself, and in the twinkling of an eye the place is open for business*)

GLOGAUER. Well! Here is the happy family! (*A general greeting*) Well, everything going fine, huh?

JERRY. Right on schedule, Mr. Glogauer.

GEORGE. That's what it is.

GLOGAUER. Well, that's wonderful—wonderful. What's going on now?

GEORGE. We're taking the last scene.

GLOGAUER. That's fine—fine! I congratulate everybody.

MISS CHASEN (*into the telephone*). Miss Chasen speaking. Mr. Glogauer is on Number Nine.

GLOGAUER. Tell 'em I will look at "Foolish Virgins" at two-fifteen.

MISS CHASEN. Mr. Glogauer will look at "Foolish Virgins" at two-fifteen.

GLOGAUER. The reason I came down—you don't mind if I interrupt you for a minute for a very special reason?

GEORGE. Why, no.

(*There is a general movement. Some of the* BRIDESMAIDS *are about to depart*)

GLOGAUER. Everybody stay here, please! I want everybody to hear this!

GEORGE. Everybody listen to Mr. Glogauer! Mr. Glogauer is probably going to say something.

KAMMERLING. Attention, everybody!

GLOGAUER. Boys and girls, as you know this is the last day of the shooting. Many of you have worked for me before, but never under such happy circumstances, and so I want you all to be here while I say something. Seventeen years ago— (*The* BISHOP, *who is no fool, sits down*) —when I went into the movie business, I made up my mind it should be run like a business, as a business, and for a business. And that is what I have tried to do. But never before have I been able to do it until today. Never since I started to make Glogauer Super-Jewels has a picture of mine been finished exactly on the schedule. And what is the reason for that? Because now for the first time we have a man who is able to make decisions, and to make them like *that*—Dr. George Lewis.

GEORGE (*as the applause dies*). Ladies and Gentlemen—

GLOGAUER. Wait a minute—I am not through yet. (GEORGE *apologetically steps back*) And so in recognition of his remarkable achievement, I take great pleasure in presenting him with a very small token of my regard. (*He gives a signal. Immediately* TWO MEN *enter, carrying a huge table on which is spread out a golden dinner set —something absolutely staggering. It is met with a chorus of delighted little gasps.* SUSAN *scampers down to gurgle over it*) A solid gold dinner set, a hundred and six pieces, and with his initials in diamonds on every piece.

MAY. What's the first prize?

(*There are calls of "Speech," and "*DR. LEWIS*"*)

GEORGE. Ladies and gentlemen—and Mr. Glogauer—this is the first solid gold dinner set I have ever received. I hardly know what to say, because this is the first solid gold dinner set I have ever received, and I hardly know what to say. All I can say is it's wonderful, Mr. Glogauer, and now let's show Mr. Glogauer the finish of the picture, and take the last scene.

KAMMERLING (*pushing the* BRIDESMAIDS *away*). All right, all right! Look at it afterwards!

GLOGAUER (*as* MISS CHASEN *starts to leave*). I will address the new playwrights on Number Eight.

MISS CHASEN. Yes, Mr. Glogauer.

KAMMERLING. Everybody take their places! Mr. Glogauer is waiting!

GEORGE. Everybody take their places!

LIGHT MAN. Hey, Spike!

BISHOP. Yah?

LIGHT MAN. They're off at Caliente. Fourth race.

BISHOP. O.K. Let me know the minute you hear.

LIGHT MAN. O.K.

KAMMERLING. All right. We are taking the scene now, Mr. Jackson. Horses come later.

GEORGE. We are taking the scene now, Mr. Glogauer.

GLOGAUER. Fine!

KAMMERLING. Are we lined? (CAMERAMEN *assent*) Phased? (*Another assent*) Red light. How are we for sound?

MIXER (*through his phone*). O.K.

KAMMERLING. All right. Are we up to speed?

VOICE. Right.

KAMMERLING. Four bells!

(*Four bells sound. There is complete silence*)

VOICE (*in the distance*). Taking on upper stage! Everybody quiet!

KAMMERLING. Hit your lights! (*Lights on*) Camera!

BISHOP. Cyril Fonsdale, dost thou take this woman to be thy wedded wife, to live together in the holy state of matrimony? Dost thou promise within sacred sight of this altar to love her, comfort her, honor and keep her in sickness and in health, and, forsaking all others, keep true only unto her, so long as ye both shall live?

THE GROOM. I do.

BISHOP. Mildred Martin, dost thou take this man to be thy wedded husband? Dost thou promise to obey him and serve him, love, honor and keep him in sickness and in health, so long as ye both shall live?

SUSAN. I do.

BISHOP. Forasmuch as these two have consented together in holy wedlock, and have witnessed the same before this company and have given and pledged their troth each to the other, I hereby pronounce them man and wife.

(SUSAN *and* THE GROOM *embrace, as camera on truck is moved up for close-up*)

KAMMERLING. Cut! One bell!

(*One bell sounds. Hammering and sawing instantly spring up all over the place again*)

LIGHT MAN. Spike! That horse ran sixth.

BISHOP. God damn it! I knew that would happen.

GEORGE. There you are, Mr. Glogauer—embrace, fade-out, the end.

GLOGAUER. I see, I see. Wait a minute—I don't understand. You said what?

GEORGE. Embrace, fade-out, the end.

GLOGAUER. End? You mean you take this scene last. But it's not really the end.

GEORGE. Sure it is. (*To* KAMMERLING *and the others*) Isn't it?

KAMMERLING. Certainly it's the end.

GLOGAUER. But how can it be? What about the backstage scene?

KAMMERLING. What?

GLOGAUER (*slightly frenzied*). On the opening night! Where her mother is dying, and she has to act anyhow!

GEORGE. That wasn't in it, Mr. Glogauer.

KAMMERLING. Why, no.

GLOGAUER. Wasn't in it! I had twelve playwrights working on that.

GEORGE. But it wasn't in it.

GLOGAUER (*dangerously calm*). This is a picture about a little country girl?

GEORGE. Yes, sir.

GLOGAUER. Who gets a job in a Broadway cabaret?

GEORGE. There isn't any Broadway cabaret.

GLOGAUER. No Broadway cabaret?

GEORGE. She doesn't come to New York in this.

GLOGAUER. Doesn't come—you mean the cabaret owner doesn't make her go out with this bootlegger?

GEORGE. Why, no, Mr. Glogauer.

GLOGAUER. Well, what happens to her? What *does* she do?

GEORGE. Why, this rich woman stops off at the farm-house and she takes her to Florida and dresses her all up.

GLOGAUER. And there is no backstage scene? Any place?

GEORGE. No. She goes out swimming and gets too far out and then Cyril Fonsdale—

GLOGAUER. Let me see that script, please.

GEORGE. It's all there, Mr. Glogauer. (GLOGAUER *looks through the script*) See? There's where she goes swimming.

GLOGAUER (*closing the script with a bang*). Do you know what you have done, Doctor Lewis? You have made the wrong picture!

(*Consternation, of course*)

GEORGE. Huh?

KAMMERLING. What is that?

GLOGAUER. That is all you have done! Made the wrong picture!

GEORGE. But—but—

JERRY. Are you sure, Mr. Glogauer?

GLOGAUER (*looking at the thing in his hand*) Where did you get such a script?

GEORGE. Why, it's the one you gave me.

GLOGAUER. I never gave you such a script. She goes swimming! Swimming! Do you know who made this picture? Biograph, in 1910! Florence Lawrence, and Maurice Costello—and even then it was no good!

JERRY. But look, Mr. Glogauer—

GLOGAUER. Sixty thousand dollars I paid for a scenario, and where is it? In swimming!

GEORGE. Well, everybody was here while we were making it.

GLOGAUER. Everybody was here! Where were their minds? Kammerling! Kammerling!

KAMMERLING. It is not my fault. Dr. Lewis gave us the script.

GLOGAUER. I had to bring you all the way from Germany for this! Miss Newton! You held the script in your hands! Where were your eyes?

MISS NEWTON. I got it from Dr. Lewis—right in his office. I'm sure I couldn't—

GLOGAUER. So, Doctor! On Wednesday night we open and

we have *got* to open! And after that it goes to four hundred exhibitors and we got signed contracts! So tell me what to do, please!

GEORGE. Well, couldn't we release it as a super-special?

GLOGAUER. Never in my life have I known such a thing! After this I make a ruling—every scenario we produce, somebody has got to read it!

JERRY. Yes, Mr. Glogauer.

GLOGAUER. You know what this does to *you*, Miss Walker! You are through! Swimming! This kills your career! And you know who you got to thank for it? Dr. Lewis! (SUSAN *meets the situation by bursting into tears*) A fine supervisor! The business is in the hands of incompetents, he says! So what do I do? I give him everything the way he wants it—his own star—his own staff— (*It is a new thought. He fixes* MAY *and* JERRY *with a malignant eye*) Oh, yes. And where were *you people* while all this was going on?

JERRY. Mr. Glogauer, I was on the cost end. I didn't have anything to do with the script. Dr. Lewis was the—

GLOGAUER. But Miss Daniels was here—all the time! Right with Dr. Lewis! What about *that*?

MAY (*not frightened*). Yes. I was here.

GLOGAUER. Well! Where was your mind?

MAY. To tell you the truth, Mr. Glogauer, I thought it was just another Super-Jewel.

GLOGAUER. Oh, you did?

MAY. I couldn't see any difference.

GLOGAUER. You couldn't, huh?

MAY. And while we're on the subject, Mr. Glogauer, just why is it all Dr. Lewis's fault?

GLOGAUER. Why is it his fault? Who did this thing? Who else is to blame?

MAY. Well, if I'm not too inquisitive, what do *you* do with yourself all the time? Play marbles?

GLOGAUER. What's that?

MAY. Where were *you* while all this was going on? Out
to lunch?

GLOGAUER (*drawing himself up with dignity*). I go to my
office. That will be all. (*About to say something else, but
changes his mind*) I go to my office. (*Notices the script
still in his hand*) Mr. Supervisor, I make you a present.

GEORGE (*Weakly, as he takes it*). Thank you.

GLOGAUER (*to the company*). And will you all please
understand that nothing about this is to get out of the
studio. That is official. Come, Hyland! Seventeen years
and this is the worst thing that has ever happened to
me!

JERRY (*following him*). Mr. Glogauer, if I'd been on the
set this never would have happened. I didn't have anything to do with the script—

(*They are gone*)

KAMMERLING (*after a moment's embarrassed pause*). That
is all for today. You will be notified.

BISHOP. Well—the wrong picture and the wrong horse!

(*A babble of talk springs up as everyone starts to go.
SUSAN has a fresh outburst of tears*)

GEORGE. Susan, don't cry like that.

SUSAN (*through sobs*). You heard what Mr. Glogauer said
—my career is ruined. I'm—through.

MRS. WALKER. Now, darling, you mustn't take on that way.
Everything'll turn out all right.

GEORGE. But, Susan, it wasn't my fault. I didn't know it
was the wrong picture.

(*All are now gone except* MAY *and* KAMMERLING)

KAMMERLING. It is too bad, Miss Daniels.

MAY. Yah. Isn't it?

KAMMERLING. But after all it is the movie business. It is
just the same in Germany.

MAY. It is, huh?

KAMMERLING. Even worse. Oh, it is terrible over there. I
think I go back.

(*He leaves.* JERRY *returns, at white heat*)

JERRY. Well, you fixed everything fine, didn't you? On top of everything else you had to go and get smart!

MAY. It was time somebody got smart, Jerry.

JERRY. Well, you *did* it! And maybe you think Glogauer isn't sore!

MAY. Well, you don't have to worry, do you, Jerry?

JERRY. What?

MAY (*very calmly*). You don't have to worry. You crawled out from under. You gave as pretty an exhibition as *I've* ever seen.

JERRY. What do you mean?

MAY. Oh, nothing. Just the way you stood up for George.

JERRY. Well, somebody's got to keep his feet on the ground around here!

MAY (*so quietly*). Yours are all right—aren't they, Jerry? Yah. Right deep in the soil of California!

JERRY. I was trying to fix things up—that's what I was trying to do.

MAY. No, Jerry. No. It's been coming on you ever since you got out here, and now it's here. You've gone Hollywood, Jerry. And as far as I'm concerned, that's that.

(*It has been said very quietly, but its very quietness gives it a definiteness.* JERRY *looks at her; senses that she means it. He turns on his heel and goes*)

(MAY *is alone for a moment. Then, in the offing, a man's voice is heard, singing, "I wanna be loved by you-ou-ou, and nobody else but you,—I wanna be kissed by you, a-lone." At the end of the song the singer comes into sight. It is the* BISHOP. *He disappears again*)

(GEORGE *comes back.*)

GEORGE. She wouldn't talk to me, May! Shut the door right in my face and wouldn't talk to me!

MAY (*abstracted*). What?

GEORGE. She just keeps on crying and won't even talk to me.

MAY. That's all right. Everything is all right. It is for me, anyhow. Just fine and dandy.

GEORGE. Fine and dandy?

MAY. Just swell.

GEORGE. Susan ought to know I didn't do it on purpose. I tried to tell her. Look, May, do you think the picture's so bad?

MAY. Bad as what, George?

GEORGE. Bad as he thinks it is?

MAY. Well, I think it's got a good chance.

GEORGE. Chance of what, May?

MAY. Of being as bad as he thinks it is.

GEORGE. Oh!

MAY. By the way, George—just to keep the record straight —how'd you come to *make* the wrong picture. Or don't you know?

GEORGE. Well, I've been trying to think. You know that thing in my office where we keep the new scenarios— well, if you're in a hurry it looks exactly like the waste-basket—and so I reached into it, only it was the waste-basket—

MAY. And thus endeth the first lesson.

GEORGE. But look, if I go to him and tell him how it happened—

MISS CHASEN (*in the distance*). Paging Dr. Lewis! Miss Daniels!

MAY. Ah, here we are! Right in here. I thought it was taking a long time. (MISS CHASEN *enters*) You're late.

MISS CHASEN (*giving her two envelopes*). Executive office! No answer! (*Turns to go*)

MAY. Wait a minute. Who else have you got? (*Examining remaining envelopes*) Kammerling, Weisskopf, Meterstein—Ah, yes. (MISS CHASEN *goes*) (MAY *turns back to* GEORGE.) Do you want yours?

GEORGE. Do you mean we're—fired, May?

MAY. Good and fired!

GEORGE (*in a daze, opening his letter*) Yah.

MAY (*looking at hers*). Me too. Well, George—we've got a solid gold dinner set, anyway. A hundred and six pieces, and every piece marked with your initials in diamonds. That's not bad for two months' work. (TWO PAGES *enter and carry off the dinner set*) No, George— you *haven't* got a solid gold dinner set.

Curtain

SCENE II

(*It is the Pullman car again, and, by a strange coincidence, the same car on which* MAY *and her companions went West. But it is* MAY *alone who is traveling back East— at all events, she is seated alone when we first behold the car. The* PORTER *enters—and, since it is the same car, it is also the same porter. He is right there with the same question, too*)

PORTER. You ready to have your berth made up?

MAY. No, thanks.

PORTER. I been meaning to ask you, Miss Daniels—how's come those two gentlemen ain't going back?

MAY. Well, that's a long story.

PORTER. Yes, ma'am.

MAY. But I wouldn't be surprised if at least one of them was with you pretty soon.

(*The train whistle blows*)

PORTER. We makes a two-minute stop here. Anything you want?

MAY. No, thanks. Where are we?

PORTER. We makes a stop at Needle's Point. That's where they got that sanitarium.

MAY. Look—is there a news stand?

PORTER. Yes, ma'am.

MAY. See if you can get hold of Thursday's Los Angeles papers, will you?

PORTER. Yes, ma'am. (*Starts off*)

MAY (*calls after him*). They've got to be Thursday's or I don't want 'em.

(MAY *is left alone. There is a single blast of the whistle; the lights no longer fly past outside the window,* MAY *tries to look out. Then she settles herself again; takes up a book; tries to read; throws it down*)

(*The* PORTER *re-enters with luggage*)

PORTER. Right this way, sir. You need any help? Just a gentleman from the sanitarium.

(LAWRENCE VAIL *enters. Instantly, of course, he recognizes* MAY)

MAY. Why, Mr. Vail!

VAIL. Hello, Miss Daniels.

MAY. So you're the gentleman from the sanitarium?

VAIL. That's right. Well, this is a good deal of a surprise!

MAY. Well—please sit down.

VAIL. Thanks. Well!

MAY. You're certainly the last person I—I hadn't heard you were ill. Nothing serious, I hope?

VAIL (*shakes his head*). Just a kind of breakdown. Underwork.

MAY. I can't quite picture that reception room without you.

VAIL. Then I heard about this place—sanitarium here. Sounded pretty good, so I came out. Fellow named Jenkins runs it. Playwright. Seems he came out here under contract, but he couldn't stand the gaff. Went mad in the eighth month. So he started this place. Doesn't take anything but playwrights.

MAY. Good, is it?

VAIL. Great. First three days they put you in a room without a chair in it. Then they have a big art gallery—life-sized portraits of all the studio executives. You see, for an hour every day you go in there and say whatever you want to any picture.

MAY (*nods*). I see.

PORTER (*passing through*). I'll get your papers right now.

VAIL. And now what's all this about? Going home on a visit?

MAY. Well—going home.

VAIL. All washed up?

MAY. Scrubbed.

VAIL. Really? I'm kind of surprised. I never quite got the hang of what you people did out there, but I had the idea you were in pretty solid. Something happened?

MAY (*taking a moment*). Did you ever meet Dr. Lewis?

VAIL. I had quite a talk with Dr. Lewis.

MAY. Well, Dr. Lewis did something that no one had ever done before. He reminded Mr. Glogauer about turning the Vitaphone down. That made him supervisor.

VAIL. Only supervisor?

MAY. And there was also Miss Susan Walker. Miss Walker is a young woman who has a chance of becoming the world's worst actress. I should say a very good chance. She's young yet—has plenty of time.

VAIL. I see.

MAY. With that to start with, the Doctor cinched things by working from the wrong scenario. Some little thing from 1910. The picture opened Wednesday. And how is *your* uncle, Mr. Vail?

VAIL. My recollection of the 1910 pictures is that they weren't so bad.

MAY. They didn't have the Doctor in those days. Most of it you can't see because the Doctor forgot to tell them to turn the lights on; Miss Walker has a set of gestures

that would do credit to a travelling derrick—and did
you ever happen to hear about the Doctor's bright
particular weakness?

VAIL. There's something else?

MAY. It's called Indian nuts. (*A glance around*) There
must be one around here somewhere. Anyhow, he eats
them. With sound. He kept cracking them right through
the picture, and they recorded swell.

VAIL. That, I take it, decided you?

MAY. That, and—other things.

VAIL. Funny—I should think there would be a great field
out there for a man who could turn out the wrong
picture.

MAY. Yes, if he could do it regularly. But sooner or later
Dr. Lewis would make the right one.

VAIL. Not the Doctor.

MAY. Well, maybe you're right.

PORTER (*re-entering with newspapers and a pillow*). Here
your papers, Miss Daniels.

MAY (*taking them*). Thanks.

PORTER (*to* VAIL). I brought you a pillow.

VAIL. Thank you. (PORTER *goes*)

MAY (*scanning the date line*). Yah. These have probably
got the notices.

VAIL (*reaching for one*). Oh, you mean the picture?

MAY. It wouldn't surprise me. (THEY *each open a paper.*
MAY *is in no hurry*)

VAIL. You're a pretty brave girl, actually sending out for
these.

MAY. Well, I might as well know the worst.

VAIL (*finding the place*) Here we are, I guess. "Gingham
and Orchids"—that the name of it?

MAY. That's it.

VAIL (*scanning the headlines as he folds the paper*). An
all-talking, all-singing—

MAY. All-lousy picture.

(*She takes the paper,* VAIL *meanwhile opening the other one*)

VAIL (*as* MAY *reads*). I guess that must be what they mean by a hundred per cent. (MAY'*s eyes slide quickly down the column, then she looks blankly up at* VAIL) What is it? (MAY *hands the paper over to him, indicating the spot.* VAIL *reads*) "Never in the history of Hollywood has so tumultuous an ovation been accorded to any picture—"

MAY (*not quite able to speak; indicates a spot further on in the review*) No. Down there.

VAIL (*reads*). "Herman Glogauer's 'Gingham and Orchids' is a welcome relief from the avalanche of backstage pictures. It marks a turning point in the motion picture industry—a return to the sweet simplicity and tender wistfulness of yesteryear."

MAY. It *does* say that?

VAIL. Indeed it does.

MAY (*as if in a daze, takes the paper from* VAIL *and reads further*). "A new star twinkled across the cinema heavens last night and the audience took her at once to its heart. Here at last is an actress who is not afraid to appear awkward and ungraceful." That word is "afraid," isn't it?

VAIL. That's right.

MAY. "In the scene on the church steps, where she waved to the onlookers below, her hands revealed a positively Duse-like quality." I'll tell you about that some day.

VAIL. I'll be there.

MAY (*still reading*). "And here is one wedding, by the way, that sets a new mark for originality and freshness. It does not use pigeons." Remind me about that one, too.

VAIL. I will.

MAY (*reads*). "Then too, the lighting of the picture is superb. Dr. Lewis has wisely seen the value of leaving

the climaxes to the imagination of the audience. In the
big scenes almost nothing was visible." (*She indicates
the other paper*) I'm afraid I haven't got strength
enough to reach for that one.

VAIL. I beg your pardon. (*He changes papers with her*)
The whole thing couldn't be a typographical error,
could it?

MAY (*looks the new paper quickly over, then looks up at
VAIL with a weak smile*). I want you to settle yourself
for this.

VAIL. I'm ready.

MAY. Put the pillow right back of you.

VAIL. All right. (*Does so*)

MAY. "In the opening sequences the audience was puzzled
by a constant knocking, and it seemed to many of us
that something might be wrong with the sound ap-
paratus. Then suddenly we realized that what was being done was what Eugene O'Neill did with the constant beating of the tom-tom in 'The Emperor Jones.'
It was the beat of the hail on the roof." (*She looks up
at VAIL, who nods*) "It is another of the masterly touches
brought to the picture by that new genius of the films,
Dr. George Lewis." (*She lowers the paper, then, as if
she cannot quite believe it, raises it and reads again*)
"That new genius of the films, Dr. George Lewis." (*For
a moment, MAY and VAIL merely look at each other.
Then VAIL leans back, crosses his legs, sighs*)

VAIL. I hear the boll weevil is getting into the cotton-
crop again.

(*The* PORTER *returns*)

PORTER. Here's a telegram for you, Miss Daniels. Caught
us right here at Needle's Point.

MAY. Oh, thanks. (*The* PORTER *goes*) My guess is that this
is from that new genius of the films.

VAIL. I wouldn't wonder.

MAY. Oh, yes. (*Reads*) "The picture is colossal. It has put the movies back where they were ten years ago. I am the Wonder Man of the Talkies. They keep coming at me to decide things. Please take next train back—Jerry is gone and I am all alone here. They have made me an Elk and Susan is an Eastern Star. Please take next train back—I need you. Where is Jerry? I am also a Shriner."

VAIL. Well, what are you going to do about that?

MAY (*looking at the telegram*). "Jerry is gone and I am all alone here." (*Letting the telegram slowly fall*) Well, it looks as if I'm going back.

VAIL. I think you have to.

MAY. Because if George is alone out there— (*She breaks off*) And then there's another thing. As long as George owns Hollywood now, there are two or three reforms that I'd like to put into effect. Do you know what I'm going to do?

VAIL. What?

MAY. I'm going to get all those page boys together and take their signs away from them—then nobody will know where anybody is. I'm going to pack up the Schlepkins and send 'em back to Brooklyn, and then I'm going to bring their mother out *here*. I'm going to take Miss Leighton out of that reception room—

VAIL. Put cushions on those chairs—

MAY. And make her ask for an appointment to get back in!

VAIL. Great!

MAY. And when I get that done, I'm going out to Mr. Glogauer's house, put the illuminated dome where the bathroom is, and then I'm going to take the bathroom and drop it into the Pacific Ocean. . . .

The curtain is down

SCENE III

*{It is again Mr. Glogauer's reception room, but altered,
as you see at first glance, in one vital particular. Over
every door, and the room is fairly fringed with doors,
there is a sizeable picture of* DR. GEORGE LEWIS. *And
that isn't all. The thoughtful* GLOGAUER *has so arranged
matters that these pictures light up whenever the cor-
responding door is opened—every last one of them
When there is plenty of dashing in and out—and that
is one of the things that there is an abundance of in* MR.
GLOGAUER'S *place of business—you see a* GEORGE *whose
beaming countenance is being constantly ringed with
incandescents.*

*It is a busy place at the moment. Half a dozen people
are talking at once, all pressing the great* DR. LEWIS
*about this matter or that. A man at an easel is sketch-
ing the* DOCTOR'S *portrait. There are two or three news-
papermen.* MISS NEWTON *is there with her eternal scripts.
There is a man who wants an indorsement for somebody's neckties, and still another man who seems, believe it or not, to be taking down the* DOCTOR'S *autobiography. A* PAGE *stands waiting with a gold box filled
with Indian nuts, and occasionally the* DOCTOR *dips a
hand in. Presiding over the whole thing is the* DOCTOR'S
*able secretary, who stands with watch in hand and arm
upraised, as though about to bring everything to halt
at any second.*

As for the DOCTOR, *he is pacing busily up and down, and
handling all comers.)*

GEORGE. So far as my plans for Mr. Glogauer are concerned, I can only say that the coming year will be a
Glogauer year. And by the time all of our plans have
been carried into effect, why, the legitimate stage had
better look to its laurels.

(METERSTEIN *dashes in*)

METERSTEIN. They're waiting for you on No. 8, Dr. Lewis!

SECRETARY. Dr. Lewis on No. 8 at three-twenty.

METERSTEIN. Right! (*Dashes out again*)

PAINTER. Dr. Lewis, will you turn your head just a little this way?

BIOGRAPHER. Dr. Lewis, we were up to Chapter 7. September, 1910.

GEORGE. Oh, yes. My biography. I was still living in Medallion then. I was but a boy, and one day an idea came to me. I decided to be an usher.

THE MAN. Dr. Lewis, your indorsement will have a hundred thousand men wearing Non-Wrinkable Ties inside of three months.

REPORTER. Dr. Lewis, can I have the rest of that statement?

SECRETARY (*watch in hand*). One minute more, Doctor!

MISS NEWTON. Dr. Lewis, I have to have a decision on these scenarios.

PAINTER. Dr. Lewis, please!

REPORTER. Doctor, it's getting late.

WEISSKOPF (*dashing in and out*). O.K. on those contracts, Doctor!

GEORGE. O.K.

REPORTER. How about a statement from Miss Walker?

GEORGE. Miss Walker is making a personal appearance in San Francisco. She'll be here pretty soon.

SECRETARY. Time! Time's up!

(MISS NEWTON *goes out as* MISS LEIGHTON *comes in*)

MISS LEIGHTON. Dr. Lewis, the Knights of Columbus are downstairs.

SECRETARY. Your time is up, gentlemen! Sorry!

REPORTER. Well, can we see him again later?

PAINTER. I'm only half finished here.

TIE MAN. If I could have just one minute—

SECRETARY (*shepherding them out*). The Doctor has no

free time this month. All requests must be submitted
in writing.

MISS LEIGHTON. What about the Knights of Columbus, Dr.
Lewis? Shall I tell them to come up?

GEORGE. Tell them I'll join later.

MISS LEIGHTON. Yes, sir. (*Goes*)

GEORGE. Now, where were we?

BIOGRAPHER. You decided to be an usher.

GEORGE. Oh, yes. I became an usher and pretty 'soon I
was put in charge of the last two rows of the mezzanine.

(SUSAN *enters*)

GEORGE. Hello, darling! (*Dismissing the others*) All right,
everybody!

SECRETARY. You are due on No. 8 in two minutes, Doctor.

GEORGE. All right.

SECRETARY. The Doctor will start Chapter 8 on Tuesday
at twelve-fifteen.

(*They all go out*—GEORGE *and* SUSAN *are alone*)

GEORGE. How was it, Susan?

SUSAN. Oh, wonderful, George! Thousands of people, and
arc lights, and my name on top of everything! Oh, it
was wonderful, George!

GEORGE. It's been wonderful here, too. I'm up to Chapter
8 in my biography, and there's a man painting my portrait, and—Oh, what do you think? I've got a surprise
for you, Susan.

SUSAN. George, what is it? Tell me quick!

GEORGE. Three guesses.

SUSAN. A swimming pool?

GEORGE. No.

SUSAN. Two swimming pools?

GEORGE. It's an aeroplane.

SUSAN. George!

GEORGE. The man gave it to me for nothing. All I had to
do was buy a few aeroplanes for Mr. Glogauer.

SUSAN. That's wonderful, George! Just what we needed!

GEORGE. First I was only going to buy a couple, but the man kept talking to me, and it worked out that if I bought a few more I'd get one free.

SUSAN. George, you're so clever! You couldn't have given me a nicer surprise! Isn't everything wonderful, George?

GEORGE. Yes, only I wish May and Jerry would get here. They always know what to do in case things come up.

SUSAN. George, you mustn't worry about it. They got your telegrams.

GEORGE. Yes, but you see, Susan, we've always been together. This is the first time in years I haven't been together, and—did you see my pictures, Susan? They light up! (*He points to one of them, and at that moment it does light up*) See?

(*Through the door comes a pretty annoyed* GLOGAUER, *followed by* MISS CHASEN)

GLOGAUER. Dr. Lewis, I want to talk to you. How do you do, Miss Walker? Dr. Lewis, did you order four hundred and sixty aeroplanes?

GEORGE. How's that?

GLOGAUER. Four hundred and sixty aeroplanes have just arrived in front of the studio. They say you ordered them.

GEORGE (*uneasily*). Well, don't you believe in aviation, Mr. Glogauer?

GLOGAUER. The question is, Dr. Lewis: why did you buy four hundred and sixty aeroplanes?

(*Enter* MISS LEIGHTON)

MISS LEIGHTON. Mr. Glogauer! Another hundred aeroplanes just arrived and there's more coming every minute!

GLOGAUER. WHAT?

MISS LEIGHTON. They're arriving in groups of fifty, Mr. Glogauer.

GLOGAUER. What is this, Doctor! Don't tell me you bought *more* than four hundred and sixty aeroplanes!

MISS LEIGHTON. The man from the aeroplane company says the order calls for two thousand!

GLOGAUER. Two thousand!

MISS LEIGHTON. That's what he said!

GLOGAUER. Is this *true*, Doctor? Can such a thing be possible?

GEORGE. Well, the man from the aeroplane company—

GLOGAUER. Two thousand! Two thousand aeroplanes! Where's Meterstein—Weisskopf!

MISS CHASEN. Mr. Weisskopf! Mr. Meterstein!

GLOGAUER. Two thousand aeroplanes! Seventeen years and never in my life— (*He storms out, followed by the others*)

MISS LEIGHTON. I told them you weren't in and that you couldn't see anybody.

SUSAN. George, is anything the matter? Shouldn't you have bought the aeroplanes?

GEORGE (*bringing up the rear of the procession*). But Mr. Glogauer, I don't see what you're so angry about! All I did was buy a few aeroplanes!

(*All are gone. A pause; then* MAY *enters. She at once becomes conscious of the pictures of* GEORGE; *looks at the lighted picture over the door through which she has entered. Closes the door, then opens and closes it again.* MISS LEIGHTON *returns*)

MISS LEIGHTON. Hello, Miss Daniels.

MAY. Hello, Miss Leighton.

MISS LEIGHTON. Have you been away?

MAY (*indicating the pictures*). I see you've got some new decorations.

MISS LEIGHTON. How's that?

MAY (*trying another door*). Is that all they do? No fireworks?

MISS LEIGHTON. Aren't they lovely? Mr. Glogauer had them put up all over the building the day after the picture opened. When Dr. Lewis came into the studio, everything lit up.

MAY. Mr. Glogauer, too?

MISS LEIGHTON. How's that?

MAY (*a change of manner*). Miss Leighton—is Mr. Hyland around?

MISS LEIGHTON. Mr. Hyland? Oh, Mr. Hyland isn't with us any more.

MAY. He isn't? Where is he?

MISS LEIGHTON. I don't know, Miss Daniels. I only know he isn't with the company. I think he went back East.

MAY. Went back East? When did he leave, Miss Leighton?

MISS LEIGHTON. Well, I really don't know, Miss Daniels—

MISS CHASEN (*entering*). Miss Leighton, Mr. Glogauer wants his coffee. He's going crazy.

MISS LEIGHTON. But he's had it twice this morning.

MISS CHASEN. He wants it over again—he's raving.

MISS LEIGHTON. Oh, dear. That's the second time this week he's raved. (*She departs with* MISS CHASEN. *Immediately* GEORGE *sticks his head in; then, seeing* MAY, *literally falls on her neck*)

GEORGE. May!

MAY. Well, if it isn't Dr. Lewis!

GEORGE. Gosh, but I'm glad to see you, May! Did you—did you get my telegrams? I've been wiring you and wiring you!

MAY. Where's Jerry, George?

GEORGE. Why—why, I don't know. Isn't he with *you*, May? —he went to find *you*.

MAY. Went where? When?

GEORGE. Why—why, right after you did. He had a big fight with Mr. Glogauer—he told him all kinds of things— and then he went looking for you, but you were gone already.

MAY. Wait a minute, George. You mean Jerry got fired?

GEORGE (*nods*). He didn't even get a letter.

MAY. Well, where is he now, George? Where did he go? Haven't you heard from him?

GEORGE. I don't know. Look, May, something terrible has happened. I bought a lot of aeroplanes—

MAY. George, where would Jerry be likely to go to? What did he say when he left here?

GEORGE. He didn't say anything, May. He just said he was going to find you and nothing else mattered.

MAY (*a smile*). Oh, he didn't say anything, eh? Just that?

GEORGE. He'll come back, May—he'll come back when he knows you're here. But May, what am I going to do about the aeroplanes? (*He breaks off as* JERRY *enters.* MAY *and* JERRY *stand looking at each other*) Hello, Jerry! Why—here's Jerry now, May!

JERRY. May, you've got to listen to me. You were right. I knew you were right the minute I walked off that set. And I went straight up to Glogauer and told him so.

GEORGE. I told her, Jerry, I told her all about it.

JERRY. And so the answer is—here I am.

GEORGE. Here he is, May. We're all together again.

JERRY. Are we together, May? What about it, May? Are we together?

MAY (*landing into him*). What the hell do you mean by leaving George alone here?

JERRY. Well, I wasn't going to stay here without you!

MAY. Then why didn't you come after me?

JERRY. I did!

MAY. All right, then!

GEORGE. Yes, sir, we're all together again.

(*Suddenly* MAY *turns away from them—averts her face*)

JERRY. What is it, kid—what's the matter?

GEORGE. Why, May!

MAY (*coming out of it*). I'm all right, gentlemen. Let a lady have her moment, for God's sake. It's just that we're together again, I guess. It's seemed so long.

JERRY. May, I can't ever forgive myself—

MAY. Don't, Jerry—you make me feel like a second act climax. Well, from now on it's the Army with Banners, no matter what happens! George is the biggest man in Hollywood and we're riding the high wave!

GEORGE. No, we aren't, May.

MAY. What?

GEORGE. Mr. Glogauer is awful mad. I bought two thousand aeroplanes.

JERRY. You did what?

GEORGE. I bought two thousand aeroplanes.

MAY. What for?

GEORGE. I don't know. The man must have been a salesman.

MAY. Let me get this straight—you bought two thousand aeroplanes?

GEORGE. That's right.

MAY. For Mr. Glogauer?

GEORGE (*nods*). I got one free.

JERRY. What! In God's name, George, what did you do it for?

GEORGE. Can't we do something with them? There ought to be some way to use two thousand aeroplanes!

MAY. Sure—make applesauce!

JERRY. Well, you can't lick that! It's all over but the shouting, May. For God's sake, George, how could you do such a thing?

MAY. Well, there you are, Jerry, and what are you going to do about it?

JERRY. Why did you do it, George?

GEORGE. Well, if somebody offered you an aeroplane—

(*And back comes* MR. GLOGAUER, *followed by* SUSAN *and about half the studio force*)

GLOGAUER (*who seems to be beaming*). Well, Doctor, we have done it again! Isn't it wonderful?

SUSAN. George!

GEORGE. Huh?

GLOGAUER. We've done it again! What a man you are, Doctor—what a man you are!

JERRY. What is this?

GLOGAUER. Miss Daniels! Mr. Hyland! Did you hear what the Doctor did? He went out and bought two thousand aeroplanes! Wasn't that wonderful?

MAY (*trying to get her bearings*). Wonderful!

JERRY. Wonderful!

GLOGAUER. The trend is changing, Miss Daniels—they just been telephoning me! Everybody wants to make aeroplane pictures, but they can't make 'em because the Doctor bought up all the aeroplanes! Every company is phoning me—offering me any amount!

GEORGE. Yes, I thought they would.

SUSAN. Isn't it wonderful?

GLOGAUER. So, Doctor, you saw the trend coming! You saw the trend!

MAY. Saw it? He *is* the trend!

JERRY. You don't realize the kind of man you've got here!

GLOGAUER. Yes, I do! Doctor—this is the way you work— always you make believe you are doing the wrong thing —and *then*! Doctor, I bow to you!

SUSAN. Oh, George!

MAY. George, you don't need us. You just go ahead and be yourself.

GEORGE. Mr. Glogauer, there's something we've got to take up.

GLOGAUER (*anxiously*). What?

GEORGE (*pointing to the door through which* GLOGAUER *has just entered*). One of my pictures doesn't light up!

GLOGAUER (*greatly upset*). What! Meterstein! Weisskopf! (METERSTEIN *and* WEISSKOPF *hurry off, to rectify the error*) Doctor, you're not angry! Tell me you're not angry!

MISS LEIGHTON (*entering*). Mr. Glogauer—

GLOGAUER. Yes?

MISS LEIGHTON. Do you know the studio's being torn down?

GLOGAUER. What?

MISS LEIGHTON. There's a lot of workmen downstairs. They have orders to tear down the studio!

GLOGAUER. Tear down the studio!

MISS LEIGHTON. Yes, sir!

GLOGAUER (*looks slowly to* GEORGE *to see if he is the man who gave the order.* GEORGE *wears a broad grin of perfect confidence. He nods.* GLOGAUER *turns back to* MISS LEIGHTON). Tell 'em to go ahead! Tell 'em to go ahead! I don't know what is it, but it'll turn out all right!

(METERSTEIN *and* WEISSKOPF *dash in, indicating the relit picture*)

METERSTEIN. O.K. now, Mr. Glogauer!

GEORGE. We're putting up a bigger one, Mr. Glogauer.

JERRY. Say, that's a good idea!

GLOGAUER. Wonderful! There's another trend coming, eh, Doctor?

GEORGE. Sure, sure!

SUSAN. Isn't he wonderful, May?

MISS LEIGHTON (*at 'phone*). Construction department, please.

The curtain is down.

YOU CAN'T TAKE IT WITH YOU

You Can't Take It with You was produced at the Booth Theatre, New York City, Monday night, December 14th, 1936, by Sam H. Harris, with the following cast:

PENELOPE SYCAMORE	JOSEPHINE HULL
ESSIE	PAULA TRUEMAN
RHEBA	RUTH ATTAWAY
PAUL SYCAMORE	FRANK WILCOX
MR. DE PINNA	FRANK CONLAN
ED	GEORGE HELLER
DONALD	OSCAR POLK
MARTIN VANDERHOF	HENRY TRAVERS
ALICE	MARGOT STEVENSON
HENDERSON	HUGH RENNIE
TONY KIRBY	JESS BARKER
BORIS KOLENKHOV	GEORGE TOBIAS
GAY WELLINGTON	MITZI HAJOS
MR. KIRBY	WILLIAM J. KELLY
MRS. KIRBY	VIRGINIA HAMMOND
	GEORGE LEACH
THREE MEN	RALPH HOLMES
	FRANKLIN HELLER
OLGA	ANNA LUBOWE

Stage Manager—WILLIAM MCFADDEN

The Scene Is the Home of Martin Vanderhof,
New York

ACT ONE

A Wednesday Evening.

*(During this act the curtain is lowered to
denote the passing of several hours.)*

ACT TWO

A Week Later.

ACT THREE

The Next Day.

ACT ONE

SCENE I

The home of MARTIN VANDERHOF—*just around the corner from Columbia University, but don't go looking for it. The room we see is what is customarily described as a living room, but in this house the term is something of an understatement. The every-man-for-himself room would be more like it. For here meals are eaten, plays are written, snakes collected, ballet steps practiced, xylophones played, printing presses operated—if there were room enough there would probably be ice skating. In short, the brood presided over by* MARTIN VAN DERHOF *goes on about the business of living in the fullest sense of the word. This is a house where you do as you like, and no questions asked.*

At the moment, GRANDPA VANDERHOF's *daughter,* MRS. PENELOPE SYCAMORE, *is doing what she likes more than anything else in the world. She is writing a play—her eleventh. Comfortably ensconced in what is affectionately known as Mother's Corner, she is pounding away on a typewriter perched precariously on a rickety card table. Also on the table is one of those plaster-of-Paris skulls ordinarily used as an ash tray, but which serves* PENELOPE *as a candy jar. And, because* PENNY *likes companionship, there are two kittens on the table, busily lapping at a saucer of milk.*

PENELOPE VANDERHOF SYCAMORE *is a round little woman in her early fifties, comfortable looking, gentle, homey.*

121

*One would not suspect that under that placid exterior
there surges the Divine Urge—but it does, it does.*

*After a moment her fingers lag on the keys; a thoughtful
expression comes over her face. Abstractedly she takes
a piece of candy out of the skull, pops it into her mouth.
As always, it furnishes the needed inspiration—with a
furious burst of speed she finishes a page and whips it
out of the machine. Quite mechanically, she picks up
one of the kittens, adds the sheet of paper to the pile
underneath, replaces the kitten.*

As she goes back to work, ESSIE CARMICHAEL, MRS. SYCA-
MORE's *eldest daughter, comes in from the kitchen. A
girl of about twenty-nine, very slight, a curious air of
the pixie about her. She is wearing ballet slippers—in
fact, she wears them throughout the play.*

ESSIE (*fanning herself*). My, that kitchen's hot.

PENNY (*finishing a bit of typing*). What, Essie?

ESSIE. I say the kitchen's awful hot. That new candy I'm
making—it just won't ever get cool.

PENNY. Do you have to make candy today, Essie? It's such
a hot day.

ESSIE. Well, I got all those new orders. Ed went out and
got a bunch of new orders.

PENNY. My, if it keeps on I suppose you'll be opening up
a store.

ESSIE. That's what Ed was saying last night, but I said
no, I want to be a dancer. (*Bracing herself against the
table, she manipulates her legs, ballet fashion*)

PENNY. The only trouble with dancing is, it takes so long.
You've been studying such a long time.

ESSIE (*slowly drawing a leg up behind her as she talks*).
Only—eight—years. After all, Mother, you've been writing plays for eight years. We started about the same
time, didn't we?

PENNY. Yes, but you shouldn't count my first two years, because I was learning to type.

(*From the kitchen comes a colored maid named* RHEBA —*a very black girl somewhere in her thirties. She carries a white tablecloth, and presently starts to spread it over the table*)

RHEBA (*as she enters*). I think the candy's hardening up now, Miss Essie.

ESSIE. Oh, thanks, Rheba. I'll bring some in, Mother—I want you to try it. (*She goes into the kitchen*)

(PENNY *returns to her work as* RHEBA *busies herself with the table*)

RHEBA. Finish the second act, Mrs. Sycamore?

PENNY. Oh, no, Rheba. I've just got Cynthia entering the monastery.

RHEBA. Monastery? How'd she get there? She was at the El Morocco, wasn't she?

PENNY. Well, she gets tired of the El Morocco, and there's this monastery, so she goes there.

RHEBA. Do they let her in?

PENNY. Yes, I made it Visitors' Day, so of course anybody can come.

RHEBA. Oh.

PENNY. So she arrives on Visitors' Day, and—just stays.

RHEBA. All night?

PENNY. Oh, yes. She stays six years.

RHEBA (*as she goes into the kitchen*). Six years? My, I bet she busts that monastery wide open.

PENNY (*half to herself, as she types*). "Six Years Later."

(PAUL SYCAMORE *comes up from the cellar. Mid-fifties, but with a kind of youthful air. His quiet charm and mild manner are distinctly engaging*)

PAUL (*turning back as he comes through the door*). Mr. De Pinna! (*A voice from below. "Yah?"*) Mr. De Pinna, will you bring up one of those new skyrockets, please?

I want to show them to Mrs. Sycamore. (*An answering monosyllable from the cellar as he turns toward* PENNY) Look, Penny—what do you think of these little fire crackers? Ten strings for a nickel. Listen. (*He puts one down on the center table and lights it. It goes off with a good bang*) Nice, huh?

PENNY. Paul, dear, were you ever in a monastery?

PAUL (*quite calmly*). No, I wasn't. . . . Wait till you see the new rockets. Gold stars, then blue stars, then some bombs, and then a balloon. Mr. De Pinna thought of the balloon.

PENNY. Sounds lovely. Did you do all that today?

PAUL. Sure. We made up—oh, here we are. (MR. DE PINNA *comes up from the cellar. A bald-headed little man with a serious manner, and carrying two good-sized sky-rockets*) Look, Penny. Cost us eighteen cents to make and we sell 'em for fifty. How many do you figure we can make before the Fourth, Mr. De Pinna?

DE PINNA. Well, we've got two weeks yet—what day you going to take the stuff up to Mount Vernon?

PAUL. Oh, I don't know—about a week. You know, we're going to need a larger booth this year—got a lot of stuff made up.

DE PINNA (*examining the rocket in his hand*). Look, Mr. Sycamore, the only thing that bothers me is, I'm afraid the powder chamber is just a little bit close to the balloon.

PAUL. Well, we've got the stars and the bombs in between.

DE PINNA. But that don't give the balloon time enough. A balloon needs plenty of time.

PAUL. Want to go down in the cellar and try it?

DE PINNA. All right.

PAUL (*as he disappears through the cellar door*). That's the only way you'll really tell.

PENNY (*halting* DE PINNA *in the cellar doorway*). Mr. De

Pinna, if a girl you loved entered a monastery, what would you do?

DE PINNA (*he wasn't expecting that one*). Oh, I don't know, Mrs. Sycamore—it's been so long. (*He goes*)

(RHEBA *returns from the kitchen, bringing a pile of plates*)

RHEBA. Miss Alice going to be home to dinner tonight, Mrs. Sycamore?

PENNY (*deep in her thinking*). What? I don't know, Rheba. Maybe.

RHEBA. Well, I'll set a place for her, but she's only been home one night this week. (*She puts down a plate or two*) Miss Essie's making some mighty good candy to-day. She's doing something new with cocoanuts. (*More plates*) Let's see—six, and Mr. De Pinna, and if Mr. Kolenkhov comes that makes eight, don't it? (*At which point a muffled sound, reminiscent of the Battle of the Marne, comes up from the cellar. It is the skyrocket, of course. The great preliminary hiss, followed by a series of explosions.* PENNY *and* RHEBA, *however, don't even notice it.* RHEBA *goes right on*) Yes, I'd better set for eight.

PENNY. I think I'll put this play away for a while, Rheba, and go back to the war play.

RHEBA. Oh, I always liked that one—the war play.

(ESSIE *returns from the kitchen, carrying a plate of freshly made candy*)

ESSIE. They'll be better when they're harder, mother, but try one—I want to know what you think.

PENNY. Oh, they look awfully good. (*She takes one*) What do you call them?

ESSIE. I think I'll call 'em Love Dreams.

PENNY. Oh, that's nice. . . . I'm going back to my war play, Essie. What do you think?

ESSIE. Oh, are you, Mother?

PENNY. Yes, I sort of got myself into a monastery and I can't get out.

ESSIE. Oh, well, it'll come to you, Mother. Remember how you got out of that brothel. . . . . Hello, boys. (*This little greeting is idly tossed toward the snake solarium, a glass structure looking something like a goldfish aquarium, but containing, believe it or not, snakes*) The snakes look hungry. Did Rheba feed them?

PENNY (*as* RHEBA *re-enters*). I don't know. Rheba, did you feed the snakes yet?

RHEBA. No, Donald's coming and he always brings flies with him.

PENNY. Well, try to feed them before Grandpa gets home. You know how fussy he is about them.

RHEBA. Yes'm.

PENNY (*handing her the kittens*). And take Groucho and Harpo into the kitchen with you. . . . I think I'll have another Love Dream.

(MR. SYCAMORE *emerges from the cellar again*)

PAUL. Mr. De Pinna was right about the balloon. It was too close to the powder.

ESSIE (*practicing a dance step*). Want a Love Dream, Father? They're on the table.

PAUL. No, thanks. I gotta wash.

PENNY. I'm going back to the war play, Paul.

PAUL. Oh, that's nice. We're putting some red stars after the blue stars, then come the bombs and *then* the balloon. That ought to do it. (*He goes up the stairs*)

ESSIE (*another dance step*). Mr. Kolenkhov says I'm his most promising pupil.

PENNY (*absorbed in her own troubles*). You know, with forty monks and one girl, something ought to happen.

(ED CARMICHAEL *comes down the stairs. A nondescript young man in his mid-thirties. In shirtsleeves at the moment*)

ED. Listen! (*He hums a snatch of melody as he heads for the far corner of the room—the xylophone corner. Arriving there, he picks up the sticks and continues the*

melody on the xylophone. Immediately ESSIE *is up on
her toes, performing intricate ballet steps to* ED's *accompaniment*)

ESSIE (*dancing*). I like that, Ed. Yours?

ED (*shakes his head*). Beethoven.

ESSIE (*never coming down off her toes*). Lovely. Got a
lot of *you* in it. . . . I made those new candies this
afternoon, Ed.

ED (*playing away*). Yah?

ESSIE. You can take 'em around tonight.

ED. All right. . . . Now, here's the finish. This is me (*He
works up to an elaborate crescendo, but* ESSIE *keeps pace
with him right to the finish*)

ESSIE. That's fine. Remember it when Kolenkhov comes,
will you?

PENNY (*who has been busy with her papers*). Ed, dear,
why don't you and Essie have a baby? I was thinking
about it just the other day.

ED. I don't know—we could have one if you wanted us to.
What about it, Essie? Do you want to have a baby?

ESSIE. Oh, I don't care. I'm willing if Grandpa is.

ED. Let's ask him.

(ESSIE *goes into the kitchen as* PENNY *goes back to her
manuscripts*)

PENNY (*running through the pile*). Labor play . . . religious play . . . sex play. I know it's here some place.

(ED, *meanwhile, has transferred his attention from the
xylophone to a printing press that stands handily by,
and now gives it a preliminary workout*)

(MR. DE PINNA *comes out of the cellar, bound for the
kitchen to wash up*)

DE PINNA. I was right about the balloon. It was too close to
the powder.

ED. Anything you want printed, Mr. De Pinna? How about
some more calling cards?

DE PINNA (*as he passes into the kitchen*). No, thanks. I've
still got the *first* thousand.

ED (*calling after him*). Well, call on somebody, will you?
(*He then gives his attention to* RHEBA, *who is busy with
the table again*) What have we got for dinner, Rheba?
I'm ready to print the menu.

RHEBA. Cornflakes, watermelon, some of those candies
Miss Essie made, and some kind of meat—I forget.

ED. I think I'll set it up in boldface Cheltenham tonight.
(*He starts to pick out the letters*) If I'm going to take
those new candies around I'd better print up some de-
scriptive matter after dinner.

PENNY. Do you think anybody reads those things, Ed—
that you put in the candy boxes? . . . Oh, here it is.
(*She pulls a manuscript out of a pile*) "Poison Gas."
(*The door bell sounds*) I guess that's Donald. (*As*
RHEBA *breaks into a broad grin*) Look at Rheba smile.

ED. The boy friend, eh, Rheba?

PENNY (*as* RHEBA *disappears into the hallway*). Donald
and Rheba are awfully cute together. Sort of like Porgy
and Bess.

(RHEBA *having opened the door, the gentleman named*
DONALD *now looms up in the doorway—darkly. He is a
colored man of no uncertain hue*)

DONALD. Good evening, everybody!

ED. Hi, Donald! How've you been?

DONALD. I'm pretty good, Mr. Ed. How you been, Mrs.
Sycamore?

PENNY. Very well, thank you. (*She looks at him, apprais-
ingly*) Donald, were you ever in a monastery?

DONALD. No-o. I don't go no place much. I'm on relief.

PENNY. Oh, yes, of course.

DONALD (*pulling a bottle out of each side pocket*). Here's
the flies, Rheba. Caught a big mess of them today.

RHEBA (*taking the jars*). You sure did.

DONALD. I see you've been working, Mrs. Sycamore.

PENNY. Yes, indeed, Donald.

DONALD. How's Grandpa?

PENNY. Just fine. He's over at Columbia this afternoon. The Commencement exercises.

DONALD. My, the years certainly do roll 'round.

ED (*with his typesetting*). M — E — A — T. . . . What's he go there for all the time, Penny?

PENNY. I don't know. It's so handy—just around the corner. (PAUL *comes downstairs*)

PAUL. Oh, Donald! Mr. De Pinna and I are going to take the fireworks up to Mount Vernon next week. Do you think you could give us a hand?

DONALD. Yes, sir, only I can't take no money for it this year, because if the Government finds out I'm working they'll get sore.

PAUL. Oh! . . . Ed, I got a wonderful idea in the bathroom just now. I was reading Trotzky. (*He produces a book from under his arm*) It's yours, isn't it?

ED. Yah, I left it there.

PENNY. *Who* is it?

PAUL. *You* know, Trotzky. The Russian Revolution.

PENNY. Oh.

PAUL. Anyhow, it struck me it was a great fireworks idea. Remember "The Last Days of Pompeii"?

PENNY. Oh, yes. Palisades Park. (*With a gesture of her arms she loosely describes a couple of arcs, indicative of the eruption of Mt. Vesuvius*) That's where we met.

PAUL. Well, I'm going to do the Revolution! A full hour display.

DONALD. Say!

PENNY. Paul, that's wonderful!

ED. The red fire is the flag, huh?

PAUL. Sure! And the Czar, and the Cossacks!

DONALD. And the freeing of the slaves?

PAUL. No, no, Donald—

(*The sound of the front door slamming. A second's pause,*

and then GRANDPA *enters the living room.* GRANDPA *is about 75, a wiry little man whom the years have treated kindly. His face is youthful, despite the lines that sear it; his eyes are very much alive. He is a man who made his peace with the world long, long ago, and his whole attitude and manner are quietly persuasive of this*)

GRANDPA (*surveying the group*). Well, sir, you should have been there. That's all I can say—you should have been there.

PENNY. Was it a nice Commencement, Grandpa?

GRANDPA. Wonderful. They get better every year. (*He peers into the snake solarium*) You don't know how lucky you are you're snakes.

ED. Big class this year, Grandpa? How many were there?

GRANDPA. Oh, must have been two acres. *Everybody* graduated. And much funnier speeches than they had last year.

DONALD. You want to listen to a good speech you go up and hear Father Divine.

GRANDPA. I'll wait—they'll have him at Columbia.

PENNY. Donald, will you tell Rheba Grandpa's home now and we won't wait for Miss Alice.

DONALD. Yes'm. . . . (*As he goes through the kitchen door*) Rheba, Grandpa's home—we can have dinner.

PAUL. Got a new skyrocket today, Grandpa. Wait till you see it. . . . Wonder why they don't have fireworks at Commencements.

GRANDPA. Don't make enough noise. You take a good Commencement orator and he'll drown out a whole carload of fireworks. And say just as much, too.

PENNY. Don't the graduates ever say anything?

GRANDPA. No, they just sit there in cap and nightgown, get their diplomas, and then along about forty years from now they suddenly say, "Where am I?"

(ESSIE *comes in from the kitchen, bringing a plate of tomatoes for the evening meal*)

ESSIE. Hello, Grandpa. Have a nice day?

GRANDPA (*watching* ESSIE *as she puts the tomatoes on the table*). Hello-have-a-nice-day. (*Suddenly he roars at the top of his voice*) Don't I even get kissed?

ESSIE (*kissing him*). Excuse me, Grandpa.

GRANDPA. I'll take a tomato, too. (ESSIE *passes the plate;* GRANDPA *takes one and sits with it in his hand, solemnly weighing it*) You know, I could have used a couple of these this afternoon. . . . Play something, Ed.

(ED *at once obliges on the xylophone—something on the dreamy side. Immediately* ESSIE *is up on her toes again, drifting through the mazes of a toe dance*)

ESSIE (*after a moment*). There was a letter came for you, Grandpa. Did you get it?

GRANDPA. Letter for me? I don't know anybody.

ESSIE. It was for you, though. Had your name on it.

GRANDPA. That's funny. Where is it?

ESSIE. I don't know. Where's Grandpa's letter, mother?

PENNY (*who has been deep in her work*). What, dear?

ESSIE (*dancing dreamily away*). Where's that letter that came for Grandpa last week?

PENNY. I don't know. (*Then, brightly*) I remember seeing the kittens on it.

GRANDPA. Who was it from? Did you notice?

ESSIE. Yes, it was on the outside.

GRANDPA. Well, who was it?

ESSIE (*first finishing the graceful flutterings of the Dying Swan*). United States Government.

GRANDPA. Really? Wonder what *they* wanted.

ESSIE. There was one before that, too, from the same people. There was a couple of them.

GRANDPA. Well, if any more come I wish you'd give them to me.

ESSIE. Yes, Grandpa.

(*A fresh flurry of dancing; the xylophone grows a little louder*)

GRANDPA. I think I'll go out to Westchester tomorrow and do a little snake-hunting.

PAUL (*who has settled down with his book some time before this*). "God is the State; the State is God."

GRANDPA. What's that?

PAUL. "God is the State; the State is God."

GRANDPA. Who says that?

PAUL. Trotzky.

GRANDPA. Well, that's all right—I thought *you* said it.

ED. It's nice for printing, you know. Good and short. (*He reaches into the type case*) G — O — D — space — I — S — space — T — H — E

(*The sound of the outer door closing, and* ALICE SYCAMORE *enters the room. A lovely, fresh young girl of about twenty-two. She is plainly* GRANDPA's *grand-daughter, but there is something that sets her apart from the rest of the family. For one thing, she is in daily contact with the world; in addition, she seems to have escaped the tinge of mild insanity that pervades the rest of them. But she is a Sycamore for all that, and her devotion and love for them are plainly apparent. At the moment she is in a small nervous flutter, but she is doing her best to conceal it*)

ALICE (*as she makes the rounds, kissing her grandfather, her father, her mother*). And so the beautiful princess came into the palace, and kissed her mother, and her father, and her grandfather—hi, Grandpa—and what do you think? They turned into the Sycamore family. Surprised?

ESSIE (*examining* ALICE's *dress*). Oh, Alice, I like it. It's new, isn't it?

PENNY. Looks nice and summery.

ESSIE. Where'd you get it?

ALICE. Oh, I took a walk during lunch hour.

GRANDPA. You've been taking a lot of walks lately. That's the second new dress this week.

ALICE. Oh, I just like to brighten up the office once in a while. I'm known as the Kay Francis of Kirby & Co. . . . Well, what's new around here? In the way of plays, snakes, ballet dancing or fireworks. Dad, I'll bet you've been down in that cellar all day.

PAUL. Huh?

PENNY. I'm going back to the war play, Alice.

ESSIE. Ed, play Alice that Beethoven thing you wrote. Listen, Alice.

(*Like a shot* ED *is at the xylophone again,* ESSIE *up on her toes*)

(GRANDPA, *meanwhile, has unearthed his stamp album from under a pile of oddments in the corner, and is now busy with his magnifying glass*)

GRANDPA. Do you know that you can mail a letter all the way from Nicaragua for two pesetos?

PENNY (*meanwhile dramatically reading one of her own deathless lines*). "Kenneth, my virginity is a priceless thing to me."

ALICE (*finding it hard to break through all this*). Listen, people. . . . Listen. (*A break in the music; she gets a scattered sort of attention*) I'm not home to dinner. A young gentleman is calling for me.

ESSIE. Really? Who is it?

PENNY. Well, isn't that nice?

ALICE (*with quiet humor*). I did everything possible to keep him from coming here, but he's calling for me.

PENNY. Why don't you both stay to dinner?

ALICE. No, I want him to take you in easy doses. I've tried to prepare him a little, but don't make it any worse than you can help. Don't read him any plays, mother, and don't let a snake bite him, Grandpa, because I like him. And I wouldn't dance for him, Essie, because we're going to the Monte Carlo ballet tonight.

GRANDPA. Can't do *anything*. Who *is* he—President of the United States?

ALICE. No, he's vice-president of Kirby & Co. Mr. Anthony
Kirby, Jr.

ESSIE. The Boss's son?

PENNY. Well!

ALICE. The Boss's son. Just like the movies.

ESSIE. That explains the new dresses.

ED. And not being home to dinner for three weeks.

ALICE. Why, you're wonderful!

PENNY (*all aglow*). Are you going to marry him?

ALICE. Oh, of course. Tonight! Meanwhile I have to go up
and put on my wedding dress.

ESSIE. Is he good looking?

ALICE (*vainly consulting her watch*). Yes, in a word. Oh,
dear! What time is it?

PENNY. I don't know. Anybody know what time it is?

PAUL. Mr. De Pinna might know.

ED. It was about five o'clock a couple of hours ago.

ALICE. Oh, I ought to know better than to ask you people.
. . . Will you let me know the minute he comes, please?

PENNY. Of course, Alice.

ALICE. Yes, I know, but I mean the *minute* he comes.

PENNY. Why, of course. (ALICE *looks apprehensively from
one to the other; then disappears up the stairs*) Well,
what do you think of that?

GRANDPA. She seems to like him, if you ask me.

ESSIE. I should say so. She's got it bad.

PENNY. Wouldn't it be wonderful if she married him? We
could have the wedding right in this room.

PAUL. Now, wait a minute, Penny. This is the first time
he's ever called for the girl.

PENNY. You only called for me once.

PAUL. Young people are different nowadays.

ESSIE. Oh, I don't know. Look at Ed and me. He came to
dinner *once* and just stayed.

PENNY. Anyhow, I think it's wonderful. I'll bet he's crazy
about her. It must be he that's been taking her out every

night. (*The door bell rings*) There he is! Never mind, Rheba, I'll answer it. (*She is fluttering to the door*) Now remember what Alice said, and be *very* nice to him.

GRANDPA (*rising*). All right—let's take a look at him.

PENNY (*at the front door; milk and honey in her voice*). Well! Welcome to our little home! I'm Alice's mother. Do come right in! Here we are! (*She reappears in the archway, piloting the stranger*) This is Grandpa, and that's Alice's father, and Alice's sister, and her husband, Ed Carmichael. (*The family all give courteous little nods and smiles as they are introduced*) Well! Now give me your hat and make yourself right at home.

THE MAN. I'm afraid you must be making a mistake.

PENNY. How's that?

THE MAN. My card.

PENNY (*reading*). "Wilbur C. Henderson. Internal Revenue Department."

HENDERSON. That's right.

GRANDPA. What can we do for you?

HENDERSON. Does a Mr. Martin Vanderhof live here?

GRANDPA. Yes, sir. That's me.

HENDERSON (*all milk and honey*). Well, Mr. Vanderhof, the Government wants to talk to you about a little matter of income tax.

PENNY. Income tax?

HENDERSON. Do you mind if I sit down?

GRANDPA. No, no. Just go right ahead.

HENDERSON (*settling himself*). Thank you.

(*From above stairs the voice of* ALICE *floats down*)

ALICE. Mother! Is that Mr. Kirby?

PENNY (*going to the stairs*). No. No, it isn't, darling. It's —an internal something or other. (*To* MR. HENDERSON) Pardon me.

HENDERSON (*pulling a sheaf of papers from his pocket*). We've written you several letters about this, Mr. Vanderhof, but have not had any reply.

GRANDPA. Oh, that's what those letters were.

ESSIE. I told you they were from the Government.

(MR. DE PINNA *comes up from the cellar, bearing a couple of giant firecrackers. He pauses as he sees a stranger*)

DE PINNA. Oh, pardon me.

PAUL. Yes, Mr. De Pinna?

DE PINNA. These things are not going off, Mr. Sycamore. Look. (*He prepares to apply a match to one of them, as a startled income tax man nearly has a conniption fit. But* PAUL *is too quick for him*)

PAUL. Ah—not here, Mr. De Pinna. Grandpa's busy.

DE PINNA. Oh. (MR. DE PINNA *and* PAUL *hurry into the hall with their firecrackers*)

HENDERSON (*now that order has been restored*). According to our records, Mr. Vanderhof, you have never paid an income tax.

GRANDPA. That's right.

HENDERSON. Why not?

GRANDPA. I don't believe in it.

HENDERSON. Well—you own property, don't you?

GRANDPA. Yes, sir.

HENDERSON. And you receive a yearly income from it?

GRANDPA. I do.

HENDERSON. Of—(*He consults his records*)—between three and four thousand dollars.

GRANDPA. About that.

HENDERSON. You've been receiving it for years.

GRANDPA. I have. 1901, if you want the exact date.

HENDERSON. Well, the Government is only concerned from 1914 on. That's when the income tax started.

GRANDPA. Well?

HENDERSON. Well—it seems, Mr. Vanderhof, that you owe the Government twenty-two years' back income tax.

ED. Wait a minute! You can't go back that far—that's outlawed.

HENDERSON (*calmly regarding him*). What's *your* name?

ED. What difference does that make?

HENDERSON. Ever file an income tax return?

ED. No, sir.

HENDERSON. What was your income last year?

ED. Ah—twenty-eight dollars and fifty cents, wasn't it, Essie?

(ESSIE *gives quick assent; the income tax man dismisses the whole matter with an impatient wave of the hand and returns to bigger game*)

HENDERSON. Now, Mr. Vanderhof, you know there's quite a penalty for not filing an income tax return.

PENNY. Penalty?

GRANDPA. Look, Mr. Henderson, let me ask you something.

HENDERSON. Well?

GRANDPA. Suppose I pay you this money—mind you, I don't say I'm going to do it—but just for the sake of argument—what's the Government going to do with it?

HENDERSON. How do you mean?

GRANDPA. Well, what do I get for my money? If I go into Macy's and buy something, there it *is*—I see it. What's the Government give me?

HENDERSON. Why, the Government gives you everything. It protects you.

GRANDPA. What from?

HENDERSON. Well—invasion. Foreigners that might come over here and take everything you've got.

GRANDPA. Oh, I don't think they're going to do that.

HENDERSON. If you didn't pay an income tax, they would. How do you think the Government keeps up the Army and Navy? All those battleships . . .

GRANDPA. Last time we used battleships was in the Spanish-American War, and what did we get out of it? Cuba—and we gave that back. I wouldn't mind paying if it were something sensible.

HENDERSON (*beginning to get annoyed*). Well, what about

Congress, and the Supreme Court, and the President?
We've got to pay *them*, don't we?

GRANDPA (*ever so calmly*). Not with my money—no, sir.

HENDERSON (*furious*). Now wait a minute! I'm not here to
argue with you. All I know is that you haven't paid an
income tax and you've got to pay it!

GRANDPA. They've got to show me.

HENDERSON (*yelling*). We *don't* have to show you! I just
told you! All those buildings down in Washington, and
Interstate Commerce, and the Constitution!

GRANDPA. The Constitution was paid for long ago. And
Interstate Commerce—what *is* Interstate Commerce,
anyhow?

HENDERSON (*with murderous calm*). There are forty-eight
states—see? And if there weren't Interstate Commerce,
nothing could go from one state to another. See?

GRANDPA. Why not? They got fences?

HENDERSON. No, they haven't got fences! They've got *laws*!
. . . My God, I never came across anything like this
before!

GRANDPA. Well, I might pay about seventy-five dollars, but
that's all it's worth.

HENDERSON. You'll pay every cent of it, like everybody else!

ED (*who has lost interest*). Listen, Essie—listen to this a
minute.

(*The xylophone again;* ESSIE *goes into her dance*)

HENDERSON (*going right ahead, battling against the music*). And let me tell you something else! You'll go to
jail if you don't pay, do you hear that? There's a law,
and if you think you're bigger than the law, you've got
another think coming! You'll hear from the United
States Government, that's all I can say! (*He is back-
ing out of the room*)

GRANDPA (*quietly*). Look out for those snakes.

HENDERSON (*jumping*). Jesus!

(*Out in the hall, and not more than a foot or two behind*

MR. HENDERSON, *the firecracker boys are now ready to
test that little bomber. It goes off with a terrific detona-
tion, and* MR. HENDERSON *jumps a full foot. He wastes
no time at all in getting out of there*)

PAUL (*coming back into the room*). How did that sound
to you folks?

GRANDPA (*quite judicially*). I liked it.

PENNY. My goodness, he was mad, wasn't he?

GRANDPA. Oh, it wasn't his fault. It's just that the whole
thing is so silly.

PENNY (*suddenly finding herself with a perfectly good
Panama in her hand*). He forgot his hat.

GRANDPA. What size is it?

PENNY (*peering into its insides*). Seven and an eighth.

GRANDPA. Just right for me.

DE PINNA. Who was that fellow, anyhow?

(*Again the door bell*)

PENNY. This *must* be Mr. Kirby.

PAUL. Better make sure this time.

PENNY. Yes, I will. (*She disappears*)

ESSIE. I hope he's good-looking.

PENNY (*heard at the door*). How do you do?

A MAN'S VOICE. Good evening.

PENNY (*taking no chances*). Is this Mr. Anthony Kirby,
Jr.?

TONY. Yes.

PENNY (*giving her all*). Well, Mr. Kirby, come right in!
We've been expecting you. Come right in! (*They come
into sight;* PENNY *expansively addresses the family*)
This is *really* Mr. Kirby! Now, I'm Alice's mother, and
that's *Mr.* Sycamore, and Alice's grandfather, and her
sister Essie, and Essie's husband. (*There are a few
mumbled greetings*) There! Now you know *all* of us,
Mr. Kirby. Give me your hat and make yourself right at
home.

(TONY KIRBY *comes a few steps into the room. He is a*

*personable young man, not long out of Yale, and, as we
will presently learn, even more recently out of Cambridge. Although he fits all the physical requirements
of a Boss's son, his face has something of the idealist in
it. All in all, a very nice young man)*

TONY. How do you do?

(*Again the voice of the vigilant* ALICE *floats down from
upstairs.* "Is that Mr. Kirby, Mother?")

PENNY (*shouting up the stairs*). Yes, Alice. He's *lovely!*

ALICE (*aware of storm signals*). I'll be right down.

PENNY. Do sit down, Mr. Kirby.

TONY. Thank you. (*A glance at the dinner table*) I hope
I'm not keeping you from dinner?

GRANDPA. No, no. Have a tomato?

TONY. No, thank you.

PENNY (*producing the candy-filled skull*). How about a
piece of candy?

TONY (*eyeing the container*). Ah—no, thanks.

PENNY. Oh, I forgot to introduce Mr. De Pinna. This is
Mr. De Pinna, Mr. Kirby.

(*An exchange of "How do you do's?"*)

DE PINNA. Wasn't I reading about your father in the newspaper the other day? Didn't he get indicted or something?

TONY (*smiling*). Hardly that. He just testified before the
Securities Commission.

DE PINNA. Oh.

PENNY (*sharply*). Yes, of course. I'm sure there was nothing crooked about it, Mr. De Pinna. As a matter of fact—
(*She is now addressing* TONY) —Alice has often told
us what a lovely man your father is.

TONY. Well, I know father couldn't get along without
Alice. She knows more about the business than any of
us.

ESSIE. You're awful young, Mr. Kirby, aren't you, to be
vice-president of a big place like that.

TONY. Well, you know what that means, vice-president. All I have is a desk with my name on it.

PENNY. Is that all? Don't you get any salary?

TONY (*with a laugh*). Well, a little. More than I'm worth, I'm afraid.

PENNY. Now you're just being modest.

GRANDPA. Sounds kind of dull to me—Wall Street. Do you like it?

TONY. Well, the hours are short. And I haven't been there very long.

GRANDPA. Just out of college, huh?

TONY. Well, I knocked around for a while first. Just sort of had fun.

GRANDPA. What did you do? Travel?

TONY. For a while. Then I went to Cambridge for a year.

GRANDPA (*nodding*). England.

TONY. That's right.

GRANDPA. Say, what's an English commencement like? Did you see any?

TONY. Oh, very impressive.

GRANDPA. They are, huh?

TONY. Anyhow, now the fun's over, and—I'm facing the world.

PENNY. You've certainly got a good start, Mr. Kirby. Vice-president, and a rich father.

TONY. Well, that's hardly my fault.

PENNY (*brightly*). So now I suppose you're all ready to settle down and—get married.

PAUL. Come now, Penny, I'm sure Mr. Kirby knows his own mind.

PENNY. I wasn't making up his mind for him—was I, Mr. Kirby?

TONY. That's quite all right, Mrs. Sycamore.

PENNY (*to the others*). You see?

ESSIE. You mustn't rush him, mother.

PENNY. Well, all I meant was he's bound to get married, and suppose the wrong girl gets him?

(*The descending* ALICE *mercifully comes to* TONY'S *rescue at this moment. Her voice is heard from the stairs*)

ALICE. Well, here I am, a vision in white. (*She comes into the room—and very lovely indeed*) Apparently you've had time to get acquainted.

PENNY. Oh, yes, indeed. We were just having a delightful talk about love and marriage.

ALICE. Oh, dear. (*She turns to* TONY) I'm sorry. I came down as fast as I could.

RHEBA (*bringing a platter of sliced watermelon*). God damn those flies in the kitchen. . . . Oh, Miss Alice, you look beautiful. Where you going?

ALICE (*making the best of it*). I'm going out, Rheba.

RHEBA (*noticing* TONY). Stepping, huh?

(*The door bell sounds*)

ESSIE. That must be Kolenkhov.

ALICE (*uneasily*). I think we'd better go, Tony.

TONY. All right.

(*Before they can escape, however,* DONALD *emerges from the kitchen, bearing a tray*)

DONALD. Grandpa, you take cream on your cornflakes? I forget.

GRANDPA. Half and half, Donald.

(*The voice of* BORIS KOLENKHOV *booms from the outer door*)

KOLENKHOV. Ah, my little Rhebishka!

RHEBA (*with a scream of laughter*). Yassuh, Mr. Kolenkhov!

KOLENKHOV. I am so hungry I could even eat my little Rhebishka! (*He appears in the archway, his great arm completely encircling the delighted* RHEBA. MR. KOLENKHOV *is one of* RHEBA'S *pets, and if you like Russians he might be one of yours. He is enormous, hairy, loud, and very, very Russian. His appearance in the archway still further traps* ALICE *and* TONY) Grandpa, what do you think? I have had a letter from Russia! The Second Five Year Plan is a failure! (*He lets out a laugh that shakes the rafters*)

ESSIE. I practiced today, Mr. Kolenkhov!

KOLENKHOV (*with a deep Russian bow*). My Pavlowa! (*Another bow*) Madame Sycamore! . . . My little Alice! (*He kisses her hand*) Never have I seen you look so magnificent.

ALICE. Thank you, Mr. Kolenkhov. Tony, this is Mr. Kolenkhov, Essie's dancing teacher. Mr. Kirby.

TONY. How do you do?

(*A click of the heels and a bow from* KOLENKHOV)

ALICE (*determined, this time*). And now we really *must* go. Excuse us, Mr. Kolenkhov—we're going to the Monte Carlo ballet.

KOLENKHOV (*at the top of his tremendous voice*). The Monte Carlo ballet! It *stinks!*

ALICE (*panicky now*). Yes. . . . Well—good-by, everybody. Good-by.

TONY. Good-by. I'm so glad to have met you all.

(*A chorus of answering "Good-bys" from the family. The young people are gone*)

KOLENKHOV (*still furious*). The Monte Carlo ballet!

PENNY. Isn't Mr. Kirby lovely? . . . Come on, everybody! Dinner's ready!

ED (*pulling up a chair*). I thought he was a nice fellow, didn't you?

ESSIE. Mm. And so good-looking.

PENNY. And he had such nice manners. Did you notice, Paul? Did you notice his manners?

PAUL. I certainly did. You were getting pretty personal with him.

PENNY. Oh, now, Paul . . . Anyhow, he's a very nice young man.

DE PINNA (*as he seats himself*). He looks kind of like a cousin of mine.

KOLENKHOV. Bakst! Diaghileff! *Then* you had the *ballet*!

PENNY. I think if they get married here I'll put the altar right where the snakes are. You wouldn't mind, Grandpa, would you?

ESSIE. Oh, they'll want to get married in a church. His family and everything.

GRANDPA (*tapping on a plate for silence*). Quiet, everybody! Quiet! (*They are immediately silent—Grace is about to be pronounced.* GRANDPA *pauses a moment for heads to bow, then raises his eyes heavenward. He clears his throat and proceeds to say Grace*) Well, Sir, we've been getting along pretty good for quite a while now, and we're certainly much obliged. Remember, all we ask is just to go along and be happy in our own sort of way. Of course we want to keep our health, but as far as anything else is concerned, we'll leave it to You. Thank You. (*The heads come up as* RHEBA *comes through the door with a steaming platter*) So the Second Five Year Plan is a failure, eh, Kolenkhov?

KOLENKHOV (*booming*). Catastrophic! (*He reaches across the table and spears a piece of bread. The family, too, is busily plunging in*)

The curtain is down

SCENE II

(*Late the same night. The house is in darkness save for a light in the hall.*

Somewhere in the back regions an accordion is being played. Then quiet. Then the stillness of the night is suddenly broken again by a good loud BANG! from the cellar. Somewhere in the nether regions, one of the Sycamores is still at work.

Once more all is quiet, then the sound of a key in the outer door. The voices of ALICE *and* TONY *drift through.*)

ALICE. I could see them dance every night of the week. I think they're marvelous.

TONY. They are, aren't they? But of course just walking inside *any* theater gives *me* a thrill.

ALICE (*as they come into sight in the hallway*). It's been *so* lovely, Tony. I hate to have it over.

TONY. Oh, is it over? Do I have to go right away?

ALICE. Not if you don't want to.

TONY. I don't.

ALICE. Would you like a cold drink?

TONY. Wonderful.

ALICE (*pausing to switch on the light*). I'll see what's in the ice-box. Want to come along?

TONY. I'd follow you to the ends of the earth.

ALICE. Oh, just the kitchen is enough. (*They go out. A pause, a ripple of gay laughter from the kitchen, then they return.* ALICE *is carrying a couple of glasses,* TONY *brings two bottles of ginger ale and an opener*) Lucky you're not hungry, Mr. K. An ice-box full of cornflakes. That gives you a rough idea of the Sycamores.

TONY (*working away with the opener*). Of course, why they make these bottle openers for Singer midgets I never *was* able to—ah! (*As the bottle opens*) All over my coat.

ALICE. I'll take mine in a glass, if you don't mind.

TONY (*pouring*). There you are. A foaming beaker.

ALICE. Anyhow, it's cold.

TONY (*pouring his own*). Now if you'll please be seated. I'd like to offer a toast.

ALICE (*settling herself*). We are seated.

TONY. Miss Sycamore— (*He raises his glass on high*) —to you.

ALICE. Thank you, Mr. Kirby. (*Lifting her own glass*) To you. (*They both drink*)

TONY (*happily*). I wouldn't trade one minute of this evening for—all the rice in China.

ALICE. Really?

TONY. Cross my heart.

ALICE (*a little sigh of contentment. Then shyly*). Is there much rice in China?

TONY. Terrific. Didn't you read "The Good Earth"? (*She laughs. They are silent for a moment*) I suppose I ought to go.

ALICE. Is it very late?

TONY (*looks at his watch*). Very. (ALICE *gives a little nod. Time doesn't matter*) I don't want to go.

ALICE. I don't want you to.

TONY. All right, I won't. (*Silence again*) When do you get your vacation?

ALICE. Last two weeks in August.

TONY. I might take mine then, too.

ALICE. Really?

TONY. What are you going to do?

ALICE. I don't know. I hadn't thought much about it.

TONY. Going away, do you think?

ALICE. I might not. I like the city in the summer time.

TONY. I do too.

ALICE. But you always go up to Maine, don't you?

TONY. Why—yes, but I'm sure I *would* like the city in the summer time. That is, I'd like it if—Oh, you know what I mean, Alice. I'd love it if *you* were here.

ALICE. Well—it'd be nice if you were here, Tony.

TONY. You know what you're saying, don't you?

ALICE. What?

TONY. That you'd rather spend the summer with me than anybody else.

ALICE. It looks that way, doesn't it?

TONY. Well, if it's true about the summer, how would you feel about—the winter?

ALICE (*seeming to weigh the matter*). Yes. I'd—like that too.

TONY .(*tremulous*). Then comes spring—and autumn. If you could—see your way clear about those, Miss Sycamore. . . .

ALICE (*again a little pause*). Yes.

TONY. I guess that's the whole year. We haven't forgotten anything, have we?

ALICE. No.

TONY. Well, then—

(*Another pause, their eyes meet. And at this moment,* PENNY *is heard from the stairway*)

PENNY. Is that you, Alice? What time is it? (*She comes into the room, wrapped in a bathrobe*) Oh! (*In sudden embarrassment*) Excuse me, Mr. Kirby. I had no idea —that is, I— (*She senses the situation*) —I didn't mean to interrupt anything.

TONY. Not at all, Mrs. Sycamore.

ALICE (*quietly*). No, Mother.

PENNY. I just came down for a manuscript— (*Fumbling at her table*) —then you can go right ahead. Ah, here it is. "Sex Takes a Holiday." Well—good night, Mr. Kirby.

TONY. Good night, Mrs. Sycamore.

PENNY. Oh, I think you can call me Penny, don't you, Alice? At least I hope so.

(*With a little laugh she vanishes up the stairs. Before* PENNY'S *rippling laugh quite dies, BANG! from the cellar.* TONY *jumps*)

ALICE (*quietly*). It's all right, Tony. That's Father.

TONY. This time of night?

ALICE (*ominously*). Any time of night. Any time of *day.*

(*She stands silent. In the pause,* TONY *gazes at her fondly*)

TONY. You're more beautiful, more lovely, more adorable than anyone else in the whole world.

ALICE (*as he starts to embrace her*). Don't, Tony. I can't.

TONY. What?

ALICE. I can't, Tony.

TONY. My dear, just because your mother—all mothers are like that, Alice, and Penny's a darling. You see, I'm even calling her Penny.

ALICE. I don't mean that. (*She faces him squarely*) Look, Tony. This is something I should have said a long time ago, but I didn't have the courage. I let myself be swept away because—because I loved you so.

TONY. Darling!

ALICE. No, wait, Tony. I want to make it clear to you. You're of a different world—a whole different kind of people. Oh, I don't mean money or socially—that's too silly. But your family and mine—it just wouldn't work, Tony. It just wouldn't work.

(*Again an interruption. This time it is* ED *and* ESSIE, *returning from the neighborhood movie. We hear their voices at the door, deep in an argument.* ED: "All right, have it your way. She can't dance. That's why they pay her all that money—because she can't dance." And then ESSIE: "Well, I don't call that dancing, what she does."*)

(*They come into sight*)

ESSIE. Oh, hello. (*There is an exchange of greetings, a note of constraint in* ALICE's *voice. But* ESSIE *goes right ahead*) Look! What do *you* think? Ed and I just saw Fred Astaire and Ginger Rogers. Do you think she can dance, Mr. Kirby?

TONY (*mildly taken aback by this*). Why, yes—I always thought so.

ESSIE. What does she do, anyhow? Now, look—you're Fred Astaire and I'm Ginger Rogers. (*She drapes herself against* TONY, *à la Ginger Rogers*)

ALICE. Essie, please.

ESSIE. I just want to use him for a minute. . . . Look, Mr. Kirby—(*Her arms go round his neck, her cheek against his*)

ALICE (*Feeling that it's time to take action*). Essie, you're just as good as Ginger Rogers. We all agree.

ESSIE (*triumphantly*). You see, Ed?

ED. Yeh. . . . Come on, Essie—we're butting in here.

ESSIE. Oh, they've been together all evening. . . . Good night, Mr. Kirby.

(*An exchange of good nights—it looks as though the* CARMICHAELS *are really going upstairs before the whole thing gets too embarrassing. Then* ED *turns casually to* ESSIE *in the doorway*)

ED. Essie, did you ask Grandpa about us having a baby?

ESSIE (*as they ascend the stairs*). Yes—he said go right ahead.

ALICE (*when they are gone*). You see? That's what it would be like, always.

TONY. But I didn't mind that. Besides, darling, we're not going to live with our families. It's just you and I.

ALICE. No, it isn't—it's never quite that. I love them, Tony —I love them deeply. Some people could cut away, but I couldn't. I know they do rather strange things—I never know what to expect next—but they're gay, and they're fun, and—I don't know—there's a kind of nobility about them. That may sound silly, but I mean—the way they just don't care about things that other people give their whole lives to. They're—really wonderful, Tony.

TONY. Alice, you talk as though only you could understand them. That's not true. Why, I fell in love with them tonight.

ALICE. But your family, Tony. I'd want *you*, and everything about you, everything about *me*, to be—one. I couldn't start out with a part of me that you didn't share, and part of you that I didn't share. Unless we were all one

—you, and *your* mother and father—I'd be miserable. And they never can be, Tony—I know it. They couldn't be.

TONY. Alice, every family has got curious little traits. What of it? My father raises orchids at ten thousand dollars a bulb. Is that sensible? My mother believes in spiritualism. That's just as bad as your mother writing plays, isn't it?

ALICE. It goes deeper, Tony. Your mother believes in spiritualism because it's fashionable. And your father raises orchids because he can afford to. My mother writes plays because eight years ago a typewriter was delivered here by mistake.

TONY. Darling, what *of* it?

ALICE. And look at Grandpa. Thirty-five years ago he just quit business one day. He started up to his office in the elevator and came right down again. He just stopped. He could have been a rich man, but he said it took too much time. So for thirty-five years he's just collected snakes and gone to circuses and commencements. It never occurs to any of them—

(*As if to prove her point, they are suddenly interrupted at this moment by the entrance of* DONALD *from the kitchen. It is a* DONALD *who has plainly not expected to encounter midnight visitors, for he is simply dressed in a long white nightgown and a somewhat shorter bathrobe—a costume that permits a generous expanse of white nightshirt down around the legs, and, below that, a couple of very black shins. His appearance, incidentally, explains where all that music had been coming from, for an accordion is slung over his shoulder*)

DONALD (*surprised, but not taken aback*). Oh, excuse me. I didn't know you folks was in here.

ALICE (*resigned*). It's all right, Donald.

DONALD. Rheba kind of fancied some candy, and— (*His*

gaze is roaming the room) oh, there it is. (*He picks up* PENNY'S *skull, if you know what we mean*) You-all don't want it, do you?

ALICE. No, Donald. Go right ahead.

DONALD. Thanks. (*He feels that the occasion calls for certain amenities*) Have a nice evening?

ALICE. Yes, Donald.

DONALD. Nice dinner?

ALICE (*restraining herself*). Yes, Donald.

DONALD. The ballet nice?

ALICE (*entirely too quietly*). Yes, Donald.

DONALD (*summing it all up*). That's nice. (*He goes—and* ALICE *bursts forth*)

ALICE. Now! Now do you see what I mean? Could you explain Donald to your father? Could you explain Grandpa? You couldn't, Tony, you couldn't! I should have known! I did know! I love you, Tony, but I love them too! And it's no use, Tony! It's no use! (*She is weeping now in spite of herself*)

TONY (*quietly*). There's only one thing you've said that matters—that makes any sense at all. You love me.

ALICE. But, Tony, I know so well . . .

TONY. My darling, don't you think other people have had the same problem? Everybody's got a family.

ALICE (*through her tears*). But not like mine.

TONY. That doesn't stop people who love each other. . . . Darling! Darling, won't you trust me, and go on loving me, and forget everything else?

ALICE. How can I?

TONY. Because nothing can keep us apart. You know that. You must know it. Just as I know it. (*He takes her in his arms*) They want you to be happy, don't they? They *must*.

ALICE. Of course they do. But they can't change, Tony. I wouldn't want them to change.

TONY. They won't have to change. They're charming, lov-able people, just as they are. You're worrying about something that may never come up.

ALICE. Oh, Tony, am I?

TONY. All that matters right now is that we love each other. That's right, isn't it?

ALICE (*whispering*). Yes.

TONY. Well, then!

ALICE (*in his arms*). Tony, Tony!

TONY. Now! I'd like to see a little gayety around here. Young gentleman calling, and getting engaged and everything.

ALICE (*smiling up into his face*). What do I say?

TONY. Well, first you thank the young man for getting en-gaged to you.

ALICE. Thank you, Mr. Kirby, for getting engaged to me.

TONY. And then you tell him what it was about him that first took your girlish heart.

ALICE. The back of your head.

TONY. Huh?

ALICE. Uh-huh. It wasn't your charm, and it wasn't your money—it was the back of your head. I just happened to like it.

TONY. What happened when I turned around?

ALICE. Oh, I got used to it after a while.

TONY. I see . . . Oh, Alice, think of it. We're pretty lucky, aren't we?

ALICE. I know that *I* am. The luckiest girl in the world.

TONY. I'm not exactly unlucky myself.

ALICE. It's wonderful, isn't it?

TONY. Yes . . . Lord, but I'm happy.

ALICE. Are you, Tony?

TONY. Terribly . . . And now—good night, my dear. Un-til tomorrow.

ALICE. Good night.

TONY. Isn't it wonderful we work in the same office? Otherwise I'd be hanging around *here* all day.

ALICE. Won't it be funny in the office tomorrow—seeing each other and just going on as though nothing had happened?

TONY. Thank God I'm vice-president. I can dictate to you all day. "Dear Miss Sycamore: I love you, I love you, I love you."

ALICE. Oh, darling! You're such a fool.

TONY (*an arm about her as he starts toward the hallway*). Why don't you meet me in the drugstore in the morning—before you go up to the office? I'll have millions of things to say to you by then.

ALICE. All right.

TONY. And then lunch, and then dinner tomorrow night.

ALICE. Oh, Tony! What will people say?

TONY. It's got to come out some time. In fact, if you know a good housetop, I'd like to do a little shouting.

(*She laughs—a happy little ripple. They are out of sight in the hallway by this time; their voices become inaudible*)

(PAUL, *at this point, decides to call it a day down in the cellar. He comes through the door, followed by* MR. DE PINNA. *He is carrying a small metal container, filled with powder*)

PAUL. Yes, sir, Mr. De Pinna, we did a good day's work.

DE PINNA. That's what. Five hundred Black Panthers, three hundred Willow Trees, and eight dozen Junior Kiddie Bombers.

(ALICE *comes back from the hallway, still under the spell of her love*)

PAUL. Why, hello, Alice. You just come in?

ALICE (*softly*). No. No, I've been home quite a while.

PAUL. Have a nice evening? Say, I'd like you to take a look at this new red fire we've got.

ALICE (*almost singing it*). I had a beautiful evening, Father.

PAUL. Will you turn out the lights, Mr. De Pinna? I want Alice to get the full effect.

ALICE (*who hasn't heard a word*). What, Father?

PAUL. Take a look at this new red fire. It's beautiful. (MR. DE PINNA *switches the lights out;* PAUL *touches a match to the powder. The red fire blazes, shedding a soft glow over the room*) There! What do you think of it? Isn't it beautiful?

ALICE (*radiant; her face aglow, her voice soft*). Yes, Father. Everything is beautiful. It's the most beautiful red fire in the world! (*She rushes to him and throws her arms about him, almost unable to bear her own happiness*)

Curtain

ACT TWO

(*A week later, and the family has just risen from the din-ner table. Two or three of them have drifted out of the room, but* GRANDPA *and* PAUL *still sit over their coffee cups*)

(*There is, however, a newcomer in the room. Her name is* GAY WELLINGTON, *and, as we will presently guess, she is an actress, a nymphomaniac, and a terrible souse. At the moment she sits with a gin bottle in one hand and a glass in the other, and is having a darned good time. Hovering over her, script in hand, is a slightly worried* PENNY. ED *is watching the proceedings from somewhere in the vicinage of the printing press, and* DONALD, *leisurely clearing the table, has paused to see if* MISS WEL-LINGTON *can really swallow that one more drink of gin that she is about to tackle. She does, and another besides*)

(PENNY *finally decides to make a try*)

PENNY. I'm ready to read the play now, Miss Wellington, if you are.

GAY WELLINGTON. Just a minute, dearie—just a minute. (*The gin again*)

PENNY. The only thing is—I hope you won't mind my mentioning this, but—you don't drink when you're act-ing, do you, Miss Wellington? I'm just asking, of course.

GAY. I'm glad you brought it up. Once a play opens, I never touch a drop. Minute I enter a stage door, this bottle gets put away till intermission.

GRANDPA (*who plainly has his doubts*). Have you been on the stage a long time, Miss Wellington?

GAY. All my life. I've played everything. Ever see "Peg o' My Heart"?

GRANDPA. Yes, indeed.

GAY (*with that fine logic for which the inebriated brain is celebrated*). I saw it too. Great show. (*She staggers backwards a bit, but recovers herself just in time*) My! Hot night, ain't it?

DONALD (*ever helpful*). Want me to open a window, Miss Wellington?

GAY. No, the hell with the weather. (*She takes a second look at the dusky* DONALD) Say, he's cute.

(RHEBA, *who has entered just in time to overhear this, gives* GAY *a look that tells her in no uncertain terms to keep out of Harlem on dark nights. Then she stalks back into the kitchen,* DONALD *close on her heels*)

DONALD (*trying to explain it all*). She's just acting, Rheba. She don't mean anything.

PENNY. Well, any time you're ready, we can go up to my room and start. I thought I'd read the play up in my room.

GAY. All right, dearie, just a minute. (*She starts to pour one more drink, then suddenly her gaze becomes transfixed. She shakes her head as though to dislodge the image, then looks again, receives verification, and starts to pour the gin back into the bottle*) When I see snakes it's time to lay down. (*She makes for a couch in the corner, and passes right out—cold*)

PENNY. Oh, but those are real, Miss Wellington. They're Grandpa's. . . . Oh, dear! I hope she's not going to— (*Shaking her*) Miss Wellington! Miss Wellington!

ED. She's out like a light.

PAUL. Better let her sleep it off.

DONALD (*carrying the news into the kitchen*). Rheba, Miss Wellington just passed out.

(*From the nether recesses we hear* RHEBA's *reaction—an emphatic "Good!"*)

PENNY. Do you think she'll be all right?

GRANDPA. Yes, but I wouldn't cast her in the religious play.

PENNY. Well, I suppose I'll just have to wait. I wonder if I shouldn't cover her up.

GRANDPA. Next time you meet an actress on the top of a bus, Penny, I think I'd *send* her the play, instead of bringing her home to read it.

ESSIE (*as* ED *starts in with the printing press*). Ed, I wish you'd stop printing and take those Love Dreams around. They're out in the kitchen.

ED. I will. I just want to finish up these circulars.

ESSIE. Well, do that later, can't you? You've got to get back in time to play for me when Kolenkhov comes.

GRANDPA. Kolenkhov coming tonight?

ESSIE. Yes, tomorrow night's his night, but I had to change it on account of Alice.

GRANDPA. Oh! . . . Big doings around here tomorrow night, huh?

PENNY. Isn't it exciting? You know, I'm so nervous—you'd think it was me he was engaged to, instead of Alice.

ESSIE. What do you think they'll *be* like—his mother and father? . . . Ed, what are you doing *now*?

ED. Penny, did you see the new mask I made last night? (*He reveals a new side of his character by suddenly holding a homemade mask before his face*) Guess who it is.

PENNY. Don't tell me now, Ed. Wait a minute . . . Cleopatra.

ED (*furious*). It's Mrs. Roosevelt. (*He goes into the kitchen*)

(PAUL, *meanwhile, has gone to a table in the corner of the room, from which he now brings a steel-like boat model, two or three feet high, puts it down on the floor, and proceeds to sit down beside it. From a large cardboard box, which he has also brought with him, he proceeds to take out additional pieces of steel and fit them into the model)*

PAUL. You know, the nice thing about these Erector Sets, you can make so many different things with them. Last week it was the Empire State Building.

GRANDPA. What is it this week?

PAUL. The Queen Mary.

PENNY (*looking it over*). Hasn't got the right hat on. (ED *comes in from the kitchen, bringing a pile of about a dozen candy boxes, neatly wrapped, and tied together for purposes of delivery*)

ED (*as* MR. DE PINNA *comes in from the hall*). Look. Mr. De Pinna, would you open the door and see if there's a man standing in front of the house?

ESSIE. Why, what for?

ED. Well, the last two days, when I've been out delivering, I think a man's been following me.

ESSIE. Ed, you're crazy.

ED. No, I'm not. He follows me, and he stands and watches the house.

DE PINNA. Really? (*Striding out*) I'll take a look and see.

GRANDPA. I don't see what anybody would follow *you* for, Ed.

PENNY. Well, there's a lot of kidnapping going on, Grandpa.

GRANDPA. Yes, but not of Ed.

ED (*as* MR. DE PINNA *returns from the hall*). Well? Did you see him?

DE PINNA. There's nobody out there at all.

ED. You're sure?

DE PINNA. Positive. I just saw him walk away.

ED. You see? I told you.

ESSIE. Oh, it might have been anybody, walking along the street. Ed, will you hurry and get back?

ED (*picking up his boxes*). Oh, all right.

DE PINNA. Want to go down now, Mr. Sycamore, and finish packing up the fireworks?

PAUL (*putting the Queen Mary back on the table*). Yeh, we've got to take the stuff up to Mt. Vernon in the morning.

(*They go into the cellar. Simultaneously the voice of* ALICE, *happily singing, is heard as she descends the stairs*)

ALICE. Mother, may I borrow some paper? I'm making out a list for Rheba tomorrow night.

PENNY. Yes, dear. Here's some.

ALICE (*as she sights* MISS WELLINGTON). Why, what happened to your actress friend? Is she giving a performance?

PENNY. No, she's not acting, Alice. She's really drunk.

ALICE. Essie, you're going to give Rheba the kitchen all day tomorrow, aren't you? Because she'll need it.

ESSIE. Of course, Alice. I'm going to start some Love Dreams now, so I'll be 'way ahead. (*She goes into the kitchen*)

ALICE. Thanks, dear . . . Look, Mother, I'm coming home at three o'clock tomorrow. Will you have everything down in the cellar by that time? The typewriter, and the snakes, and the xylophone, and the printing press . . .

GRANDPA. And Miss Wellington.

ALICE. And Miss Wellington. That'll give me time to arrange the table, and fix the flowers.

GRANDPA. The Kirbys are certainly going to get the wrong impression of this house.

ALICE. You'll *do* all that, won't you, Mother?

PENNY. Of course, dear.

ALICE. And I think we'd better have cocktails ready by seven-fifteen, in case they happen to come a little early. . . . I wonder if I ought to let Rheba cook the dinner. What do you think, Grandpa?

GRANDPA. Now, Alice, I wouldn't worry. From what I've

seen of the boy I'm sure the Kirbys are very nice people, and if everything isn't so elaborate tomorrow night, it's all right too.

ALICE. Darling, I'm not trying to impress them, or pretend we're anything that we aren't. I just want everything to—to go off well.

GRANDPA. No reason why it shouldn't, Alice.

PENNY. We're all going to do everything we can to make it a nice party.

ALICE. Oh, my darlings, I love you. You're the most wonderful family in the world, and I'm the happiest girl in the world. I didn't know anyone could *be* so happy. He's so wonderful, Grandpa. Why, just seeing him— you don't know what it does to me.

GRANDPA. Just seeing him. Just seeing him for lunch, and dinner, and until four o'clock in the morning, and at nine o'clock *next* morning you're at the office again and there he is. You just see him, huh?

ALICE. I don't care! I'm in love! (*She swings open the kitchen door*) Rheba! Rheba! (*She goes into the kitchen*)

GRANDPA. Nice, isn't it? Nice to see her so happy.

PENNY. I remember when I was engaged to Paul—how happy I was. And you know, I still feel that way.

GRANDPA. I know . . . Nice the way Ed and Essie get along too, isn't it?

PENNY. And Donald and Rheba, even though they're *not* married. . . . Do you suppose Mr. De Pinna will ever marry anyone, Grandpa?

GRANDPA (*a gesture toward the couch*). Well, there's Miss Wellington.

PENNY. Oh, dear, I *wish* she'd wake up. If we're going to read the play tonight—

(MR. DE PINNA *comes up from the cellar, bringing along a rather large-sized unframed painting*)

DE PINNA. Mrs. Sycamore, look what I found! (*He turns*

*the canvas around, revealing a portrait of a somewhat
lumpy discus thrower, in Roman costume—or was it
Greek?) Remember?*

PENNY. Why, of course. It's my painting of you as The
Discus Thrower. Look, Grandpa.

GRANDPA. I remember it. Say, you've gotten a little bald,
haven't you, Mr. De Pinna?

DE PINNA (*running a hand over his completely hairless
head*). Is it very noticeable?

PENNY. Well, it was a long time ago—just before I stopped
painting. Let me see—that's eight years.

DE PINNA. Too bad you never finished it, Mrs. Sycamore.

PENNY. I always meant to finish it, Mr. De Pinna, but I
just started to write a play one day and that was that.
I never painted again.

GRANDPA. Just as well, too. *I* was going to have to strip
next.

DE PINNA (*meditatively*). Who would have thought, that
day I came to deliver the ice, that I was going to stay
here for eight years?

GRANDPA. The milkman was here for five, just ahead of
you.

DE PINNA. Why did he leave, anyhow? I forget.

GRANDPA. He didn't leave. He died.

PENNY. He was such a nice man. Remember the funeral,
Grandpa? We never knew his name and it was kind
of hard to get a certificate.

GRANDPA. What was the name we finally made up for him?

PENNY. Martin Vanderhof. We gave him *your* name.

GRANDPA. Oh, yes, I remember.

PENNY. It was a lovely thought, because otherwise he
never would have got all those flowers.

GRANDPA. Certainly was. And it didn't hurt *me* any. Not
bothered with mail any more, and I haven't had a telephone call from that day to this. (*He catches an un-
wary fly and drops it casually into the snake solarium*)

PENNY. Yes, it was really a wonderful idea.

DE PINNA (*with the picture*). I wish you'd finish this some-time, Mrs. Sycamore. I'd kind of like to have it.

PENNY. You know what, Mr. De Pinna? I think I'll do some work on it. Right tonight.

DE PINNA. Say! Will you?

(*The door bell rings*)

PENNY (*peering at the prostrate* GAY). I don't think she's going to wake up anyhow. . . . Look, Mr. De Pinna! You go down in the cellar and bring up the easel and get into your costume. Is it still down there?

DE PINNA (*excited*). I think so! (*He darts into the cellar*)

PENNY. Now, where did I put my palette and brushes? (*She dashes up the stairs as the voice of* KOLENKHOV *is heard at the door, booming, of course*)

KOLENKHOV. Rhebishka! My little Rhebishka!

RHEBA (*delighted, as usual*). Yassuh, Mr. Kolenkhov!

PENNY (*as she goes up the stairs*). Hello, Mr. Kolenkhov. Essie's in the kitchen.

KOLENKHOV. Madame Sycamore, I greet you! (*His great arm again encircling* RHEBA, *he drags her protestingly into the room*) Tell me, Grandpa—what should I do about Rhebishka! I keep telling her she would make a great toe dancer, but she laughs only!

RHEBA (*breaking away*). No, suh! I couldn't get up on my toes, Mr. Kolenkhov! I got corns! (*She goes into the kitchen*)

KOLENKHOV (*calling after her*). Rhebishka, you could wear diamonds! (*Suddenly he sights the portrait of* MR. DE PINNA) What is that?

GRANDPA (*who has taken up his stamp album again*). It's a picture of Mr. De Pinna. Penny painted it.

KOLENKHOV (*summing it up*). It stinks.

GRANDPA. I know. (*He indicates the figure on the couch*) How do you like that?

KOLENKHOV (*peering over*). What is *that*?

GRANDPA. She's an actress. Friend of Penny's.

KOLENKHOV. She is drunk—no?

GRANDPA. She is drunk—yes. . . . How are *you*, Kolen-khov?

KOLENKHOV. Magnificent! Life is chasing around inside of me, like a squirrel.

GRANDPA. 'Tis, huh? . . . What's new in Russia? Any more letters from your friend in Moscow?

KOLENKHOV. I have just heard from him. I saved for you the stamp. (*He hands it over*)

GRANDPA (*receiving it with delight*). Thanks, Kolenkhov.

KOLENKHOV. They have sent him to Siberia.

GRANDPA. That so? How's he like it?

KOLENKHOV. He has escaped. He has escaped and gone back to Moscow. He will get them yet, if they do not get him. The Soviet Government! I could take the whole Soviet Government and—grrah! (*He crushes Stalin and all in one great paw, just as* ESSIE *comes in from the kitchen*)

ESSIE. I'm sorry I'm late, Mr. Kolenkhov. I'll get into my dancing clothes right away.

KOLENKHOV. Tonight you will really work, Pavlowa. (*As Essie goes up the stairs*) Tonight we will take something new.

GRANDPA. Essie making any progress, Kolenkhov?

KOLENKHOV (*first making elaborately sure that* ESSIE *is gone*). Confidentially, she stinks.

GRANDPA. Well, as long as she's having fun. . . .

(DONALD *ambles in from the kitchen, chuckling*)

DONALD. You sure do tickle Rheba, Mr. Kolenkhov. She's laughing her head off out there.

KOLENKHOV. She is a great woman. . . . Donald, what do you think of the Soviet Government?

DONALD. The what, Mr. Kolenkhov?

KOLENKHOV. I withdraw the question. What do you think of *this* Government?

DONALD. Oh, I like it fine. I'm on relief, you know.

KOLENKHOV. Oh, yes. And you like it?

DONALD. Yassuh, it's fine. Only thing is you got to go round to the place every week and collect it, and sometimes you got to stand in line pretty near half an hour. Government ought to be run better than that—don't you think, Grandpa?

GRANDPA (*as he fishes an envelope out of his pocket*). Government ought to stop sending me letters. Want me to be at the United States Marshal's office Tuesday morning at ten o'clock.

KOLENKHOV (*peering at the letter*). Ah! Income tax! They have got you, Grandpa.

GRANDPA. Mm. I'm supposed to give 'em a lot of money so as to keep Donald on relief.

DONALD. You don't say, Grandpa? You going to pay it now?

GRANDPA. That's what they want.

DONALD. You mean I can come right *here* and get it instead of standing in that line?

GRANDPA. No, Donald. You will have to waste a full half hour of your time every week.

DONALD. Well, I don't like it. It breaks up my week. (*He goes into the kitchen*)

KOLENKHOV. He should have been in Russia when the Revolution came. Then he would have stood in line—a bread line. (*He turns to* GRANDPA) Ah, Grandpa, what they have done to Russia. Think of it! The Grand Duchess Olga Katrina, a cousin of the Czar, she is a waitress in Childs' restaurant! I ordered baked beans from her only yesterday. It broke my heart. A crazy world, Grandpa.

GRANDPA. Oh, the world's not so crazy, Kolenkhov. It's the people *in* it. Life's pretty simple if you just relax.

KOLENKHOV. How can you relax in times like these?

GRANDPA. Well, if they'd relaxed there wouldn't *be* times like these. That's just my point. Life is simple and kind of beautiful if you let it come to you. But the trouble is people forget that. I know I did. I was right in the thick of it—fighting, and scratching, and clawing. Regular jungle. One day it just kind of struck me. I wasn't having any fun.

KOLENKHOV. So you did what?

GRANDPA. Just relaxed. Thirty-five years ago, that was. And I've been a happy man ever since.

(*From somewhere or other* GRANDPA *has brought one of those colored targets that one buys at Schwartz's. He now hangs it up on the cellar door, picks up a handful of feathered darts, and carefully throws one at the target*)

(*At the same time* ALICE *passes through the room, en route from kitchen to the upstairs region*)

ALICE. Good evening, Mr. Kolenkhov.

KOLENKHOV (*bowing low over her hand*). Ah, Miss Alice! I have not seen you to present my congratulations. May you be very happy and have many children. That is my prayer for you.

ALICE. Thank you, Mr. Kolenkhov. That's quite a thought. (*Singing gayly, she goes up the stairs*)

KOLENKHOV (*looking after her*). Ah, love! That is all that is left in the world, Grandpa.

GRANDPA. Yes, but there's plenty of that.

KOLENKHOV. And soon Stalin will take that away, too. I tell you, Grandpa—

(*He stops as* PENNY *comes down the stairs—a living example of what the well-dressed artist should wear. She has on an artist's smock over her dress, a flowing black tie, and a large black velvet tam-o'-shanter, worn at a rakish angle. She carries a palette and an assortment of paints and brushes*)

PENNY. Seems so nice to get into my art things again. They still look all right, don't they, Grandpa?

GRANDPA. Yes, indeed.

KOLENKHOV. You are a breath of Paris, Madame Sycamore.

PENNY. Oh, thank you, Mr. Kolenkhov.

DONALD (*coming in from the kitchen*). I didn't know you was working for the WPA.

PENNY. Oh, no, Donald. You see, I used to paint all the time, and then one day—

(*The outer door slams and* ED *comes in*)

ED (*in considerable excitement*). It happened again! There was a fellow following me every place I went!

PENNY. Nonsense, Ed. It's your imagination.

ED. No, it isn't. It happens every time I go out to deliver candy.

GRANDPA. Maybe he wants a piece of candy.

ED. It's all right for you to laugh, Grandpa, but he keeps following me.

KOLENKHOV (*somberly*). You do not know what following is. In Russia *everybody* is followed. I was followed right out of Russia.

PENNY. Of course. You see, Ed—the whole thing is just imagination. (MR. DE PINNA *comes up from the cellar, ready for posing. He wears the traditional Roman costume, and he certainly cuts a figure. He is carrying* PENNY'S *easel, a discus, and a small platform for posing purposes*) Ah, here we are! . . . Right here, Mr. De Pinna.

DONALD (*suddenly getting it*). Oh, is that picture supposed to be Mr. De Pinna?

PENNY (*sharply*). Of course it is, Donald. What's it look like—me?

DONALD (*studying the portrait*). Yes, it does—a little bit.

PENNY. Nonsense! What would I be doing with a discus?

KOLENKHOV. Ed, for tonight's lesson we use the first movement of Scheherazade.

ED. Okay.

DE PINNA (*about to mount the platform*). I hope I haven't forgotten how to pose. (*He takes up the discus and strikes the classic pose of the Discus Thrower. Somehow, it is not quite convincing)*

DONALD. What's he going to do with that thing? Throw it?

PENNY. No, no, Donald. He's just posing. . . . Mr. De Pinna, has something happened to your figure during these eight years?

DE PINNA *(pulling in his stomach)*. No, I don't think it's any different.

(With a sudden snort, GAY WELLINGTON comes to)

PENNY *(immediately alert)*. Yes, Miss Wellington?

(For answer, GAY peers first at PENNY, then at MR. DE PINNA. Then, with a strange snort, she just passes right out again)

PENNY. Oh, dear.

(ESSIE comes tripping down the stairs—very much the bal-let dancer. She is in full costume—ballet skirt, tight white satin bodice, a garland of roses in her hair)

ESSIE. Sorry, Mr. Kolenkhov, I couldn't find my slippers.

KOLENKHOV *(having previously removed his coat, he now takes off his shirt, displaying an enormous hairy chest beneath his undershirt)*. We have a hot night for it, my Pavlowa, but art is only achieved through perspiration.

PENNY. Why, that's wonderful, Mr. Kolenkhov. Did you hear that, Grandpa—art is only achieved through per-spiration.

GRANDPA. Yes, but it helps if you've got a little talent with it. *(He returns to his dart throwing)* Only made two bull's-eyes last night. Got to do better than that. *(He hurls a dart at the board, then his eye travels to MISS WELLINGTON, whose posterior offers an even easier tar-get)* Mind if I use Miss Wellington, Penny?

PENNY. What, Grandpa?

GRANDPA *(shakes his head)*. Never mind. . . . Too easy.

(GRANDPA throws another dart at the target)

KOLENKHOV. You are ready? We begin! *(With a gesture he orders the music started; under KOLENKHOV's critical eye*

ESSIE *begins the mazes of the dance*) Fouettée, temps, élevée. (ESSIE *obliges with her own idea of fouettée, temps, élevée*) Pirouette! . . . Come, come! You can do that! It's eight years now. Pirouette! . . . At last! . . . Entrechat! . . . Entrechat! (ESSIE *leaps into the air, her feet twirling*) No, Grandpa, you cannot relax with Stalin in Russia. The Czar relaxed, and what happened to *him*?

GRANDPA. He was too late.

ESSIE (*still leaping away*). Mr. Kolenkhov! Mr. Kolenkhov!

KOLENKHOV. If he had not relaxed the Grand Duchess Olga Katrina would not be selling baked beans today.

ESSIE (*imploringly*). Mr. Kolenkhov!

KOLENKHOV. I am sorry. (*The door bell rings*) We go back to the pirouette.

PENNY. Could you pull in your stomach, Mr. De Pinna? . . . That's right.

KOLENKHOV. A little freer. A little freer with the hands. The whole body must work. Ed, help us with the music. The music must be free, too.

(*By way of guiding* ED, KOLENKHOV *hums the music at the pace that it should go. He is even pirouetting a bit himself*)

(*From the front door comes the murmur of voices, not quite audible over the music. Then the stunned figure of* RHEBA *comes into the archway, her eyes popping*)

RHEBA. Mrs. Sycamore. . . . Mrs. Sycamore. (*With a gesture that has a grim foreboding in it, she motions toward the still invisible reason for her panic*)

(*There is a second's pause, and then the reason is revealed in all its horror. The* KIRBYS, *in full evening dress, stand in the archway. All three of them.* MR. AND MRS. KIRBY, *and* TONY)

(PENNY *utters a stifled gasp; the others are too stunned even to do that. Their surprise at seeing the* KIRBYS, *however, is no greater than that of the* KIRBYS *at the sight that is spread before them*)

(GRANDPA, *alone of them all, rises to the situation. With a kind of old world grace, he puts away his darts and makes the guests welcome*)

GRANDPA. How do you do?

KIRBY (*uncertainly*). How do you do?

(*Not that it helps any, but* MR. DE PINNA *is squirming into his bathrobe,* KOLENKHOV *is thrusting his shirt into his trousers, and* ED *is hastily getting into his coat*)

TONY. Are we too early?

GRANDPA. No, no. It's perfectly all right—we're glad to see you.

PENNY (*getting rid of the smock and tam*). Why—yes. Only—we thought it was to be tomorrow night.

MRS. KIRBY. Tomorrow night!

KIRBY. What!

GRANDPA. Now, it's perfectly all right. Please sit right down and make yourselves at home. (*His eyes still on the* KIRBYS, *he gives* DONALD *a good push toward the kitchen, by way of a hint.* DONALD *goes, promptly, with a quick little stunned whistle that sums up HIS feelings*)

KIRBY. Tony, how could you possibly—

TONY. I—I don't know. I thought—

MRS. KIRBY. Really, Tony! This is most embarrassing.

GRANDPA. Not at all. Why, we weren't doing a thing.

PENNY. Just spending the evening at home.

GRANDPA. That's all. . . . Now, don't let it bother you. This is Alice's mother, Mrs. Sycamore . . . Alice's sister, Mrs. Carmichael. . . . *Mr.* Carmichael. . . . Mr. Kolenkhov. . . . (*At this point* MR. DE PINNA *takes an anticipatory step forward, and* GRANDPA *is practically compelled to perform the introduction*) And—Mr. De Pinna. Mr. De Pinna, would you tell Mr. Sycamore to come right up? Tell him that Mr. and Mrs. Kirby are here.

PENNY (*her voice a heavy whisper*). And be sure to put his
pants on.

DE PINNA (*whispering right back*). All right. . . . Excuse
me. (*He vanishes—discus and all*)

GRANDPA. Won't you sit down?

PENNY (*first frantically trying to cover the prostrate* GAY
WELLINGTON). I'll tell Alice that you're— (*She is at the
foot of the stairs*) —Alice! Alice, dear! (*The voice of*
ALICE *from above*, "*What is it?*") Alice, will you come
down, dear? We've got a surprise for you. (*She comes
back into the room, summoning all her charm*) Well!

GRANDPA. Mrs. Kirby, may I take your wrap?

MRS. KIRBY. Well—thank you. If you're perfectly sure that
we're not— (*Suddenly she sees the snakes and lets out
a scream*)

GRANDPA. Oh, don't be alarmed, Mrs. Kirby. They're perfectly harmless.

MRS. KIRBY (*edging away from the solarium*). Thank you.
(*She sinks into a chair, weakly*)

GRANDPA. Ed. take 'em into the kitchen.

(ED *at once obeys*)

PENNY. Of course we're so used to them around the house—

MRS. KIRBY. I'm sorry to trouble you, but snakes happen to
be the one thing—

KIRBY. I feel very uncomfortable about this. Tony, how
could you have done such a thing?

TONY. I'm sorry, Dad. I thought it was tonight.

KIRBY. It was very careless of you. *Very!*

GRANDPA. Now, now, Mr. Kirby—we're delighted.

PENNY. Oh, now, anybody can get mixed up, Mr. Kirby.

GRANDPA. Penny, how about some dinner for these folks?
They've come for dinner, you know.

MRS. KIRBY. Oh, please don't bother. We're really not hungry at all.

PENNY. But it's not a bother. Ed!— (*Her voice drops to a
loud whisper*) Ed, tell Donald to run down to the A. and

P. and get half a dozen bottles of beer, and—ah—some canned salmon—(*her voice comes up again*)—do you like canned salmon, Mr. Kirby?

KIRBY. Please don't trouble, Mrs. Sycamore. I have a little indigestion, anyway.

PENNY. Oh, I'm sorry . . . How about you, Mrs. Kirby? Do you like canned salmon?

MRS. KIRBY (*you just know that she hates it*). Oh, I'm very fond of it.

PENNY. You can have frankfurters if you'd rather.

MRS. KIRBY (*regally*). Either one will do.

PENNY (*to ED again*). Well, make it frankfurters, and some canned corn, and Campbell's Soup.

ED (*going out the kitchen door*). Okay!

PENNY (*calling after him*). And tell him to hurry! (PENNY *again addresses the* KIRBYS) The A. and P. is just at the corner, and frankfurters don't take *any* time to boil.

GRANDPA (*as* PAUL *comes through the cellar door*). And this is Alice's father, *Mr.* Sycamore. Mr. and Mrs. Kirby.

THE KIRBYS. How do you do?

PAUL. I hope you'll forgive my appearance.

PENNY. This is Mr. Sycamore's busiest time of the year. Just before the Fourth of July—

(*And then* ALICE *comes down. She is a step into the room before she realizes what has happened; then she fairly freezes in her tracks*)

ALICE. Oh!

TONY. Darling, will you ever forgive me? I'm the most dull witted person in the world. I thought it was tonight.

ALICE (*staggered*). Why, Tony, I thought you— (*To the* KIRBYS) —I'm so sorry I can't imagine—why, I wasn't —have you all met each other?

KIRBY. Yes, indeed.

MRS. KIRBY. How do you do, Alice?

ALICE (*not even yet in control of herself*). How do you do, Mrs. Kirby? I'm afraid I'm not very—presentable.

TONY. Darling, you look lovely.

KIRBY. Of course she does. Don't let this upset you, my dear—we've all just met each other a night sooner, that's all.

MRS. KIRBY. Of course.

ALICE. But I was planning such a nice party tomorrow night . . .

KIRBY (*being the good fellow*). Well, we'll come again to-morrow night.

TONY. There you are, Alice. Am I forgiven?

ALICE. I guess so. It's just that I—we'd better see about getting you some dinner.

PENNY. Oh, that's all done, Alice. That's all been attended to.

(DONALD, *hat in hand, comes through the kitchen door; hurries across the room and out the front way. The* KIRBYS *graciously pretend not to see*)

ALICE. But mother—what are you—what did you send out for? Because Mr. Kirby suffers from indigestion—he can only eat certain things.

KIRBY. Now, it's quite all right.

TONY. Of course it is, darling.

PENNY. I asked him what he wanted, Alice.

ALICE (*doubtfully*). Yes, but—

KIRBY. Now, now, it's not as serious as all that. Just because I have a little indigestion.

KOLENKHOV (*helping things along*). Perhaps it is not indigestion at all, Mr. Kirby. Perhaps you have stomach ulcers.

ALICE. Don't be absurd, Mr. Kolenkhov!

GRANDPA. You mustn't mind Mr. Kolenkhov, Mr. Kirby. He's a Russian, and Russians are inclined to look on the dark side.

KOLENKHOV. All right, I am a Russian. But a friend of mine, a Russian, *died* from stomach ulcers.

KIRBY. Really, I—

ALICE (*desperately*). Please, Mr. Kolenkhov! Mr. Kirby has indigestion and that's all.

KOLENKHOV (*with a Russian shrug of the shoulders*). All right. Let him wait.

GRANDPA (*leaping into the breach*). Tell me, Mr. Kirby, how do you find business conditions? Are we pretty well out of the depression?

KIRBY. What? . . . Yes, yes, I think so. Of course, it all depends.

GRANDPA. But you figure that things are going to keep on improving?

KIRBY. Broadly speaking, yes. As a matter of fact, industry is now operating at sixty-four per cent. of full capacity, as against eighty-two per cent. in 1925. Of course in 1929, a peak year—

(*Peak year or no peak year,* GAY WELLINGTON *chooses this moment to come to life. With a series of assorted snorts, she throws the cover back and pulls herself to a sitting position, blinking uncertainly at the assemblage. Then she rises, and weaves unsteadily across the room. The imposing figure of* MR. KIRBY *intrigues her*)

GAY (*playfully rumpling* MR. KIRBY'S *hair as she passes him*). Hello, Cutie. (*And with that she lunges on her way—up the stairs*)

(*The* KIRBYS, *of course, are considerably astounded by this exhibition; the* SYCAMORES *have watched it with varying degrees of frozen horror.* ALICE, *in particular, is speechless; it is* GRANDPA *who comes to her rescue*)

GRANDPA. That may seem a little strange to you, but she's not quite accountable for her actions. A friend of Mrs. Sycamore's. She came to dinner and was overcome by the heat.

PENNY. Yes, some people feel it, you know, more than others. Perhaps I'd better see if she's all right. Excuse me, please. (*She goes hastily up the stairs*)

ALICE. It *is* awfully hot. (*A fractional pause*) You usually escape all this hot weather, don't you, Mrs. Kirby? Up in Maine?

MRS. KIRBY (*on the frigid side*). As a rule. I had to come down this week, however, for the Flower Show.

TONY. Mother wouldn't miss that for the world. That blue ribbon is the high spot of her year.

ESSIE. I won a ribbon at a Flower Show once. For raising onions. Remember?

ALICE (*quickly*). That was a Garden Show, Essie.

ESSIE. Oh, yes.

(PENNY *comes bustling down the stairs again*)

PENNY. I'm so sorry, but I think she'll be all right now. . . . Has Donald come back yet?

ALICE. No, he hasn't.

PENNY. Well, he'll be right back, and it won't take any time at all. I'm afraid you must be starved.

KIRBY. Oh, no. Quite all right. (*Pacing the room, he suddenly comes upon* PAUL'S *Erector Set*) Hello! What's this? I didn't know there were little children in the house.

PAUL. Oh, no. That's mine.

KIRBY. Really? Well, I suppose every man has his hobby. Or do you use this as a model of some kind?

PAUL. No, I just play with it.

KIRBY. I see.

TONY. Maybe you'd be better off if *you* had a hobby like that, Dad. Instead of raising orchids.

KIRBY (*indulgently*). Yes, I wouldn't be surprised.

ALICE (*leaping on this as a safe topic*). Oh, *do* tell us about your orchids, Mr. Kirby. (*She addresses the others*) You know, they take six years before they blossom. Think of that!

KIRBY (*warming to his subject*). Oh, some of them take longer than that. I've got one coming along now that I've waited ten years for.

PENNY (*making a joke*). Believe it or not, I was waiting for an orchid.

KIRBY. Ah—yes. Of course during that time they require the most scrupulous care. I remember a bulb that I was very fond of—

(DONALD *suddenly bulges through the archway, his arms full. The tops of beer bottles and two or three large cucumbers peep over the edge of the huge paper bag*)

PENNY. Ah, here we are! Did you get everything, Donald?

DONALD. Yes'm. Only the frankfurters didn't look very good, so I got pickled pigs' feet.

(MR. KIRBY *blanches at the very idea*)

ALICE (*taking command*). Never mind, Donald—just bring everything into the kitchen. (*She turns at the kitchen door*) Mr. Kirby, please tell them *all* about the orchids —I know they'd love to hear it. And—excuse me. (*She goes*)

GRANDPA. Kind of an expensive hobby, isn't it, Mr. Kirby— raising orchids?

KIRBY. Yes, it is, but I feel that if a hobby gives one sufficient pleasure, it's never expensive.

GRANDPA. That's very true.

KIRBY. You see, I need something to relieve the daily nerve strain. After a week in Wall Street I'd go crazy if I didn't have something like that. Lot of men I know have yachts—just for that very reason.

GRANDPA (*mildly*). Why don't they give up Wall Street?

KIRBY. How's that?

GRANDPA. I was just joking.

MRS. KIRBY. I think it's necessary for everyone to have a hobby. Of course it's more to me than a hobby, but my great solace is—spiritualism.

PENNY. Now, Mrs. Kirby, don't tell me you fell for that. Why, everybody knows it's a fake.

MRS. KIRBY (*freezing*). To me, Mrs. Sycamore, spiritualism is—I would rather not discuss it, Mrs. Sycamore.

PAUL. Remember, Penny, you've got one or two hobbies of your own.

PENNY. Yes, but not silly ones.

GRANDPA (*with a little cough*). I don't think it matters what the hobby is—the important thing is to have one.

KOLENKHOV. To be ideal, a hobby should improve the body as well as the mind. The Romans were a great people! Why! What was their hobby? Wrestling. In wrestling you have to think quick with the mind and act quick with the body.

KIRBY. Yes, but I'm afraid wrestling is not very practical for most of us. (*He gives a deprecating little laugh*) I wouldn't make a very good showing as a wrestler.

KOLENKHOV. You could be a *great* wrestler. You are built for it. Look!

(*With a startlingly quick movement* KOLENKHOV *grabs* MR. KIRBY'S *arms, knocks his legs from under him with a quick movement of a foot, and presto!* MR. KIRBY *is flat on his whatsis. Not only that, but instantaneously* KO-LENKHOV *is on top of him*)

(*Just at this moment* ALICE *re-enters the room—naturally, she stands petrified. Several people, of course, rush immediately to the rescue,* TONY *and* PAUL *arriving at the scene of battle first. Amidst the general confusion they help* MR. KIRBY *to his feet*)

ALICE. Mr. Kirby! Are you—hurt?

TONY. Are you all right, Father?

KIRBY (*pulling himself together*). I—I—uh—(*He blinks, uncertainly*)—where are my glasses?

ALICE. Here they are, Mr. Kirby. . . . Oh, Mr. Kirby, they're broken.

KOLENKHOV (*full of apology*). Oh, I am sorry. But when you wrestle again, Mr. Kirby, you will of course not wear glasses.

KIRBY (*coldly furious*). I do not intend to wrestle again, Mr. Kolenkhov. (*He draws himself up, stiffly, and in return gets a sharp pain in the back. He gives a little gasp*)

TONY. Better sit down, father.

ALICE. Mr. Kolenkhov, how could you do such a thing? Why didn't somebody stop him?

MRS. KIRBY. I think, if you don't mind, perhaps we had better be going.

TONY. Mother!

ALICE (*close to tears*). Oh, Mrs. Kirby—please! Please don't go! Mr. Kirby—please! I—I've ordered some scrambled eggs for you, and—plain salad—Oh, please don't go!

KOLENKHOV. I am sorry if I did something wrong. And I apologize.

ALICE. I can't tell you how sorry I am, Mr. Kirby. If I'd been here—

KIRBY (*from a great height*). That's quite all right.

TONY. Of course it is. It's all right, Alice. We're not going. (*The* KIRBYS *reluctantly sit down again*)

(*A moment's silence—no one knows quite what to say*)

PENNY (*brightly*). Well! That was exciting for a minute, wasn't it?

GRANDPA (*quickly*). You were talking about your orchids, Mr. Kirby. Do you raise many different varieties?

KIRBY (*still unbending*). I'm afraid I've quite forgotten about my orchids.

(*More silence, and everyone very uncomfortable*)

ALICE. I'm—awfully sorry, Mr. Kirby.

KOLENKHOV (*exploding*). What did I do that was so terrible? I threw him on the floor! Did it kill him?

ALICE. Please, Mr. Kolenkhov.

(*An annoyed gesture from* KOLENKHOV; *another general pause*)

PENNY. I'm sure dinner won't be any time at all now.

(*A pained smile from* MRS. KIRBY)

ESSIE. Would you like some candy while you're waiting? I've got some freshly made.

KIRBY. My doctor does not permit me to eat candy. Thank you.

ESSIE. But these are nothing, Mr. Kirby. Just cocoanut and marshmallow fudge.

ALICE. Don't, Essie.

(RHEBA *appears in the kitchen doorway, beckoning violently to* ALICE)

RHEBA (*in a loud whisper*). Miss Alice! Miss Alice! (ALICE *quickly flies to* RHEBA's *side*) The eggs fell down the sink.

ALICE (*desperately*). Make some more! Quick!

RHEBA. I ain't got any.

ALICE. Send Donald out for some!

RHEBA (*disappearing*). All right.

ALICE (*calling after her*). Tell him to run! (*She turns back to the* KIRBYS) I'm so sorry. There'll be a little delay, but everything will be ready in just a minute.

(*At this moment* DONALD *fairly shoots out of the kitchen door and across the living room, beating the Olympic record for all time*)

(PENNY *tries to ease the situation with a gay little laugh. It doesn't quite come off, however*)

TONY. I've certainly put you people to a lot of trouble, with my stupidity.

GRANDPA. Not at all, Tony.

PENNY. Look! Why don't we all play a game of some sort while we're waiting?

TONY. Oh, that'd be fine.

ALICE. Mother, I don't think Mr. and Mrs. Kirby—

KOLENKHOV. *I* have an idea. I know a wonderful trick with a glass of water. (*He reaches for a full glass that stands on the table*)

ALICE (*quickly*). No, Mr. Kolenkhov.

GRANDPA (*shaking his head*). No-o.

PENNY. But I'm sure Mr. and Mrs. Kirby would love this game. It's perfectly harmless.

ALICE. Please, Mother. . . .

KIRBY. I'm not very good at games, Mrs. Sycamore.

PENNY. Oh, but *any* fool could play this game, Mr. Kirby. (*She is bustling around, getting paper and pencil*) All you do is write your name on a piece of paper—

ALICE. But Mother, Mr. Kirby doesn't want—

PENNY. Oh, he'll love it! (*Going right on*) Here you are, Mr. Kirby. Write your name on this piece of paper. And Mrs. Kirby, you do the same on this one.

ALICE. Mother, what *is* this game?

PENNY. I used to play it at school. It's called Forget-Me-Not. Now, I'm going to call out five words—just anything at all—and as I say each word, you're to put down the first thing that comes into your mind. Is that clear? For instance, if I say "grass," you might put down "green"—just whatever you think of, see? Or if I call out "chair," you might put down "table." It shows the reactions people have to different things. You see how simple it is, Mr. Kirby?

TONY. Come on, father! Be a sport!

KIRBY (*stiffly*). Very well. I shall be happy to play it.

PENNY. You see, Alice? He *does* want to play.

ALICE (*uneasily*). Well—

PENNY. Now, then? Are we ready?

KOLENKHOV. Ready!

PENNY. Now, remember—you must play fair. Put down the first thing that comes into your mind.

KIRBY (*pencil poised*). I understand.

PENNY. Everybody ready? . . . The first word is "potatoes." (*She repeats it*) "Potatoes." . . . Ready for the next one? . . . "Bathroom." (ALICE *shifts rather uneasily, but seeing that no one else seems to mind, she relaxes again*) Got that?

KOLENKHOV. Go ahead.

PENNY. All ready? . . . "Lust."

ALICE. Mother, this is not exactly what you—

PENNY. Nonsense, Alice—that word's all right.

ALICE. Mother, it's *not* all right.

MRS. KIRBY (*unexpectedly*). Oh, I don't know. It seems to me that's a perfectly fair word.

PENNY (*to* ALICE). You see? Now, you mustn't interrupt the game.

KIRBY. May I have that last word again, please?

PENNY. "Lust," Mr. Kirby.

KIRBY (*writing*). I've got it.

GRANDPA. This is quite a game.

PENNY. Sssh, Grandpa. . . . All ready? . . . "Honeymoon." (ESSIE *snickers a little, which is all it takes to start* PENNY *off. Then she suddenly remembers herself*) Now, Essie! . . . All right. The last word is "sex."

ALICE (*under her breath*). Mother!

PENNY. Everybody got "sex?" . . . All right—now give me all the papers.

GRANDPA. What happens now?

PENNY. Oh, this is the best part. Now I read out your reactions.

KIRBY. I see. It's really quite an interesting game.

PENNY. I knew you'd like it. I'll read your paper first, Mr. Kirby. (*To the others*) I'm going to read Mr. Kirby's paper first. Listen, everybody! This is Mr. Kirby's. . . . "Potatoes—steak." That's very good. See how they go together? Steak and potatoes?

KIRBY (*modestly, but obviously pleased with himself*). I just happened to think of it.

PENNY. It's *very* good. . . . "Bathroom—toothpaste." Uh-huh. "Lust—unlawful." Isn't that nice? "Honeymoon—trip." Yes. And "sex—male." Yes, of course . . . That's really a wonderful paper, Mr. Kirby.

KIRBY (*taking a curtain call*). Thank you . . . It's more

than just a game, you know. It's sort of an experiment in psychology, isn't it?

PENNY. Yes, it is—it shows just how your *mind* works. Now we'll see how *Mrs.* Kirby's mind works. . . . Ready? . . This is *Mrs.* Kirby. . . . "Potatoes—starch." I know just what you mean, Mrs. Kirby. . . . "Bathroom —Mr. Kirby."

KIRBY. What's that?

PENNY. "Bathroom—Mr. Kirby."

KIRBY (*turning to his wife*). I don't quite follow that, my dear.

MRS. KIRBY. I don't know—I just thought of you in connection with it. After all, you *are* in there a good deal, Anthony. Bathing, and shaving—well, you *do* take a long time.

KIRBY. Indeed? I hadn't realized that I was being selfish in the matter. . . . Go on, Mrs. Sycamore.

ALICE (*worried*). I think it's a very silly game and we ought to stop it.

KIRBY. No, no. Please go on, Mrs. Sycamore.

PENNY. Where was I . . . Oh, yes. . . . "Lust—human."

KIRBY. Human? (*Thin-lipped*) Really!

MRS. KIRBY. I just meant, Anthony, that lust is after all a— human emotion.

KIRBY. I don't agree with you, Miriam. Lust is not a human emotion. It is depraved.

MRS. KIRBY. Very well, Anthony. I'm wrong.

ALICE. Really, it's the most pointless game. Suppose we play Twenty Questions?

KIRBY. No, I find this game rather interesting. Will you go on, Mrs. Sycamore? What was the next word?

PENNY (*reluctantly*). Honeymoon.

KIRBY. Oh, yes. And what was Mrs. Kirby's answer.

PENNY. Ah—"Honeymoon—dull."

KIRBY (*murderously calm*). Did you say—dull?

MRS. KIRBY. What I meant, Anthony, was that Hot Springs was not very gay that season. All those old people sitting on the porch all afternoon, and—nothing to do at night.

KIRBY. That was not your reaction at the time, as I recall it.

TONY. Father, this is only a *game*.

KIRBY. A very illuminating game. Go on, Mrs. Sycamore!

PENNY (*brightly, having taken a look ahead*). This one's all right, Mr. Kirby. "Sex—Wall Street."

KIRBY. Wall Street? What do you mean by that, Miriam?

MRS. KIRBY (*nervously*). I don't know what I meant, Anthony. Nothing.

KIRBY. But you must have meant something, Miriam, or you wouldn't have put it down.

MRS. KIRBY. It was just the first thing that came into my head, that's all.

KIRBY. But what does it mean? Sex—Wall Street.

MRS. KIRBY (*annoyed*). Oh, I don't know what it means, Anthony. It's just that you're always talking about Wall Street, even when— (*She catches herself*) I don't know what I meant . . . Would you mind terribly, Alice, if we didn't stay for dinner? I'm afraid this game has given me a headache.

ALICE (*quietly*). I understand, Mrs. Kirby.

KIRBY (*clearing his throat*). Yes, possibly we'd better postpone the dinner, if you don't mind.

PENNY. But you're coming tomorrow night, aren't you?

MRS. KIRBY (*quickly*). I'm afraid we have an engagement tomorrow night.

KIRBY. Perhaps we'd better postpone the whole affair a little while. This hot weather, and—ah—

TONY (*smoldering*). I think we're being very ungracious, Father. Of *course* we'll stay to dinner—tonight.

MRS. KIRBY (*unyielding*). I have a very bad headache, Tony.

KIRBY. Come, come, Tony, I'm sure everyone understands.

TONY (*flaring*). Well, *I* don't. I think we ought to stay to dinner.

ALICE (*very low*). No, Tony.

TONY. What?

ALICE. We were fools, Tony, ever to think it would work. It won't. Mr. Kirby, I won't be at the office tomorrow. I —won't be there at all any more.

TONY. Alice, what are you talking about?

KIRBY (*to* ALICE), I'm sorry, my dear—very sorry . . . Are you ready, Miriam?

MRS. KIRBY (*with enormous dignity*). Yes, Anthony.

KIRBY. It's been very nice to have met you all. . . . Are you coming, Anthony?

TONY. No, Father. I'm not.

KIRBY. I see. . . . Your mother and I will be waiting for you at home. . . . Good night. (*With* MRS. KIRBY *on his arm, he sweeps toward the outer door*)

(*Before the* KIRBYS *can take more than a step toward the door, however, a new* FIGURE *looms up in the archway. It is a quiet and competent-looking individual with a steely eye, and two more just like him loom up behind him*)

THE MAN (*very quietly*). Stay right where you are, everybody. (*There is a little scream from* MRS. KIRBY, *an exclamation from* PENNY) Don't move.

PENNY. Oh, good heavens!

KIRBY. How dare you? Why, what does this mean?

GRANDPA. What *is* all this?

KIRBY. I demand an explanation!

THE MAN. Keep your mouth shut, you! (*He advances slowly into the room, looking the group over. Then he turns to one of his men*) Which one is it?

ANOTHER MAN (*goes over and puts a hand on* ED's *shoulder*). This is him.

ESSIE. Ed!

ED (*terrified*). Why, what do you mean?

ALICE. Grandpa, what is it?

KIRBY. This is an outrage!

THE MAN. Shut up! (*He turns to* ED) What's your name?

ED. Edward—Carmichael. I haven't done anything.

THE MAN. You haven't, huh?

GRANDPA (*not at all scared*). This seems rather high-handed to me. What's it all about?

THE MAN. Department of Justice.

PENNY. Oh, my goodness! J-men!

ESSIE. Ed, what have you done?

ED. I haven't done anything.

GRANDPA. What's the boy done, Officer?

ALICE. What is it? What's it all about?

THE MAN (*taking his time, and surveying the room*). That door lead to the cellar?

PENNY. Yes, it does.

PAUL. Yes.

THE MAN (*ordering a man to investigate*). Mac . . . (MAC *goes into the cellar*) . . . Jim!

JIM. Yes, sir.

THE MAN. Take a look upstairs and see what you find.

JIM. Okay. (JIM *goes upstairs*)

ED (*panicky*). I haven't done anything!

THE MAN. Come here, you! (*He takes some slips of paper out of his pocket*) Ever see these before?

ED (*gulping*). They're my—circulars.

THE MAN. You print this stuff, huh?

ED. Yes, sir.

THE MAN. And you put 'em into boxes of candy to get 'em into people's homes.

ESSIE. The Love Dreams!

ED. But I didn't mean anything!

THE MAN. You didn't, huh? (*He reads the circulars*) "Dynamite the Capitol!" "Dynamite the White House!" "Dynamite the Supreme Court!" "God is the State; the State is God!"

ED. But I didn't mean that. I just like to print. Don't I, Grandpa?

(DONALD *returns with the eggs at this point, and stands quietly watching the proceedings*)

GRANDPA. Now, Officer, the government's in no danger from Ed. Printing is just his hobby, that's all. He prints anything.

THE MAN. He does, eh?

PENNY. I never heard of such nonsense.

KIRBY. I refuse to stay here and—

(MR. DE PINNA, *at this point, is shoved through the cellar door by* MAC, *protesting as he comes*)

DE PINNA. Hey, let me get my pipe, will you? Let me get my pipe!

MAC. Shut up, you! . . . We were right, Chief. They've got enough gunpowder down there to blow up the whole city.

PAUL. But we only use that—

THE MAN. Keep still! . . . Everybody in this house is under arrest.

KIRBY. What's that?

MRS. KIRBY. Oh, good heavens!

GRANDPA. Now look here, Officer—this is all nonsense.

DE PINNA. You'd better let me get my pipe. I left it—

THE MAN. Shut up, all of you!

KOLENKHOV. It seems to me, Officer—

THE MAN. Shut up!

(*From the stairs comes the sound of drunken singing— "There was a young lady," etc.* GAY WELLINGTON, *wrapped in* PENNY'S *negligee, is being carried down the stairway by a somewhat bewildered* G-MAN)

THE G-MAN. Keep still, you! Stop that! Stop it!

THE LEADER (*after* GAY *has been persuaded to quiet down*). Who's that?

GRANDPA (*pretty tired of the whole business*). That—is my mother.

(*And then, suddenly, we hear from the cellar.* MR. DE
PINNA *seems to have been right about his pipe, to judge
from the sounds below. It is a whole year's supply of
fireworks—bombs, big crackers, little crackers, skyrockets, pin wheels, everything. The house is fairly rocked
by the explosion*)

(*In the room, of course, pandemonium reigns.* MRS. KIRBY
screams; the G-MAN *drops* GAY *right where he stands and
dashes for the cellar, closely followed by* MR. DE PINNA
and PAUL; PENNY *dashes for her manuscripts and* ED
rushes to save his xylophone. KOLENKHOV *waves his arms
wildly and dashes in all directions at once; everyone is
rushing this way and that*)

(*All except one. The exception, of course, is* GRANDPA, *who
takes all things as they come.* GRANDPA *just says* "Well,
well, well!"—*and sits down. If a lot of people weren't in
the way, in fact, you feel he'd like to throw a few darts*)

Curtain

ACT THREE

The following day.

RHEBA *is in the midst of setting the table for dinner, pausing occasionally in her labors to listen to the Edwin C. Hill of the moment—*DONALD. *With intense interest and concentration, he is reading aloud from a nowopaper)*

DONALD. ". . . for appearance in the West Side Court this morning. After spending the night in jail, the defendants, thirteen in all, were brought before Judge Callahan and given suspended sentences for manufacturing fireworks without a permit."

RHEBA. Yah. Kept me in the same cell with a strip teaser from a burlesque show.

DONALD. I was in the cell with Mr. Kirby. My, he was mad!

RHEBA. Mrs. Kirby and the strip teaser—they were fighting all night.

DONALD. Whole lot about *Mr.* Kirby here. (*Reading again*) "Anthony W. Kirby, head of Kirby & Co., 62 Wall Street, who was among those apprehended, declared he was in no way interested in the manufacture of fireworks, but refused to state why he was on the premises at the time of the raid. Mr. Kirby is a member of the Union Club, the Racquet Club, the Harvard Club, and the National Geographic Society." My, he certainly is a joiner!

RHEBA. All those rich men are Elks or something.

DONALD (*looking up from his paper*). I suppose, after all this, Mr. Tony ain't ever going to marry Miss Alice, huh?

187

RHEBA. No, suh, and it's too bad, too. Miss Alice sure loves that boy.

DONALD. Ever notice how white folks always getting themselves in trouble?

RHEBA. Yassuh, I'm glad I'm colored. (*She sighs, heavily*) I don't know what I'm going to do with all that food out in the kitchen. Ain't going to be no party tonight, that's sure.

DONALD. Ain't we going to eat it anyhow?

RHEBA. Well, I'm cooking it, but I don't think anybody going to have an appetite.

DONALD. *I'm* hungry.

RHEBA. Well, *they* ain't. They're all so broke up about Miss Alice.

DONALD. What's she want to go 'way for? Where's she going?

RHEBA. I don't know—mountains some place. And she's *going*, all right, no matter what they say. I know Miss Alice when she gets that look in her eye.

DONALD. Too bad, ain't it?

RHEBA. Sure is.

(MR. DE PINNA *comes up from the cellar, bearing the earmarks of the previous day's catastrophe. There is a small bandage around his head and over one eye, and another around his right hand. He also limps slightly*)

DE PINNA. Not even a balloon left. (*He exhibits a handful of exploded firecrackers*) Look.

RHEBA. How's your hand, Mr. De Pinna? Better?

DE PINNA. Yes, it's better. (*A step toward the kitchen*) Is there some more olive oil out there?

RHEBA (*nods*). It's in the salad bowl.

DE PINNA. Thanks. (*He goes out the kitchen door as* PENNY *comes down the stairs. It is a new and rather subdued* PENNY)

PENNY (*with a sigh*). Well, she's going. Nothing anybody said could change her.

RHEBA. She ain't going to stay away long, is she, Mrs. Sycamore?

PENNY. I don't know, Rheba. She won't say.

RHEBA. My, going to be lonesome around here without her. (*She goes into the kitchen*)

DONALD. How *you* feel, Mrs. Sycamore?

PENNY. Oh, I'm all right, Donald. Just kind of upset. (*She is at her desk*) Perhaps if I do some work maybe I'll feel better.

DONALD. Well, I won't bother you then, Mrs. Sycamore. (*He goes into the kitchen*)

(PENNY *puts a sheet of paper into the typewriter; stares at it blankly for a moment; types in desultory fashion, gives it up. She leans back and sits staring straight ahead*)

(PAUL *comes slowly down the stairs; stands surveying the room a moment; sighs. He goes over to the Erector Set; absentmindedly pulls out the flag. Then, with another sigh, he drops into a chair*)

PAUL. She's going, Penny.

PENNY. Yes. (*She is quiet for a moment; then she starts to weep, softly*)

PAUL (*going to her*). Now, now, Penny.

PENNY. I can't help it, Paul. Somehow I feel it's our fault.

PAUL. It's mine more than yours, Penny. All these years I've just been—going along, enjoying myself, when maybe I should have been thinking more about Alice.

PENNY. Don't say that, Paul. You've been a wonderful father. And husband, too.

PAUL. No, I haven't. Maybe if I'd gone ahead and been an architect—I don't know—something Alice could have been proud of. I felt that all last night, looking at Mr. Kirby.

PENNY. But we've been so happy, Paul.

PAUL. I know, but maybe that's not enough. I used to think it was, but—I'm kind of all mixed up now.

PENNY (*after a pause*). What time is she going?

PAUL. Pretty soon. Train leaves at half past seven.

PENNY. Oh, if only she'd see Tony. I'm sure he could persuade her.

PAUL. But she won't, Penny. He's been trying all day.

PENNY. Where is he now?

PAUL. I don't know—I suppose walking around the block again. Anyhow, she won't talk to him.

PENNY. Maybe Tony can catch her as she's leaving.

PAUL. It won't help, Penny.

PENNY. No, I don't suppose so. . . . I feel so sorry for Tony, too. (GRANDPA *comes down the stairs—unsmiling, but not too depressed by the situation. Anxiously*) Well?

GRANDPA. Now, Penny, let the girl alone.

PENNY. But, Grandpa—

GRANDPA. Suppose she *goes* to the Adirondacks? She'll be back. You can take just so much Adirondacks, and then you come home.

PENNY. Oh, but it's all so terrible, Grandpa.

GRANDPA. In a way, but it has its bright side, too.

PAUL. How do you mean?

GRANDPA. Well, Mr. Kirby getting into the patrol wagon, for one thing, and the expression on his face when he and Donald had to take a bath together. I'll never forget that if I live to be a hundred, and I warn you people I intend to. If I can have things like that going on.

PENNY. Oh, it was even worse with Mrs. Kirby. When the matron stripped her. There was a burlesque dancer there and she kept singing a strip song while Mrs. Kirby undressed.

GRANDPA. I'll bet you Bar Harbor is going to seem pretty dull to the Kirbys for the rest of the summer.

(*With a determined step,* ALICE *comes swiftly down the stairs. Over her arm she carries a couple of dresses. Looking neither to right nor left, she heads for the kitchen*)

GRANDPA. Need any help, Alice?

ALICE (*in a strained voice*). No, thanks, Grandpa. Ed is helping with the bags. I'm just going to press these.

PENNY. Alice, dear—

GRANDPA. Now, Penny.

(ED *has appeared in the hallway with a couple of hatboxes,* ESSIE *behind him*)

ED. I'll bring the big bag down as soon as you're ready, Alice.

ESSIE. Do you want to take some candy along for the train, Alice?

ALICE. No, thanks, Essie.

PENNY. Really, Alice, you could be just as alone here as you could in the mountains. You could stay right in your room all the time.

ALICE (*quietly*). No, Mother, I want to be by myself— away from everybody. I love you all—you know that. But I just have to go away for a while. I'll be all right. . . . Father, did you 'phone for a cab?

PAUL. No, I didn't know you wanted one.

PENNY. Oh, I told Mr. De Pinna to tell you, Paul. Didn't he tell you?

ED. Oh, he told *me*, but I forgot.

ALICE (*the final straw*). Oh, I wish I lived in a family that didn't always forget everything. That—that behaved the way *other* people's families do. I'm sick of corn-flakes, and—Donald, and—(*Unconsciously, in her impatience, she has picked up one of* GRANDPA's *darts; is surprised to find it suddenly in her hand*)—everything! (*She dashes the dart to the floor*) Why can't we be like other people? Roast beef, and two green vegetables, and—doilies on the table, and—a place you could bring your friends to—without— (*Unable to control herself further, she bursts out of the room, into the kitchen*)

ESSIE. I'll—see if I can do anything. (*She goes into the kitchen*)

(*The others look at each other for a moment, helplessly.*
PENNY, *with a sigh, drops into her chair again.* PAUL
also sits. GRANDPA *mechanically picks up the dart from
the floor; smooths out the feathers.* ED, *with a futile
gesture, runs his fingers idly over the xylophone keys.
He stops quickly as every head turns to look at him*)

(*The sound of the door opening, and* TONY *appears in the
archway. A worried and disheveled* TONY)

PENNY (*quickly*). Tony, talk to her! She's in the kitchen!

TONY. Thanks. (*He goes immediately into the kitchen.
The family, galvanized, listen intently. Almost immediately,* ALICE *emerges from the kitchen again, followed
by* TONY. *She crosses the living room and starts quickly
up the stairs*) Alice, won't you listen to me? Please!

ALICE (*not stopping*). Tony, it's no use.

TONY (*following her*). Alice, you're not being fair. At
least let me talk to you.

(*They are both gone—up the stairs*)

PENNY. Perhaps if I went upstairs with them . . .

GRANDPA. Now, Penny. Let them alone.

(ESSIE *comes out of the kitchen*)

ESSIE. Where'd they go? (ED *with a gesture, indicates the
upstairs region*) She walked right out the minute he
came in.

(MR. DE PINNA *also emerges from the kitchen*)

MR. DE PINNA. Knocked the olive oil right out of my hand.
I'm going to smell kind of fishy.

GRANDPA. How're you feeling, Mr. De Pinna? Hand still
hurting you?

DE PINNA. No, it's better.

PAUL. Everything burnt up, huh? Downstairs?

DE PINNA (*nodding, sadly*). Everything. And my Roman
costume, too.

GRANDPA (*to* PENNY). I told you there was a bright side
to everything. All except my twenty-two years back

income tax. (*He pulls an envelope out of his pocket*) I get another letter every day.

DE PINNA. Say, what are you going to do about that, Grandpa?

GRANDPA. Well, I had a kind of idea yesterday. It may not work, but I'm trying it, anyhow.

DE PINNA (*eagerly*). What is it?

(*Suddenly* KOLENKHOV *appears in the doorway*)

KOLENKHOV (*even he is subdued*). Good evening, everybody!

PENNY. Why, Mr. Kolenkhov!

GRANDPA. Hello, Kolenkhov.

KOLENKHOV. Forgive me. The door was open.

GRANDPA. Come on in.

KOLENKHOV. You will excuse my coming today. I realize you are—upset.

PENNY. That's all right, Mr. Kolenkhov.

ESSIE. I don't think I can take a lesson, Mr. Kolenkhov. I don't feel up to it.

KOLENKHOV (*uncertainly*). Well, I—ah—

PENNY. Oh, but do stay to dinner, Mr. Kolenkhov. We've got all that food out there, and somebody's got to eat it.

KOLENKHOV. I will be happy to, Madame Sycamore.

PENNY. Fine.

KOLENKHOV. Thank you. . . . Now, I wonder if I know you well enough to ask of you a great favor.

PENNY. Why, of course, Mr. Kolenkhov. What is it?

KOLENKHOV. You have heard me talk about my friend the Grand Duchess Olga Katrina.

PENNY. Yes?

KOLENKHOV. She is a great woman, the Grand Duchess. Her cousin was the Czar of Russia, and today she is waitress in Childs' Restaurant. Columbus Circle.

PENNY. Yes, I know. If there's anything at all that we can do, Mr. Kolenkhov . . .

KOLENKHOV. I tell you. The Grand Duchess Olga Katrina has not had a good meal since before the Revolution.

GRANDPA. She must be hungry.

KOLENKHOV. And today the Grand Duchess not only has her day off—Thursday—but it is also the anniversary of Peter the Great. A remarkable man!

PENNY. Mr. Kolenkhov, if you mean you'd like the Grand Duchess to come to dinner, why, we'd be honored.

ESSIE. Oh, yes!

KOLENKHOV (*with a bow*). In the name of the Grand Duchess, I thank you.

PENNY. I can hardly wait to meet her. When will she be here?

KOLENKHOV. She is outside in the street, waiting. I bring her in. (*And he goes out*)

GRANDPA. You know, if this keeps on I want to live to be a hundred and *fifty*.

PENNY (*feverishly*). Ed, straighten your tie. Essie, look at your dress. How do *I* look? All right?

(KOLENKHOV *appears in the hallway and stands at rigid attention*)

KOLENKHOV (*his voice booming*). The Grand Duchess Olga Katrina! (*And the* GRAND DUCHESS OLGA KATRINA, *wheat cakes and maple syrup out of her life for a few hours, sweeps into the room. She wears a dinner gown that has seen better days, and the whole is surmounted by an extremely tacky-looking evening wrap, trimmed with bits of ancient and moth-eaten fur. But once a Grand Duchess, always a Grand Duchess. She rises above everything—Childs', evening wrap, and all*) Your Highness, permit me to present Madame Sycamore— (*PENNY, having seen a movie or two in her time, knows just what to do. She curtsies right to the floor, and catches hold of a chair just in time*) Madame Carmichael— (*ESSIE does a curtsey that begins where all others leave off. Starting on her toes, she merges the*

Dying Swan with an extremely elaborate genuflection)
Grandpa—

GRANDPA (*with a little bow*). Madame.

KOLENKHOV. Mr. Sycamore, Mr. Carmichael, and Mr. De Pinna.

(PAUL *and* ED *content themselves with courteous little bows, but not so the social-minded* MR. DE PINNA. *He bows to the floor—and stays there for a moment*)

GRANDPA! All right now, Mr. De Pinna.

(MR. DE PINNA *gets to his feet again*)

PENNY. Will you be seated, Your Highness?

THE GRAND DUCHESS. Thank you. You are most kind.

PENNY. We are honored to receive you, Your Highness.

THE GRAND DUCHESS. I am most happy to be here. What time is dinner?

PENNY (*a little startled*). Oh, it'll be quite soon, Your Highness—very soon.

THE GRAND DUCHESS. I do not mean to be rude, but I must be back at the restaurant by eight o'clock. I am substituting for another waitress.

KOLENKHOV. I will make sure you are on time, Your Highness.

DE PINNA. You know, Highness, I think you waited on me in Childs' once. The Seventy-Second Street place?

THE GRAND DUCHESS. No, no. That was my sister.

KOLENKHOV. The Grand Duchess Natasha.

THE GRAND DUCHESS. I work in Columbus Circle.

GRANDPA. Quite a lot of your family living over here now, aren't there?

THE GRAND DUCHESS. Oh, yes—many. My uncle, the Grand Duke Sergei—he is an elevator man at Macy's. A very nice man. Then there is my cousin, Prince Alexis. He will not speak to the rest of us because he works at Hattie Carnegie's. He has cards printed—Prince Alexis of Hattie Carnegie. Bah!

KOLENKHOV. When he was selling Eskimo Pies at Luna
.Park he was willing tó talk to you.

THE GRAND DUCHESS. Ah, Kolenkhov, our time is coming.
My sister Natasha is studying to be a manicure, Uncle
Sergei they have promised to make floor-walker, and
next month I get transferred to the Fifth Avenue Childs'.
From there it is only a step to Schraffts', and *then* we
will see what Prince Alexis says!

GRANDPA (*nodding*). I think you've got him.

THE GRAND DUCHESS. You are telling *me*? (*She laughs a
triumphant Russian laugh, in which* KOLENKHOV *joins*)

PENNY. Your Highness—did you know the Czar? Personally, I mean.

THE GRAND DUCHESS. Of course—he was my cousin. It was
terrible, what happened, but perhaps it was for the best.
Where could he get a job now?

KOLENKHOV. That is true.

THE GRAND DUCHESS (*philosophically*). Yes. And poor relations are poor relations. It is the same in every family.
My cousin, the King of Sweden—he was very nice to us
for about ten years, but then he said, I just cannot go
on. I am not doing so well, either. . . . I do not blame
him.

PENNY. No, of course not. . . . Would you excuse me for
just a moment? (*She goes to the foot of the stairs and
stands peering up anxiously, hoping for news of* ALICE)

DE PINNA (*the historian at heart*). Tell me, Grand Duchess,
is it true what they say about Rasputin?

THE GRAND DUCHESS. Everyone wants to know about Rasputin. . . . Yes, my dear sir, it is true. In spades.

DE PINNA. You don't say?

KOLENKHOV. Your Highness, we have to watch the time.

THE GRAND DUCHESS. Yes, I must not be late. The manager
does not like me. He is a Communist.

PENNY. We'll hurry things up. Essie, why don't you go out
in the kitchen and give Rheba a hand?

THE GRAND DUCHESS (*rising*). I will help, too. I am a very good cook.

PENNY. Oh, but Your Highness! Not on your day off!

THE GRAND DUCHESS. I do not mind. Where is your kitchen?

ESSIE. Right through here, but you're the guest of honor, Your Highness.

THE GRAND DUCHESS. But I love to cook! Come, Kolenkhov! If they have got sour cream and pot cheese I will make you some blintzes!

KOLENKHOV. Ah! Blintzes! . . . Come, Pavlowa! We show you something! (*With* ESSIE, *he goes into the kitchen*)

DE PINNA. Say! The Duchess is all right, isn't she? Hey, Duchess! Can I help? (*And into the kitchen*)

PENNY. Really, she's a very nice woman, you know. Considering she's a Grand Duchess.

GRANDPA. Wonderful what people go through, isn't it? And still keep kind of gay, too.

PENNY. Mm. She made me forget about everything for a minute. (*She returns to the stairs and stands listening*)

PAUL. I'd better call that cab, I suppose.

PENNY. No, wait, Paul. I think I hear them. Maybe Tony has— (*She stops as* ALICE's *step is heard on the stair. She enters—dressed for traveling.* TONY *looms up behind her*)

ALICE. Ed, will you go up and bring my bag down?

TONY (*quickly*). Don't you do it, Ed!

(ED *hesitates, uncertain*)

ALICE. Ed, please!

TONY (*a moment's pause; then he gives up*). All right, Ed. Bring it down. (ED *goes up the stairs as* TONY *disconsolately stalks across the room. Then he faces the Sycamores*) Do you know that you've got the stubbornest daughter in all forty-eight states?

(*The door bell rings*)

ALICE. That must be the cab. (*She goes to the door*)

GRANDPA. If it is, it's certainly wonderful service.

(*To the considerable surprise of everyone, the voice of* MR. KIRBY *is heard at the front door*)

KIRBY. Is Tony here, Alice?

ALICE. Yes. Yes, he is.

(MR. KIRBY *comes in*)

KIRBY (*uncomfortably*). Ah—good afternoon. Forgive my intruding . . . Tony, I want you to come home with me. Your mother is very upset.

TONY (*he looks at* ALICE). Very well, Father . . . Good-bye, Alice.

ALICE (*very low*). Good-bye, Tony.

KIRBY (*trying to ease the situation*). I need hardly say that this is as painful to Mrs. Kirby and myself as it is to you people. I—I'm sorry, but I'm sure you understand.

GRANDPA. Well, yes—and in a way, no. Now, I'm not the kind of person tries to run other people's lives, but the fact is, Mr. Kirby, I don't think these two young people have got as much sense as—ah—you and I have.

ALICE (*tense*). Grandpa, will you please not do this?

GRANDPA (*disarmingly*). I'm just talking to Mr. Kirby. A cat can look at a king, can't he?

(ALICE, *with no further words, takes up the telephone and dials a number. There is finality in her every movement*)

PENNY. You—you want me to do that for you, Alice?

ALICE. No, thanks, Mother.

PAUL. You've got quite a while before the train goes, Alice.

ALICE (*into the phone*). Will you send a cab to 761 Claremont, right away, please? . . . That's right, thank you. (*She hangs up*)

KIRBY. And now if you'll excuse us . . . are you ready, Tony?

GRANDPA. Mr. Kirby, I suppose after last night you think this family is crazy, don't you?

KIRBY. No, I would not say that, although I am not accustomed to going out to dinner and spending the night in jail.

GRANDPA. Well, you've got to remember, Mr. Kirby, you came on the wrong night. Now tonight, I'll bet you, nothing'll happen at all. (*There is a great burst of Russian laughter from the kitchen—the mingled voices of* KOLENKHOV *and the* GRAND DUCHESS. GRANDPA *looks off in the direction of the laughter, then decides to play safe*) Maybe.

KIRBY. Mr. Vanderhof, it was not merely last night that convinced Mrs. Kirby and myself that this engagement would be unwise.

TONY. Father, I can handle my own affairs. (*He turns to* ALICE) Alice, for the last time, will you marry me?

ALICE. No, Tony. I know exactly what your father means, and he's right.

TONY. No, he's *not*, Alice.

GRANDPA. Alice, you're in love with this boy, and you're not marrying him because we're the kind of people we are.

ALICE. Grandpa—

GRANDPA. I know. You think the two families wouldn't get along. Well, maybe they wouldn't—but who says they're right and we're wrong?

ALICE. I didn't say that, Grandpa. I only feel—

GRANDPA. Well, what *I* feel is that Tony's too nice a boy to wake up twenty years from now with nothing in his life but stocks and bonds.

KIRBY. How's that?

GRANDPA (*turning to* MR. KIRBY). Yes. Mixed up and unhappy, the way you are.

KIRBY (*outraged*). I beg your pardon, Mr. Vanderhof, I am a very happy man.

GRANDPA. Are you?

KIRBY. Certainly I am.

GRANDPA. I don't think so. What do you think you get your indigestion from? Happiness? No, sir. You get it because

most of your time is spent in doing things you don't
want to do.

KIRBY. I don't do anything I don't want to do.

GRANDPA. Yes, you do. You said last night that at the end
of a week in Wall Street you're pretty near crazy. Why
do you keep on doing it?

KIRBY. Why do I keep on—why, that's my *business*. A man
can't give up his business.

GRANDPA. Why not? You've got all the money you need.
You can't take it with you.

KIRBY. That's a very easy thing to say, Mr. Vanderhof.
But I have spent my entire life building up my business.

GRANDPA. And what's it got you? Same kind of mail every
morning, same kind of deals, same kind of meetings,
same dinners at night, same indigestion. Where does
the fun come in? Don't you think there ought to be
something *more*, Mr. Kirby? You must have wanted
more than that when you started out. We haven't got
too much time, you know—any of us.

KIRBY. What do you expect me to do? Live the way *you*
do? Do nothing?

GRANDPA. Well, I have a lot of fun. Time enough for everything—read, talk, visit the zoo now and then, practice
my darts, even have time to notice when spring comes
around. Don't see anybody I don't want to, don't have
six hours of things I *have* to do every day before I get
one hour to do what I like in—and I haven't taken bi-
carbonate of soda in thirty-five years. What's the matter
with that?

KIRBY. The matter with that? But suppose we *all* did it?
A fine world we'd have, everybody going to zoos. Don't
be ridiculous, Mr. Vanderhof. Who would do the work?

GRANDPA. There's always people that like to work—you
can't *stop* them. Inventions, and they fly the ocean.
There're always people to go down to Wall Street, too
—because they *like* it. But from what I've seen of you,

I don't think you're one of them. I think you're missing something.

KIRBY. I am not aware of missing anything.

GRANDPA. I wasn't either, till I quit. I used to get down to that office nine o'clock sharp, no matter how I felt. Lay awake nights for fear I wouldn't get that contract. Used to worry about the world, too. Got *all* worked up about whether Cleveland or Blaine was going to be elected President—seemed awful important at the time, but who cares now? What I'm trying to say, Mr. Kirby, is that I've had thirty-five years that nobody can take away from me, no matter what they do to the world. See?

KIRBY. Yes, I do see. And it's a very dangerous philosophy, Mr. Vanderhof. It's—it's un-American. And it's exactly why I'm opposed to this marriage. I don't want Tony to come under its influence.

TONY (*a gleam in his eye*). What's the matter with it, Father?

KIRBY. Matter with it? Why, it's—it's downright Communism, that's what it is.

TONY. You didn't always think so.

KIRBY. I most certainly did. What are you talking about?

TONY. I'll tell you what I'm talking about. You didn't always think so, because there was a time when you wanted to be a trapeze artist.

KIRBY. Why—why, don't be an idiot, Tony.

TONY. Oh, yes, you did. I came across those letters you wrote to Grandfather. Do you remember those?

KIRBY. NO! . . . How dared you read those letters? How dared you?

PENNY. Why, isn't that wonderful? Did you wear tights, Mr. Kirby?

KIRBY. Certainly not! The whole thing is absurd. I was fourteen years old at the time.

TONY. Yes, but at *eighteen* you wanted to be a saxophone player, didn't you?

KIRBY. Tony!

TONY. And at twenty-one you ran away from home because Grandfather wanted you to go into the business. It's all down there in black and white. You didn't *always* think so.

GRANDPA. Well, well, well!

KIRBY. I may have had silly notions in my youth, but thank God my father knocked them out of me. I went into the business and forgot about them.

TONY. Not altogether, Father. There's still a saxophone in the back of your clothes closet.

GRANDPA. There is?

KIRBY (*quietly*). That's enough, Tony. We'll discuss this later.

TONY. No, I want to talk about it *now*. I think Mr. Vanderhof is right—dead right. I'm never going back to that office. I've always hated it, and I'm not going on with it. And I'll tell you something else. I didn't make a mistake last night. I knew it was the wrong night. I brought you here on purpose.

ALICE. Tony!

PENNY. Well, for heaven's—

TONY. Because I wanted you to wake up. I wanted you to see a real family—as they really *were*. A family that loved and understood each other. You don't understand *me*. You've never had time. Well, I'm not going to make *your* mistake. I'm clearing out.

KIRBY. Clearing out? What do you mean?

TONY. I mean I'm not going to be pushed into the business just because I'm your son. I'm getting out while there's still time.

KIRBY (*stunned*). Tony, what are you going to do?

TONY. I don't know. Maybe I'll be a bricklayer, but at least I'll be doing something I want to do.

(*Whereupon the door bell rings*)

PENNY. That must be the cab.

GRANDPA. Ask him to wait a minute, Ed.

ALICE. Grandpa!

GRANDPA. Do you mind, Alice? . . . You know, Mr. Kirby, Tony is going through just what you and I did when we were his age. I think, if you listen hard enough, you can hear yourself saying the same things to *your* father twenty-five years ago. We all did it. And we were right. How many of us would be willing to settle when we're young for what we eventually get? All those plans we make . . . what happens to them? It's only a handful of the lucky ones that can look back and say that they even came close. (GRANDPA *has hit home.* MR. KIRBY *turns slowly and looks at his son, as though seeing him for the first time.* GRANDPA *continues*) So . . . before they clean out that closet, Mr. Kirby, I think I'd get in a few good hours on that saxophone.

(*A slight pause, then* THE GRAND DUCHESS, *an apron over her evening dress, comes in from the kitchen*)

THE GRAND DUCHESS. I beg your pardon, but before I make the blintzes, how many will there be for dinner?

PENNY. Why, I don't know—ah—

GRANDPA. Your Highness, may I present Mr. Anthony Kirby, and Mr. Kirby, Junior? The Grand Duchess Olga Katrina.

KIRBY. How's that?

THE GRAND DUCHESS. How do you do? Before I make the blintzes, how many will there be to dinner?

GRANDPA. Oh, I'd make quite a stack of them, Your Highness. Can't ever tell.

THE GRAND DUCHESS. Good! The Czar always said to me, Olga, do not be stingy with the blintzes. (*She returns to the kitchen, leaving a somewhat stunned* MR. KIRBY *behind her*)

KIRBY. Ah—who did you say that was, Mr. Vanderhof?

GRANDPA (*very offhand*). The Grand Duchess Olga Katrina, of Russia. She's cooking the dinner.

KIRBY. Oh!

GRANDPA. And speaking of dinner, Mr. Kirby, why don't you and Tony both stay?

PENNY. Oh, please do, Mr. Kirby. We've got all that stuff we were going to have last night. I mean tonight.

GRANDPA. Looks like a pretty good dinner, Mr. Kirby, and'll kind of give us a chance to get acquainted. Why not stay?

KIRBY. Why—I'd like to very much. (*He turns to* TONY, *with some trepidation*) What do you say, Tony? Shall we stay to dinner?

TONY. Yes, father. I think that would be fine. If—(*His eyes go to* ALICE)—if Alice will send away that cab.

GRANDPA. How about it, Alice? Going to be a nice crowd. Don't you think you ought to stay for dinner?

ALICE. Mr. Kirby—Tony—oh, Tony! (*And she is in his arms*)

TONY. Darling!

ALICE. Grandpa, you're wonderful!

GRANDPA. I've been telling you that for years. (*He kisses her*)

(ESSIE *enters from the kitchen, laden with dishes*)

ESSIE. Grandpa, here's a letter for you. It was in the icebox.

GRANDPA (*looks at the envelope*). The Government again.

TONY (*happily*). Won't you step into the office, Miss Sycamore? I'd like to do a little dictating.

GRANDPA (*with his letter*). Well, well, well!

PENNY. What is it, Grandpa?

GRANDPA. The United States Government apologizes. I don't owe 'em a nickel. It seems I died eight years ago.

ESSIE. Why, what do they mean, Grandpa?

GRANDPA. Remember Charlie, the milkman? Buried under my name?

PENNY. Yes.

GRANDPA. Well, I just told them they made a mistake and I was Martin Vanderhof, Jr. So they're very sorry and I may even get a refund.

ALICE. Why, Grandpa, you're an old crook.

GRANDPA. Sure!

KIRBY (*interested*). Pardon me, how did you say you escaped the income tax, Mr. Vanderhof?

KOLENKHOV (*bursting through the kitchen door, bringing a chair with him*). Tonight, my friends, you are going to eat. . . . (*He stops short as he catches sight of* KIRBY)

KIRBY (*heartily*). Hello, there!

KOLENKHOV (*stunned*). How do you do?

KIRBY. Fine! Fine! Never was better.

KOLENKHOV (*to* GRANDPA). What has happened?

GRANDPA. He's relaxing. (ED *strikes the keys of the xylophone*) That's right. Play something, Ed.

(*He starts to play.* ESSIE *is immediately up on her toes*)

THE GRAND DUCHESS (*entering from the kitchen*). Everything will be ready in a minute. You can sit down.

PENNY. Come on, everybody. Dinner! (*They start to pull up chairs*) Come on, Mr. Kirby!

KIRBY (*still interested in the xylophone*). Yes, yes, I'm coming.

PENNY. Essie, stop dancing and come to dinner.

KOLENKHOV. You will like Russian food, Mr. Kirby.

PENNY. But you must be careful of your indigestion.

KIRBY. Nonsense! I haven't any indigestion.

TONY. Well, Miss Sycamore, how was your trip to the Adirondacks?

ALICE. Shut your face, Mr. Kirby!

KOLENKHOV. In Russia, when they sit down to dinner . . .

GRANDPA (*tapping on his plate*). Quiet! Everybody! Quiet! (*Immediately the talk ceases. All heads are lowered as* GRANDPA *starts to say Grace*) Well, Sir, here we are again. We want to say thanks once more for everything You've done for us. Things seem to be going along fine. Alice is going to marry Tony, and it looks as if they're going to be very happy. Of course the fireworks blew up, but that was Mr. De Pinna's fault, not Yours. We've all got our health and as far as anything else is concerned, we'll leave it to You. Thank You.

(*The heads come up again.* RHEBA *and* DONALD *come through the kitchen door with stacks and stacks of blintzes. Even the Czar would have thought there were enough*)

Curtain

THE MAN WHO CAME TO DINNER

The Man Who Came to Dinner was produced by Sam H. Harris at the Music Box Theatre, New York, on Monday night, October 16, 1939, with the following cast:

MRS. ERNEST W. STANLEY	VIRGINIA HAMMOND
MISS PREEN	MARY WICKES
RICHARD STANLEY	GORDON MERRICK
JUNE STANLEY	BARBARA WOODDELL
JOHN	GEORGE PROBERT
SARAH	MRS. PRIESTLEY MORRISON
MRS. DEXTER	BARBARA ADAMS
MRS. MCCUTCHEON	EDMONIA NOLLEY
MR. STANLEY	GEORGE LESSEY
MAGGIE CUTLER	EDITH ATWATER
DR. BRADLEY	DUDLEY CLEMENTS
SHERIDAN WHITESIDE	MONTY WOOLLEY
HARRIET STANLEY	RUTH VIVIAN
BERT JEFFERSON	THEODORE NEWTON
PROFESSOR METZ	LE ROI OPERTI
THE LUNCHEON GUESTS	PHIL SHERIDAN CHARLES WASHINGTON WILLIAM POSTANCE
MR. BAKER	CARL JOHNSON
EXPRESSMAN	HAROLD WOOLF
LORRAINE SHELDON	CAROL GOODNER
SANDY	MICHAEL HARVEY
BEVERLY CARLTON	JOHN HOYSRADT
WESTCOTT	EDWARD FISHER
RADIO TECHNICIANS	RODNEY STEWART CARL JOHNSON

	{	DANIEL LEONE
		JACK WHITMAN
SIX YOUNG BOYS		DANIEL LANDON
		DONALD LANDON
		DEWITT PURDUE
		ROBERT REA
BANJO		DAVID BURNS
TWO DEPUTIES	{	CURTIS KARPE
		PHIL SHERIDAN
A PLAINCLOTHES MAN		WILLIAM POSTANCE

Stage Manager—BERNARD HART
Setting by DONALD OENSLAGER

With thanks to Cole Porter for the music and lyrics.

SYNOPSIS OF SCENES

The scene is the home of Mr. and Mrs. Stanley, in a small town in Ohio.

ACT ONE

Scene I—A December morning
Scene II—About a week later

ACT TWO

Another week has passed
Christmas Eve

ACT THREE

Christmas morning

ACT ONE

SCENE I

The curtain rises on the attractive living room in the home of MR. *and* MRS. ERNEST W. STANLEY, *in a small town in Ohio. The* STANLEYS *are obviously people of means. The room is large, comfortable, tastefully furnished. Double doors lead into a library; there is a glimpse of a dining room at the rear, and we see the first half dozen steps of a handsome curved staircase. At the other side, bay windows, the entrance hall, the outer door.*

MRS. STANLEY *is hovering nervously near the library doors, which are tightly closed. She advances a step or two, retreats, advances again and this time musters up enough courage to listen at the door. Suddenly the doors are opened and she has to leap back.*

A NURSE *in full uniform emerges—scurries, rather, out of the room.*

An angry voice from within speeds her on her way: "Great dribbling cow!"

MRS. STANLEY (*eagerly*). How is he? Is he coming out?.

(*But the* NURSE *has already disappeared into the dining room*)

(*Simultaneously the door bell rings—at the same time a young lad of twenty-one,* RICHARD STANLEY, *is descending the stairs*)

RICHARD. I'll go, Mother.

(JOHN, *a white-coated servant, comes hurrying in from the dining room and starts up the stairs, two at a time*)

MRS. STANLEY. What's the matter? What is it?

JOHN. They want pillows. (*And he is out of sight*)

(*Meanwhile the* NURSE *is returning to the sick room. The voice is heard again as she opens the doors. "Don't call yourself a doctor in my presence! You're a quack if I ever saw one!"*)

(RICHARD *returns from the hall, carrying two huge packages and a sheaf of cablegrams*)

RICHARD. Four more cablegrams and more packages. . . . Dad is going crazy upstairs, with that bell ringing all the time.

(*Meanwhile* JUNE, *the daughter of the house, has come down the stairs. An attractive girl of twenty. At the same time the telephone is ringing*)

MRS. STANLEY. Oh, dear! . . . June, will you go? . . . What did you say, Richard?

RICHARD (*examining the packages*). One's from New York and one from San Francisco.

MRS. STANLEY. There was something from Alaska early this morning.

JUNE (*at the telephone*). Yes? . . . Yes, that's right.

MRS. STANLEY. Who is it?

(*Before* JUNE *can answer, the double doors are opened again and the* NURSE *appears. The voice calls after her: "Doesn't that bird-brain of yours ever function?"*)

THE NURSE. I—I'll get them right away. . . . He wants some Players Club cigarettes.

MRS. STANLEY. Players Club?

RICHARD. They have 'em at Kitchener's. I'll run down and get 'em. (*He is off*)

JUNE (*still at the phone*). Hello. . . . Yes, I'm waiting.

MRS. STANLEY. Tell me, Miss Preen, is he—are they bringing him out soon?

MISS PREEN (*wearily*). We're getting him out of bed now. He'll be out very soon . . . Oh, thank you.

(*This last is to* JOHN, *who has descended the stairs with three or four pillows*)

MRS. STANLEY. Oh, I'm so glad. He must be very happy.

(*And again we hear the invalid's voice as* MISS PREEN *passes into the room. "Trapped like a rat in this hell-hole! Take your fish-hooks off me!"*)

JUNE (*at the phone*). Hello. . . . Yes, he's here, but he can't come to the phone right now . . . London? (*She covers the transmitter with her hand*) It's London calling Mr. Whiteside.

MRS. STANLEY. London? My, my!

JUNE. Two o'clock? Yes, I think he could talk then. All right. (*She hangs up*) Well, who do you think that was? Mr. H. G. Wells.

MRS. STANLEY (*wild-eyed*). H. G. Wells? On our telephone?

(*The door bell again*)

JUNE. I'll go. This is certainly a busy house.

(*In the meantime* SARAH, *the cook, has come from the dining room with a pitcher of orange juice*)

MRS. STANLEY (*as* SARAH *knocks on the double doors*). Oh, that's fine, Sarah. Is it fresh?

SARAH. Yes, ma'am.

(*The doors are opened;* SARAH *hands the orange juice to the nurse. The voice roars once more: "You have the touch of a sex-starved cobra!"*)

SARAH (*beaming*). His voice is just the same as on the radio.

(*She disappears into the dining room as* JUNE *returns from the entrance hall, ushering in two friends of her mother's,* MRS. DEXTER *and* MRS. MCCUTCHEON. *One is carrying a flowering plant, partially wrapped; the other is holding, with some care, what turns out to be a jar of calf's-foot jelly*)

THE LADIES. Good morning!

MRS. STANLEY. Girls, what do you think? He's getting up and coming out today!

MRS. MCCUTCHEON. You don't mean it!

MRS. DEXTER. Can we stay and see him?

MRS. STANLEY. Why, of course—he'd love it. Girls, do you know what just happened?

JUNE (*departing*). I'll be upstairs, Mother, if you want me.

MRS. STANLEY. What? . . . Oh, yes. June, tell your father he'd better come down, will you? Mr. Whiteside is coming out.

MRS. DEXTER. Is he really coming out today? I brought him a plant— Do you think it's all right if I give it to him?

MRS. STANLEY. Why, I think that would be lovely.

MRS. MCCUTCHEON. And some calf's-foot jelly.

MRS. STANLEY. Why, how nice! Who do you think was on the phone just now? H. G. Wells, from London. And look at those cablegrams. He's had calls and messages from all over this country and Europe. The New York *Times*, and Radio City Music Hall—I don't know why *they* called—and Felix Frankfurter, and Dr. Dafoe, the Mount Wilson Observatory—I just can't tell you what's been going on.

MRS. DEXTER. There's a big piece about it in this week's *Time*. Did you see it? (*Drawing it out of her bag*)

MRS. STANLEY. No—really?

MRS. MCCUTCHEON. Your name's in it too, Daisy. It tells all about the whole thing. Listen: "Portly Sheridan Whiteside, critic, lecturer, wit, radio orator, intimate friend of the great and near great, last week found his celebrated wit no weapon with which to combat a fractured hip. The Falstaffian Mr. Whiteside, trekking across the country on one of his annual lecture tours, met his Waterloo in the shape of a small piece of ice on the doorstep of Mr. and Mrs. Ernest W. Stanley, of Mesalia, Ohio. Result: Cancelled lectures and disappointment to thousands of adoring clubwomen in Omaha, Denver, and points west. Further result: The idol of the air waves rests until further notice in home of surprised Mr. and Mrs. Stanley. Possibility: Christmas may be postponed this year." What's *that* mean?

MRS. STANLEY. Why, what do you think of that? (*She takes the magazine; reads*) "A small piece of ice on the door-step of Mr. and Mrs. Ernest—" think of it!

MRS. MCCUTCHEON. Of course if it were *my* house, Daisy, I'd have a bronze plate put on the step, right where he fell.

MRS. STANLEY. Well, of course I felt terrible about it. He just never goes to dinner anywhere, and he finally agreed to come here, and then *this* had to happen. Poor Mr. Whiteside! But it's going to be so wonderful having him with us, even for a little while. Just think of it! We'll sit around in the evening and discuss books and plays, all the great people he's known. And he'll talk in that wonderful way of his. He may even read *Good-bye, Mr. Chips* to us.

(MR. STANLEY, *solid, substantial—the American business man—is descending the stairs*)

STANLEY. Daisy, I can't wait any longer. If—ah, good morning, ladies.

MRS. STANLEY. Ernest, he's coming out any minute, and H. G. Wells telephoned from London, and we're in *Time*. Look!

STANLEY (*taking the magazine*). I don't like this kind of publicity at all, Daisy. When do you suppose he's going to leave?

MRS. STANLEY. Well, he's only getting up this morning—after all, he's had quite a shock, and he's been in bed for two full weeks. He'll certainly have to rest a few days, Ernest.

STANLEY. Well, I'm sure it's a great honor, his being in the house, but it *is* a little upsetting—phone going all the

time, bells ringing, messenger boys running in and out—
(*Out of the sick room comes a business-like-looking young woman about thirty. Her name is* MARGARET CUTLER—MAGGIE *to her friends*)

MAGGIE. Pardon me, Mrs. Stanley—have the cigarettes come yet?

MRS. STANLEY. They're on the way, Miss Cutler. My son went for them.

MAGGIE. Thank you.

MRS. STANLEY. Ah—this is Miss Cutler, Mr. Whiteside's secretary.

(*An exchange of "How do you do's?"*)

MAGGIE. May I move this chair?

MRS. STANLEY (*all eagerness*). You mean he's—coming out now?

MAGGIE (*quietly*). He is indeed.

MRS. STANLEY. Ernest, call June. June! June! Mr. Whiteside is coming out!

(JOHN, *visible in the dining room, summons* SARAH *to attend the excitement. "Sarah! Sarah!"*)

(SARAH *and* JOHN *appear in the dining-room entrance,* JUNE *on the stairs.* MRS. STANLEY *and the two other ladies are keenly expectant; even* MR. STANLEY *is on the qui vive*)

(*The double doors are opened once more, and* DR. BRADLEY *appears, bag in hand. He has taken a good deal of punishment, and speaks with a rather false heartiness*)

DR. BRADLEY. Well, here we are, merry and bright. Good morning, good morning. Bring our little patient out, Miss Preen.

(*A moment's pause, and then a wheelchair is rolled through the door. It is full of pillows, blankets, and* SHERIDAN WHITESIDE. SHERIDAN WHITESIDE *is indeed portly and Falstaffian. He is wearing an elaborate velvet smoking jacket and a very loud tie, and he looks like every caricature ever drawn of him*)

(*There is a hush as the wheelchair rolls into the room.*

Welcoming smiles break over every face. The chair comes to a halt; MR. WHITESIDE *looks slowly around, into each and every beaming face. His fingers drum for a moment on the arm of the chair. He looks slowly around once more. And then he speaks)*

WHITESIDE (*quietly, to* MAGGIE). I may vomit.

MRS. STANLEY (*with a nervous little laugh*). Good morning, Mr. Whiteside. I'm Mrs. Ernest Stanley—remember? And this is Mr. Stanley.

STANLEY. How do you do, Mr. Whiteside? I hope that you are better.

WHITESIDE. Thank you. I am suing you for a hundred and fifty thousand dollars.

STANLEY. How's that? What?

WHITESIDE. I said I am suing you for a hundred and fifty thousand dollars.

MRS. STANLEY. You mean—because you fell on our steps, Mr. Whiteside?

WHITESIDE. Samuel J. Liebowitz will explain it to you in court. . . . Who are those two harpies standing there like the kiss of death?

(MRS. MCCUTCHEON, *with a little gasp, drops the calf's-foot jelly. It smashes on the floor*)

MRS. MCCUTCHEON. Oh, dear! My calf's-foot jelly.

WHITESIDE. Made from your own foot, I have no doubt. And now, Mrs. Stanley, I have a few small matters to take up with you. Since this corner druggist at my elbow tells me that I shall be confined in this mouldy mortuary for at least another ten days, due entirely to your stupidity and negligence, I shall have to carry on my activities as best I can. I shall require the exclusive use of this room, as well as that drafty sewer which you call the library. I want no one to come in or out while I am in this room.

STANLEY. What do you mean, sir?

MRS. STANLEY (*stunned*). But we have to go up the stairs to get to our rooms, Mr. Whiteside.

WHITESIDE. Isn't there a back entrance?

MRS. STANLEY. Why—yes.

WHITESIDE. Then use that. I shall also require a room for my secretary, Miss Cutler. I shall have a great many incoming and outgoing calls, so please do not use the telephone. I sleep until noon and require quiet through the house until that hour. There will be five for lunch today. Where is the cook?

STANLEY. Mr. Whiteside, if I may interrupt for a moment—

WHITESIDE. You may not, sir. . . . Will you take your clammy hand off my chair? (*This last to the nurse*) . . . And now will you all leave quietly, or must I ask Miss Cutler to pass among you with a baseball bat?

(MRS. DEXTER *and* MRS. MCCUTCHEON *are beating a hasty retreat, their gifts still in hand*)

MRS. MCCUTCHEON. Well—good-bye, Daisy. We'll call you— Oh, no, we mustn't use the phone. Well—we'll see you.

(*And they are gone*)

STANLEY (*boldly*). Now look here, Mr. Whiteside—

WHITESIDE. There is nothing to discuss, sir. Considering the damage I have suffered at your hands, I am asking very little. Good day.

STANLEY (*controlling himself*). I'll call you from the office later, Daisy.

WHITESIDE. Not on this phone, please.

(STANLEY *gives him a look, but goes*)

WHITESIDE. Here is the menu for lunch. (*He extends a slip of paper to* MRS. STANLEY)

MRS. STANLEY. But—I've already ordered lunch.

WHITESIDE. It will be sent up to you on a tray. I am using the dining room for my guests. . . . Where are those cigarettes?

MRS. STANLEY. Why—my son went for them. I don't know

why he—here, Sarah. (*She hands* SARAH *the luncheon slip*) I'll—have mine upstairs on a tray.

(SARAH *and* JOHN *depart*)

WHITESIDE (*to* JUNE, *who has been posed on the landing during all this*). Young lady, will you either go up those stairs or come down them? I cannot stand indecision.

(JUNE *is about to speak, decides against it, and ascends the stairs with a good deal of spirit*)

(MRS. STANLEY *is hovering uncertainly on the steps as* RICHARD *returns with the cigarettes*)

RICHARD. Oh, good morning. I'm sorry I was so long—I had to go to three different stores.

WHITESIDE. How did you travel? By ox-cart?

(RICHARD *is considerably taken aback. His eyes go to his mother, who motions to him to come up the stairs. They disappear together, their eyes unsteadily on* WHITESIDE)

WHITESIDE. Is there a man in the world who suffers as I do from the gross inadequacies of the human race! (*To the* NURSE, *who is fussing around the chair again*) Take those canal boats away from me! (*She obeys, hastily*) Go in and read the life of Florence Nightingale and learn how unfitted you are for your chosen profession.

(MISS PREEN *glares at him, but goes*)

DR. BRADLEY (*heartily*). Well, I think I can safely leave you in Miss Cutler's capable hands. Shall I look in again this afternoon?

WHITESIDE. If you do, I shall spit right in your eye.

DR. BRADLEY. What a sense of humor you writers have! By the way, it isn't really worth mentioning, but—I've been doing a little writing myself. About my medical experiences.

WHITESIDE (*quietly*). Am I to be spared nothing?

DR. BRADLEY. Would it be too much to ask you to—glance over it while you're here?

WHITESIDE (*eyes half closed, as though the pain were too exquisite to bear*). Trapped.

DR. BRADLEY (*delving into his bag*). I just happen to have a copy with me. (*He brings out a tremendous manuscript*) "Forty Years an Ohio Doctor. The Story of a Humble Practitioner."

WHITESIDE. I shall lose no time in reading it, if you know what I mean.

DR. BRADLEY. Much obliged, and I hope you like it. Well, see you on the morrow. Keep that hip quiet and don't forget those little pills. (*He goes*)

WHITESIDE (*handing the manuscript to* MAGGIE). Maggie, will you take *Forty Years Below the Navel* or whatever it's called?

MAGGIE (*surveying him*). I must say you have certainly behaved with all of your accustomed grace and charm.

WHITESIDE. Look here, Puss—I am in no mood to discuss my behavior, good or bad. I did not wish to cross their cheerless threshold. I was hounded and badgered into it. I now find myself, after two weeks of racking pain, accused of behaving without charm. What would you have me do? Kiss them?

MAGGIE (*giving up*). Very well, Sherry. After ten years I should have known better than to try to do anything about your manners. But when I finally give up this job I may write a book about it all. *Cavalcade of Insult*, or *Through the Years with Prince Charming*.

WHITESIDE. Listen, Repulsive, you are tied to me with an umbilical cord made of piano wire. And now if we may dismiss the subject of my charm, for which, incidentally, I receive fifteen hundred dollars per appearance, possibly we can go to work . . . Oh, no, we can't. Yes?

(*This last is addressed to a wraith-like lady of uncertain years, who has more or less floated into the room. She is carrying a large spray of holly, and her whole manner suggests something not quite of this world*)

THE LADY (*her voice seems to float, too*). My name is Harriet Stanley. I know you are Sheridan Whiteside. I saw this holly, framed green against the pine trees. I remembered what you had written, about *Tess* and *Jude the Obscure*. It was the nicest present I could bring you. (*She places the holly in his lap, and drifts out of the room again*)

WHITESIDE (*his eyes following her*). For God's sake, what was that?

MAGGIE. That was Mr. Stanley's sister, Harriet. I've talked to her a few times—she's quite strange.

WHITESIDE. Strange? She's right out of *The Hound of the Baskervilles*. . . . You know, I've seen that face before somewhere.

MAGGIE. Nonsense. You couldn't have.

WHITESIDE (*dismissing it*). Oh, well! Let's get down to work. (*He hands her the armful of holly*) Here! Press this in the doctor's book. (*He picks up the first of a pile of papers*) I see no reason why I should indorse Maidenform Brassières. (*He tears up the letter and drops the pieces on the floor*)

MAGGIE (*who has picked up the little sheaf of messages from the table*). Here are some telegrams.

WHITESIDE (*a letter in his hand*). What date is this?

MAGGIE. December tenth.

WHITESIDE. Send a wire to Columbia Broadcasting. "You can schedule my Christmas Eve broadcast from the New York studio, as I shall return East instead of proceeding to Hollywood. Stop. For special New Year's Eve broadcast will have as my guests Jascha Heifetz, Katharine Cornell, Schiaparelli, the Lunts, and Dr. Alexis Carrel, with Haille Selassie on short wave from England. Whiteside."

MAGGIE. Are you sure you'll be all right by Christmas, Sherry?

WHITESIDE. Of course I will. . . . Send a cable to Ma-

hatma Gandhi, Bombay, India. "Dear Boo-Boo: Sched-
ule changed. Can you meet me Calcutta July twelfth?
Dinner eight-thirty. Whiteside." . . . Wire to editor of
the *Christian Science Monitor*: "Do not worry, Stinkie.
Copy will arrive. Whiteside." . . . Arturo Toscanini.
Where is he?

MAGGIE. I'll find him.

WHITESIDE. "Counting on you January 4th Metropolitan
Opera House my annual benefit Home for Paroled Convicts. As you know this is a very worthy cause and close
to my heart. Tibbett, Rethberg, Martinelli and Flagstad
have promised me personally to appear. Will you have
quiet supper with me and Ethel Barrymore afterwards? .
Whiteside." (*The telephone rings*) If that's for Mrs.
Stanley tell them she's too drunk to talk.

MAGGIE. Hello . . . Hollywood?

WHITESIDE. If it's Goldwyn, hang up.

MAGGIE. Hello . . . Banjo! (*Her face lights up*)

WHITESIDE. Banjo! Give me that phone!

MAGGIE. Banjo, you old so-and-so! How are you, darling?

WHITESIDE. Come on—give me that!

MAGGIE. Shut up, Sherry! . . . Are you coming East,
Banjo? I miss you . . . No, we're not going to Hollywood . . . Oh, he's going to live.

WHITESIDE. Stop driveling and give me the phone.

MAGGIE. In fact, he's screaming at me now. Here he is.

WHITESIDE (*taking the phone*). How are you, you fawn's
behind? And what are you giving me for Christmas?
(*He roars with laughter at* BANJO's *answer*) What news,
Banjo, my boy? How's the picture coming? . . . How
are Wacko and Sloppo? . . . No, no, I'm all right. . . .
Yes, I'm in very good hands. Dr. Crippen is taking care
of me. . . . What about you? Having any fun? . . .
Playing any cribbage? . . . What? (*Again he laughs
loudly*) . . . Well, don't take all his money—leave a
little bit for me . . . You're what? . . . Having your

portrait painted? By whom? Milt Gross? . . . No, I'm
going back to New York from here. I'll be there for
twelve days, and then I go to Dartmouth for the Drama
Festival. You wouldn't understand . . . Well, I can't
waste my time talking to Hollywood riffraff. Kiss Louella
Parsons for me. Good-bye. (*He hangs up and turns to*
MAGGIE) He took fourteen hundred dollars from Sam
Goldwyn at cribbage last night, and Sam said, "Banjo, I
will never play garbage with you again."

MAGGIE. What's all this about his having his portrait
painted?

WHITESIDE. Mm. Salvador Dali. That's all that face of his
needs—a surrealist to paint it. . . . Now what do *you*
want, Miss Bed Pan?

(*This is addressed to the* NURSE, *who has returned somewhat apprehensively to the room*)

MISS PREEN. It's—it's your pills. One every—forty-five minutes. (*She drops them into his lap and hurries out of the
room*)

WHITESIDE. Now where were we?

MAGGIE (*the messages in her hand*). Here's a cable from
that dear friend of yours, Lorraine Sheldon.

WHITESIDE. Let me see it.

MAGGIE (*reading the message in a tone that gives* MISS
SHELDON *none the better of it*). "Sherry, my poor sweet
lamb, have been in Scotland on a shooting party with
Lord and Lady Cunard and only just heard of your
poor hip." (MAGGIE *gives a faint raspberry, then reads
on*) "Am down here in Surrey with Lord Bottomley.
Sailing Wednesday on the *Normandie* and cannot wait
to see my poor sweet Sherry. Your blossom girl, Lorraine." . . . In the words of the master, I may vomit.

WHITESIDE. Don't be bitter, Puss, just because Lorraine is
more beautiful than you are.

MAGGIE. Lorraine Sheldon is a very fair example of that
small but vicious circle you move in.

WHITESIDE. Pure sex jealousy if ever I saw it . . . Give
me the rest of those.

MAGGIE (*mumbling to herself*). Lorraine Sheldon . . .
Lord Bottomley . . . My Aunt Fanny.

WHITESIDE (*who has opened the next message*). Ah! It's
from Destiny's Tot.

MAGGIE (*peering over his shoulder*). England's little Rover
Boy?

WHITESIDE. Um-hm. (*He reads*) "Dear Baby's Breath,
what is this I hear about a hip fractured in some bor-
dello brawl? Does this mean our Hollywood Christmas
party is off? Finished the new play in Pago-Pago and
it's superb. Myself and a ukulele leave Honolulu tomorrow, in that order. By the way, the Sultan of Zanzibar
wants to meet Ginger Rogers. Let's face it. Oscar Wilde."

MAGGIE. He does travel, doesn't he? You know, it'd be nice
if the world went around Beverly Carlton for a change.

WHITESIDE. Hollywood next week—why couldn't he stop
over on his way to New York? Send him a cable: "Beverly Carlton, Royal Hawaiian Hotel, Honolulu—" (*The
door bell rings. MR. WHITESIDE is properly annoyed*) If
these people intend to have their friends using the front
door—

MAGGIE. What do you want them to use—a rope ladder?

WHITESIDE. I will not have a lot of mildewed pus-bags
rushing in and out of this house— (*He stops as the
voice of JOHN is heard at the front door. "Oh, good
morning, Mr. Jefferson." The answering voice of MR.
JEFFERSON is not quite audible*)

WHITESIDE (*roaring*). There's nobody home! The Stanleys
have been arrested for white slavery! Go away!

(*But the visitor, meanwhile, has already appeared in the
archway. MR. JEFFERSON is an interesting-looking young
man in his early thirties*)

JEFFERSON. Good morning, Mr. Whiteside. I'm Jefferson,
of the Mesalia *Journal*.

WHITESIDE (*sotto voce, to* MAGGIE). Get rid of him.

MAGGIE (*brusquely*). I'm sorry—Mr. Whiteside is seeing no one.

JEFFERSON. Really?

MAGGIE. So will you please excuse us? Good day.

JEFFERSON (*not giving up*). Mr. Whiteside seems to be sitting up and taking notice.

MAGGIE. I'm afraid he isn't taking notice of the Mesalia *Journal*. Do you mind?

JEFFERSON. You know, if I'm going to be insulted I'd like it to be by Mr. Whiteside himself. I never did like carbon copies.

WHITESIDE (*looking around, interested*). Mm. Touché if I ever heard one. And in Mesalia too, Maggie dear.

MAGGIE (*still on the job*). Will you please leave?

JEFFERSON (*ignoring her*). How about an interview, Mr. Whiteside?

WHITESIDE. I never give them. Go away.

JEFFERSON. Mr. Whiteside, if I don't get this interview, I lose my job.

WHITESIDE. That would be quite all right with me.

JEFFERSON. Now you don't mean that, Mr. Whiteside. You used to be a newspaper man yourself. You know what editors are like. Well, mine's the toughest one that ever lived.

WHITESIDE. You won't get around me that way. If you don't like him, get off the paper.

JEFFERSON. Yes, but I happen to think it's a good paper. William Allen White could have got out of Emporia, but he didn't.

WHITESIDE. You have the effrontery, in my presence, to compare yourself with William Allen White?

JEFFERSON. Only in the sense that William Allen White stayed in Emporia, and I want to stay here and say what I want to say.

WHITESIDE. Such as what?

JEFFERSON. Well, I can't put it into words, Mr. Whiteside
—it'd sound like an awful lot of hooey. But the *Journal*
was my father's paper. It's kind of a sentimental point
with me, the paper. I'd like to carry on where he left off.

WHITESIDE. Ah—just a minute. Then this terrifying editor,
this dread journalistic Apocalypse is—you?

JEFFERSON. Ah—yes, in a word.

(WHITESIDE *chuckles with appreciation*)

MAGGIE (*annoyed*). In the future, Sherry, I wish you
would let me know when you don't want to talk to
people. I'll usher them right in. (*She goes into the
library*)

WHITESIDE. Young man, that kind of journalistic trick went
out with Richard Harding Davis . . . Come over here.
I suppose you've written that novel?

JEFFERSON. No, I've written that play.

WHITESIDE. Well, I don't want to read it. But you can
send me your paper—I'll take a year's subscription. Do
you write the editorials, too?

JEFFERSON. Every one of them.

WHITESIDE. I know just what they're like. Ah, me! I'm
afraid you're that noble young newspaper man—cru-
sading, idealistic, dull. (*He looks him up and down*)
Very good casting, too.

JEFFERSON. You're not bad casting yourself, Mr. Whiteside.

WHITESIDE. We won't discuss it. . . . Do these old eyes
see a box of goodies over there? Hand them to me on
your way out.

JEFFERSON (*as he passes over the candy*). The trouble is,
Mr. Whiteside, that your being in this town comes
under the heading of news. Practically the biggest
news since the depression.

WHITESIDE (*examining the candy*). Mm. Pecan butternut
fudge.

(MISS PREEN, *on her way to the kitchen from the library,*

stops short as she sees MR. WHITESIDE *with a piece of candy in his hand*)

MISS PREEN. Oh, my! You mustn't eat candy, Mr. Whiteside. It's very bad for you.

WHITESIDE (*turning*). My great-aunt Jennifer ate a whole box of candy every day of her life. She lived to be a hundred and two, and when she had been dead three days she looked better than you do now. (*He swings blandly back to his visitor*) What were you saying, old fellow?

JEFFERSON (*as* MISS PREEN *makes a hasty exit*). I can at least report to my readers that chivalry is not yet dead.

WHITESIDE. We won't discuss it. . . . Well, now that you have won me with your pretty ways, what do you want?

JEFFERSON. Well, how about a brief talk on famous murders? You're an authority on murder as a fine art.

WHITESIDE. My dear boy, when I talk about murder I get paid for it. I have made more money out of the Snyder-Gray case than the lawyers did. So don't expect to get it for nothing.

JEFFERSON. Well, then, what do you think of Mesalia, how long are you going to be here, where are you going, things like that?

WHITESIDE. Very well. (a) Mesalia is a town of irresistible charm, (b) I cannot wait to get out of it, and (c) I am going from here to Crockfield, for my semi-annual visit to the Crockfield Home for Paroled Convicts, for which I have raised over half a million dollars in the last five years. From there I go to New York. . . . Have you ever been to Crockfield, Jefferson?

JEFFERSON. No, I haven't. I always meant to.

WHITESIDE. As a newspaper man you ought to go, instead of wasting your time with me. It's only about seventy-five miles from here. Did you ever hear how Crockfield started?

JEFFERSON. No, I didn't.

WHITESIDE. Ah! Sit down, Jefferson. It is one of the most endearing and touching stories of our generation. One misty St. Valentine's Eve—the year was 1901—a little old lady who had given her name to an era, Victoria, lay dying in Windsor Castle. Maude Adams had not yet caused every young heart to swell as she tripped across the stage as Peter Pan; Irving Berlin had not yet written the first note of a ragtime rigadoon that was to set the nation's feet a-tapping, and Elias P. Crockfield was just emerging from the State penitentiary. Destitute, embittered, cruel of heart, he wandered, on this St. Valentine's Eve, into a little church. But there was no godliness in his heart that night, no prayer upon his lips. In the faltering twilight, Elias P. Crockfield made his way toward the poor box. With callous fingers he ripped open this poignant testimony of a simple people's faith. Greedily he clutched at the few pitiful coins within. And then a child's wavering treble broke the twilight stillness. "Please, Mr. Man," said a little girl's voice, "won't you be my Valentine?" Elias P. Crockfield turned. There stood before him a bewitching little creature of five, her yellow curls cascading over her shoulders like a golden Niagara, in her tiny outstretched hand a humble valentine. In that one crystal moment a sealed door opened in the heart of Elias P. Crockfield, and in his mind was born an idea. Twenty-five years later three thousand ruddy-cheeked convicts were gamboling on the broad lawns of Crockfield Home, frolicking in the cool depths of its swimming pool, broadcasting with their own symphony orchestra from their own radio station. Elias P. Crockfield has long since gone to his Maker, but the little girl of the golden curls, now grown to lovely womanhood, is known as the Angel of Crockfield, for she is the wife of the warden, and in the main hall of Crockfield, between a Rembrandt and an

El Greco, there hangs, in a simple little frame, a humble valentine.

MAGGIE (*who has emerged from the library in time to hear the finish of this*). And in the men's washroom, every Christmas Eve, the ghost of Elias P. Crockfield appears in one of the booths . . . Will you sign these, please? (*The door bell is heard*)

WHITESIDE. This aging debutante, Mr. Jefferson, I retain in my employ only because she is the sole support of her two-headed brother.

JEFFERSON. I understand. . . . Well, thank you very much, Mr. Whiteside—you've been very kind. By the way, I'm a cribbage player, if you need one while you're here.

WHITESIDE. Fine. How much can you afford to lose?

JEFFERSON. I usually win.

WHITESIDE. We won't discuss that. Come back at eight-thirty. We'll play three-handed with Elsie Dinsmore . . . Metz!

(JOHN, *who has answered the door bell, has ushered in a strange-looking little man in his fifties. His hair runs all over his head and his clothes are too big for him*)

WHITESIDE. Metz, you incredible beetle-hound! What are you doing here?

METZ (*with a mild Teutonic accent*). I explain, Sherry. First I kiss my little Maggie.

MAGGIE (*embracing him*). Metz darling, what a wonderful surprise!

WHITESIDE. The enchanted Metz! Why aren't you at the university? . . . Jefferson, you are standing in the presence of one of the great men of our time. When you write that inevitable autobiography, be sure to record the day that you met Professor Adolph Metz, the world's greatest authority on insect life. Metz, stop looking at me adoringly and tell me why you're here.

METZ. You are sick, Sherry, so I come to cheer you.

MAGGIE. Metz, you tore yourself away from your little insects and came here? Sherry, you don't deserve it.

WHITESIDE. How are all your little darlings, Metz? Jefferson, would you believe that eight volumes could be written on the mating instinct of the female white ant? He did it.

METZ. Seven on the female, Sherry. One on the male.

WHITESIDE. Lived for two years in a cave with nothing but plant lice. He rates three pages in the *Encyclopaedia Britannica*. Don't you, my little hookworm?

METZ. Please, Sherry, you embarrass me. Look—I have brought you a present to while away the hours. (*He motions to* JOHN, *who comes forward bearing a great box, wrapped in brown paper. He unwraps it as he speaks*) I said to my students: "Boys and girls, I want to give a present to my sick friend, Sheridan Whiteside." So you know what we did? We made for you a community of *Periplaneta Americana*, commonly known as the American cockroach. Behold, Sherry! (*He strips off the paper*) Roach City! Inside here are ten thousand cockroaches.

JOHN. Ten thousand— (*Heading for the kitchen in great excitement*) Sarah! Sarah!

METZ. And in one week, Sherry, if all goes well, there will be fifty thousand.

MAGGIE. Well, what can go wrong? They're *in* there, aren't they?

WHITESIDE. Quiet, please.

METZ. Here in Roach City they play, they make love, they mate, they die. See—here is the graveyard. They even bury their own dead.

MAGGIE. I'm glad of that, or I'd have to do it.

WHITESIDE (*glaring at her*). Ssh!

METZ. Look! Here is where they store their grain, here is the commissary of the aristocracy, here is the maternity hospital. It is fascinating. They do everything that human beings do.

MAGGIE. Well!

WHITESIDE. Please, Maggie! These are *my* cockroaches.

METZ. With these ear-phones, Sherry, you listen to the mating calls. There are microphones down inside. Listen (*He puts the ear-phones over* WHITESIDE's *head*)

WHITESIDE (*listening, rapt*). Mm. How long has this been going on?

(MRS. STANLEY *starts timorously to descend the stairs. She tiptoes as far as the landing, then pauses as she sees the group below*)

(*Meanwhile* PROF. METZ, *his mind ever on his work, has moved in the direction of the dining room*)

METZ (*suddenly his face lights up*). Aha! *Periplaneta Americana!* There are cockroaches in this house!

MRS. STANLEY (*shocked into speech*). I beg your pardon! (*The doorbell rings*) Mr. Whiteside, I don't know who this man is, but I will not stand here and—

WHITESIDE. Then go upstairs. These are probably my luncheon guests. Metz, you're staying for the day, of course? Jefferson, stay for lunch? Maggie, tell 'em there'll be two more. Ah, come right in, Baker. Good morning, gentlemen. (*The gentlemen addressed are three in number—two white, one black. They are convicts, and they look the part. Prison gray, handcuffed together.* BAKER, *in uniform, is a prison guard. He carries a rifle*) Jefferson, here are the fruits of that humble valentine. These men, now serving the final months of their prison terms, have chosen to enter the ivy-covered walls of Crockfield. They have come here today to learn from me a little of its tradition . . . Gentlemen, I envy you your great adventure.

JOHN (*in the dining-room doorway*). Lunch is ready, Mr. Whiteside.

WHITESIDE. Good! Let's go right in. (*To one of the convicts, as they pass*) You're Michaelson, aren't you? Butcher-shop murders?

MICHAELSON. Yes, sir.

WHITESIDE. Thought I recognized you. . . . After you, Baker. . . . The other fellow, Jefferson—(*He lowers his tone*)—is Henderson, the hatchet fiend. Always chopped them up in a salad bowl—remember? (*His voice rises as he wheels himself into the dining room*) We're having chicken livers Tetrazzini, and Cherries Jubilee for dessert. I hope every little tummy is a-flutter with gastric juices. Serve the white wine with the fish, John, and close the doors. I don't want a lot of people prying on their betters.

(*The doors close. Only* MRS. STANLEY *is left outside. She collapses quietly into a chair*)

The curtain falls

SCENE II

Late afternoon, a week later. Only a single lamp is lit. The room, in the week that has passed, has taken on something of the character of its occupant. Books and papers everywhere. Stacks of books on the tables, some of them just half out of their cardboard boxes. Half a dozen or so volumes, which apparently have not appealed to the Master, have been thrown onto the floor. A litter of crumpled papers around the WHITESIDE *wheelchair; an empty candy box has slid off his lap. An old pair of pants have been tossed over one chair, a seedy bathrobe over another. A handsome Chinese vase has been moved out of its accustomed spot and is doing duty as an ash receiver.*

THE MAN WHO CAME TO DINNER

MR. WHITESIDE *is in his wheelchair, asleep. Roach City is on a stand beside him, the ear-phones, over his head. He has apparently dozed off while listening to the mating calls of* Periplaneta Americana.

For a moment only his rhythmic breathing is heard. Then MISS PREEN *enters from the library. She brings some medicine—a glass filled with a murky mixture. She pauses when she sees that he is asleep, then, after a good deal of hesitation, gently touches him on the shoulder. He stirs a little; she musters up her courage and touches him again.*

WHITESIDE (*slowly opening his eyes*). I was dreaming of Lillian Russell, and I awake to find *you.*

MISS PREEN. Your—your medicine, Mr. Whiteside.

WHITESIDE (*taking the glass*). What time is it?

MISS PREEN. About half-past six.

WHITESIDE. Where is Miss Cutler?

MISS PREEN. She went out.

WHITESIDE. Out?

MISS PREEN. With Mr. Jefferson. (*She goes into the library*) (JOHN, *meanwhile, has entered from the dining room*)

JOHN. All right if I turn the lights up, Mr. Whiteside?

WHITESIDE. Yes. Go right ahead, John.

JOHN. And Sarah has something for you, Mr. Whiteside. Made it special.

WHITESIDE. She has? Where is she? My Soufflé Queen!

SARAH (*proudly entering with a tray on which reposes her latest delicacy*). Here I am, Mr. Whiteside.

WHITESIDE. She walks in beauty like the night, and in those deft hands there is the art of Michelangelo. Let me taste the new creation. (*With one hand he pours the medicine into the Chinese vase, then swallows at a gulp one of* SARAH's *not so little cakes. An ecstatic expression comes over his face*) Poetry! Sheer poetry!

SARAH (*beaming*). I put a touch of absinthe in the dough. Do you like it?

WHITESIDE (*rapturously*). Ambrosia!

SARAH. And I got you your terrapin Maryland for dinner.

WHITESIDE. I have known but three great cooks in my
time. The Khedive of Egypt had one, my great-aunt
Jennifer another, and the third, Sarah, is you.

SARAH. Oh, Mr. Whiteside!

WHITESIDE (*lowering his voice*). How would you like to
come to New York and work for me? You and John.

SARAH. Why, Mr. Whiteside!

JOHN. Sarah! . . . It would be wonderful, Mr. Whiteside,
but what would we say to Mr. and Mrs. Stanley?

WHITESIDE. Just "good-bye."

SARAH. But—but they'd be awfully mad, wouldn't they?
They've been very kind to us.

WHITESIDE (*lightly*). Well, if they ever come to New York
we can have them for dinner, if I'm not in town. Now
run along and think it over. This is our little secret—
just between us. And put plenty of sherry in that terrapin . . . Miss Preen! (SARAH *and* JOHN *withdraw in
considerable excitement.* WHITESIDE *raises his voice to
a roar*) Miss Preen!

MISS PREEN (*appearing, breathless*). Yes? Yes?

WHITESIDE. What have you got in there, anyway? A sailor?

MISS PREEN. I was—just washing my hands.

WHITESIDE. What time did Miss Cutler go out?

MISS PREEN. A couple of hours ago.

WHITESIDE. Mr. Jefferson called for her?

MISS PREEN. Yes, sir.

WHITESIDE (*impatiently*). All right, all right. Go back to
your sex life.

(MISS PREEN *goes.* WHITESIDE *tries to settle down to his
book, but his mind is plainly troubled. He shifts a little,
looks anxiously toward the outer door*)

(HARRIET STANLEY *comes softly down the steps. She seems
delighted to find* MR. WHITESIDE *alone*)

HARRIET (*opening an album that she has brought with*

her). Dear Mr. Whiteside, may I show you a few me-
mentoes of the past? I somehow feel that you would
love them as I do.

WHITESIDE. I'd be delighted. (*Observing her*) Miss Stanley, haven't we met somewhere before?

HARRIET. Oh, no. I would have remembered it. It would
have been one of my cherished memories—like these.
(*She spreads the portfolio before him*) Look! Here I am
with my first sweetheart, under our lovely beechwood
tree. I was eight and he was ten. I have never forgotten
him. What happy times we had! What— (*She stops
short as she hears footsteps on the stairway*) There's
someone coming! I'll come back! . . . (*She gathers up
her album and vanishes into the dining room*)

(WHITESIDE *looks after her, puzzled*)

(*It is* MR. STANLEY *who comes down the stairs. He is
carrying a slip of paper in his hand, and he is obviously
at the boiling point*)

(*A few steps behind comes* MRS. STANLEY, *apprehensive
and nervous*)

MRS. STANLEY. Now, Ernest, please—

STANLEY. Be quiet, Daisy. . . . Mr. Whiteside, I want to
talk to you. I don't care whether you're busy or not. I
have stood all that I'm going to stand.

WHITESIDE. Indeed?

STANLEY. This is the last straw. I have just received a bill
from the telephone company for seven hundred and
eighty-four dollars. (*He reads from the slip in his
hand*) Oklahoma City, Calcutta, Hollywood, Australia,
Rome, New York, New York, New York, New York,
New York, New York— (*His voice trails off in an endless succession of New Yorks*) Now I realize, Mr. Whiteside, that you are a distinguished man of letters—

MRS. STANLEY. Yes, of course. We both do.

STANLEY. Please . . . But in the past week we have not
been able to call our souls our own. We have not had a

meal in the dining room *once*. I have to tiptoe out of
the house in the mornings.

MRS. STANLEY. Now, Ernest—

STANLEY (*waving her away*). I come home to find convicts sitting at my dinner table—butcher-shop mur-
derers. A man putting cockroaches in the kitchen.

MRS. STANLEY. They just escaped, Ernest.

STANLEY. That's not the point. I don't like coming home
to find twenty-two Chinese students using my bathroom. I tell you I won't stand for it, no matter *who* you
are.

WHITESIDE. Have you quite finished?

STANLEY. No, I have not. I go down into the cellar this
morning and trip over that octopus that William Beebe
sent you. I tell you I won't stand it. Mr. Whiteside, I
want you to leave this house as soon as you can and go
to a hotel. . . . Stop pawing me, Daisy. . . . That's all
I've got to say, Mr. Whiteside.

WHITESIDE. And quite enough, I should say. May I remind
you again, Mr. Stanley, that I am not a willing guest in
this house? I am informed by my doctor that I must
remain quiet for another ten days, at which time I shall
get out of here so fast that the wind will knock you
over, I hope. If, however, you insist on my leaving before that, thereby causing me to suffer a relapse, I shall
sue you for every additional day that I am held inactive,
which will amount, I assure you, to a tidy sum.

STANLEY (*to his wife*). This is outrageous. Do we have to—

WHITESIDE. As for the details of your petty complaints,
those twenty-two Chinese students came straight from
the White House, where I assure you they used the
bathroom too.

MRS. STANLEY. Mr. Whiteside, my husband didn't mean—

STANLEY. Yes, I did. I meant every word of it.

WHITESIDE. There is only one point that you make in which
I see some slight justice. I do not expect you to pay for

my telephone calls, and I shall see to it that restitution is made. Can you provide me with the exact amount?

STANLEY. I certainly can, and I certainly will.

WHITESIDE. Good. I shall instruct my lawyers to deduct it from the hundred and fifty thousand dollars that I am suing you for.

(MR. STANLEY *starts to speak, but simply chokes with rage. Furious, he storms up the steps again,* MRS. STANLEY *following*)

WHITESIDE (*calling after him*). And I'll thank you not to trip over that octopus, which once belonged to Chauncey Depew. (*Left alone,* MR. WHITESIDE *enjoys his triumph for a moment, then his mind jumps to more important matters. He looks at his watch, considers a second, then wheels himself over to the telephone*)

WHITESIDE. Give me the Mesalia *Journal*, please. (*He peers at Roach City while waiting*) Hello, *Journal*? . . . Is Mr. Jefferson there? . . . When do you expect him? . . . No. No message. (*He hangs up, drums impatiently on the arm of his chair*)

(*Then he turns sharply at the sound of the outer door opening. But it is the younger Stanleys,* RICHARD *and* JUNE, *who enter. They are in winter togs, with ice skates under their arms. In addition,* RICHARD *has a camera slung over his shoulder*)

(*Their attitudes change as they see that* WHITESIDE *is in the room. They slide toward the stairs, obviously trying to be as unobtrusive as possible*)

WHITESIDE. Come here, you two. . . . Come on, come on. I'm not going to bite you. . . . Now look here. I am by nature a gracious and charming person. If I err at all it is on the side of kindness and amiability. I have been observing you two for this past week, and you seem to me to be extremely likeable young people. I am afraid that when we first met I was definitely unpleasant to you. For that I am sorry, and I wish that in the future you would not treat me like something out of Edgar Allan Poe. How do you like my new tie?

JUNE. Thank you, Mr. Whiteside. This makes things much pleasanter. And I think the tie is very pretty.

RICHARD. Well, now that we're on speaking terms, Mr. Whiteside, I don't mind telling you that I have been admiring all your ties.

WHITESIDE. Do you like this one?

RICHARD. I certainly do.

WHITESIDE. It's yours. (*He takes it off and tosses it to him*) Really, this curious legend that I am a difficult person is pure fabrication. . . . Ice-skating, eh? Ah, me! I used to cut figure eights myself, arm in arm with Betsy Ross, waving the flag behind us.

JUNE. It was wonderful on the ice today. Miss Cutler and Mr. Jefferson were there.

WHITESIDE. Maggie? Skating?

RICHARD. Yes, and she's good, too. I got a marvelous picture of her.

WHITESIDE. Were they still there when you left?

RICHARD. I think so. Say, Mr. Whiteside, mind if I take a picture of you? I'd love to have one.

WHITESIDE. Very well. Do you want my profile? (*He indicates his stomach*)

JUNE (*starting up the stairs*). I'm afraid you're done for, Mr. Whiteside. My brother is a camera fiend.

RICHARD (*clicking his camera*). Thank you, Mr. Whiteside. I got a great one. (*He and* JUNE *go up the stairs as* MAGGIE *enters from the hallway. They call a "Hello, Miss Cutler!" as they disappear*)

MAGGIE. Hello, there. . . . Good evening, Sherry. Really Sherry, you've got this room looking like an old parrot-cage. . . . Did you nap while I was out? (WHITESIDE *merely glowers at her*) What's the matter, dear? Cat run away with your tongue? (*She is on her knees, gathering up debris*)

WHITESIDE (*furious*). Don't look up at me with those great cow-eyes, you sex-ridden hag. Where have you been all afternoon? Alley-catting around with Bert Jefferson?

MAGGIE (*her face aglow*). Sherry—Bert read his play to me this afternoon. It's superb. It isn't just that play written by a newspaper man. It's superb. I want you to read it *tonight*. (*She puts it in his lap*) It just cries out for Cornell. If you like it, will you send it to her, Sherry? And will you read it tonight?

WHITESIDE. No, I will not read it tonight or any other time. And while we're on the subject of Mr. Jefferson, you might ask him if he wouldn't like to pay your salary, since he takes up all your time.

MAGGIE. Oh, come now, Sherry. It isn't as bad as that.

WHITESIDE. I have not even been able to reach you, not knowing what haylofts you frequent.

MAGGIE. Oh, stop behaving like a spoiled child, Sherry.

WHITESIDE. Don't take that patronizing tone with me, you flea-bitten Cleopatra. I am sick and tired of your sneaking out like some lovesick high-school girl every time my back is turned.

MAGGIE. Well, Sherry—(*She pulls together the library doors and faces* WHITESIDE)—I'm afraid you've hit the nail on the head. (*With a little flourish, she removes her hat*)

WHITESIDE. Stop acting like Zasu Pitts and explain your-self.

MAGGIE. I'll make it quick, Sherry. I'm in love.

WHITESIDE. Nonsense. This is merely delayed puberty.

MAGGIE. No, Sherry, I'm afraid this is it. You're going to lose a very excellent secretary.

WHITESIDE. You are out of your mind.

MAGGIE. Yes, I think I am, a little. But I'm a girl who's waited a long time for this to happen, and now it has. Mr. Jefferson doesn't know it yet, but I'm going to try my darnedest to marry him.

WHITESIDE (*as she pauses*). Is that all?

MAGGIE. Yes, except that—well—I suppose this is what might be called my resignation—as soon as you've got someone else.

WHITESIDE (*there is a slight pause*). Now listen to me, Maggie. We have been together for a long time. You are indispensable to me, but I think I am unselfish enough not to let that stand in the way where your happiness is concerned. Because, whether you know it or not, I have a deep affection for you.

MAGGIE. I know that, Sherry.

WHITESIDE. That being the case, I will not stand by and allow you to make a fool of yourself.

MAGGIE. I'm not, Sherry.

WHITESIDE. You are, my dear. You are behaving like Tillie the Toiler. It's—it's incredible. I cannot believe that a girl who for the past ten years has had the great of the world served up on a platter before her—I cannot believe that it is anything but a kind of temporary insanity when you are swept off your feet in seven days by a second-rate, small-town newspaper man.

MAGGIE. Sherry, I can't explain what's happened. I can only tell you that it's so. It's hard for me to believe too, Sherry. Here I am, a hard-bitten old cynic, behaving like *True Story Magazine*, and liking it. Discovering the moon, and ice-skating—I keep laughing to myself all the time, but there it is. What can I do about it, Sherry? I'm in love.

WHITESIDE (*with sudden decision*). We're leaving here tomorrow. Hip or no hip, we're leaving here tomorrow. I don't care if I fracture the other one. Get me a train schedule and start packing. *I*'ll pull you out of this, Miss Stardust. *I*'ll get the ants out of those moonlit pants.

MAGGIE. It's no good, Sherry. I'd be back on the next streamlined train.

WHITESIDE. It's completely unbelievable. Can you see your-self, the wife of the editor of the Mesalia *Journal*, hav-ing an evening at home for Mr. and Mrs. Stanley, Mr. and Mrs. Poop-Face, and the members of the Book-of-the-Month Club?

MAGGIE. Sherry, I've had ten years of the great figures of our time, and don't think I'm not grateful to you for it. I've loved every minute of it. They've been wonderful years, Sherry. Gay and stimulating—why, I don't think anyone has every had the fun we've had. But a girl can't laugh all the time, Sherry. There comes a time when she wants—Bert Jefferson. You don't know Bert, Sherry. He's gentle, and he's unassuming, and—well, I love him, that's all.

WHITESIDE. I see. Well, I remain completely unconvinced. You are drugging yourself into this Joan Crawford fan-tasy, and before you become completely anesthetized I shall do everything in my power to bring you to your senses.

MAGGIE (*wheeling on him*). Now listen to me, Whiteside. I know you. Lay off. I know what a devil you can be. I've seen you do it to other people, but don't you dare to do it to me. Don't drug *yourself* into the idea that all you're thinking of is my happiness. You're thinking of yourself a little bit, too, and all those months of break-ing in somebody new. I've seen you in a passion before when your life has been disrupted, and you couldn't dine in Calcutta on July twelfth with Boo-Boo. Well, that's too bad, but there it is. I'm going to marry Bert if he'll have me, and don't you dare try any of your tricks. I'm on to every one of them. So lay off. That's my message to *you*, Big Lord Fauntleroy. (*And she is up the stairs*)

(*Left stewing in his own juice*, MR. WHITESIDE *is in a per-fect fury. He bangs the arm of his chair, then slaps at the manuscript in his lap. As he does so, the dawn of*

*an idea comes into his mind. He sits perfectly still for
a moment, thinking it over. Then, with a slow smile, he
takes the manuscript out of its envelope. He looks at
the title page, ruffles through the script, then stops and
thinks again. His face breaks out into one great smile.
Then he quickly wheels himself over to the table and
hunts hurriedly through a pile of old cablegrams and
letters, until he finds the one he wants. With this in his
hand, he takes up the telephone receiver)*

WHITESIDE *(in a lowered voice)*. Long distance, please. I
want to put in a trans-Atlantic call. *(He looks at the
cablegram again for confirmation)* Hello. Trans-Atlantic
operator? . . . This is Mesalia one four two. I want to
talk to Miss Lorraine Sheldon—S-h-e-l-d-o-n. She's on
the *Normandie*. It sailed from Southampton day before
yesterday. . . . Will it take long? . . . All right. My
name is Whiteside. . . . Thank you. *(He hangs up as
the door bell rings. He goes back to the manuscript
again and looks through it.* JOHN *then ushers in* DR.
BRADLEY)

DR. BRADLEY *(hearty, as usual)*. Well, well! Good evening,
Mr. Whiteside!

WHITESIDE. Come back tomorrow—I'm busy.

DR. BRADLEY *(turning cute)*. Now what would be the best
news that I could possibly bring you?

WHITESIDE. You have hydrophobia.

DR. BRADLEY *(laughing it off)*. No, no. . . . Mr. Whiteside, you are a well man. You can get up and walk *now*.
You can leave here tomorrow.

WHITESIDE. What do you mean?

DR. BRADLEY. Well, sir! I looked at those X-rays again this
morning, and do you know what? I had been looking
at the wrong X-rays. I had been looking at old Mrs.
Moffat's X-rays. You are perfectly, absolutely well!

WHITESIDE. Lower your voice, will you?

DR. BRADLEY. What's the matter? Aren't you pleased?

WHITESIDE. Delighted. . . . Naturally. . . . Ah—this is a very unexpected bit of news, however. It comes at a very curious moment. (*He is thinking fast; suddenly he gets an idea. He clears his throat and looks around apprehensively*) Dr. Bradley, I—ah—I have some good news for you, too. I have been reading your book—ah —*Forty Years*—what is it?

DR. BRADLEY (*eagerly*). *An Ohio Doctor*—yes?

WHITESIDE. I consider it extremely close to being one of the great literary contributions of our time.

DR. BRADLEY. Mr. Whiteside!

WHITESIDE. So strongly do I feel about it, Dr. Bradley, that I have a proposition to make to you. Just here and there the book is a little uneven, a little rough. What I would like to do is to stay here in Mesalia and work with you on it.

DR. BRADLEY (*all choked up*). Mr. Whiteside, I would be so terribly honored—

WHITESIDE. Yes. But there is just one difficulty. You see, if my lecture bureau and my radio sponsors were to learn that I am well, they would insist on my fulfilling my contracts, and I would be forced to leave Mesalia. Therefore, we must not tell anyone—not anyone at all —that I am well.

DR. BRADLEY. I see. I see.

WHITESIDE. Not even Miss Cutler, you understand.

DR. BRADLEY. No, I won't. Not a soul. Not even my wife.

WHITESIDE. That's fine.

DR. BRADLEY. When do we start work—tonight? I've got just one patient that's dying and then I'll be perfectly free.

(*The phone rings*)

WHITESIDE (*waving him away*). Ah—tomorrow morning. This is a private call—would you forgive me? . . . Hello. . . . Yes, I'm on. (*He turns again to the* DOCTOR) Tomorrow morning.

DR. BRADLEY. Tomorrow morning it is. Good night. You've made me very proud, Mr. Whiteside. (*He goes*)

WHITESIDE (*again on the phone*). Yes, yes, this is Mr. Whiteside on the phone. Put them through. . . . Hello. Is this my Blossom Girl? How are you, my lovely? . . . No, no, I'm all right. . . . Yes, still out here. . . . Lorraine dear, when do you land in New York? . . . Tuesday? That's fine. . . . Now listen closely, my pet. I've great news for you. I've discovered a wonderful play with an enchanting part in it for you. Cornell would give her eye teeth to play it, but I think I can get it for you. . . . Now wait, wait. Let me tell you. The author is a young newspaper man in this town. Of course he wants Cornell, but if you jump on a train and get right out here, I think you could swing it, if you play your cards right. . . . No, he's young, and very attractive, and just your dish, my dear. It just takes a little doing, and you're the girl that can do it. Isn't that exciting, my pet? . . . Yes. . . . Yes, that's right. . . . And look. Don't send me any messages. Just get on a train and arrive. . . . Oh, no, don't thank me, my darling. It's perfectly all right. Have a nice trip and hurry out here. Good-bye, my blossom. (*He hangs up and looks guiltily around. Then he straightens up and gleefully rubs his hands together*)

(MISS PREEN *enters, medicine in hand, and frightened, as usual*)

WHITESIDE (*jovial as hell*). Hello, Miss Preen. My, you're looking radiant this evening.

MISS PREEN (*staggered*). What?

(WHITESIDE *takes the medicine from her and swallows it at one gulp.* MISS PREEN, *still staggered, retreats into the library, just as* MAGGIE *comes down the stairs. She is dressed for the street*)

MAGGIE (*pausing on the landing*). Sherry, I'm sorry for what I said before. I'm afraid I was a little unjust.

WHITESIDE (*all nobility*). That's all right, Maggie dear.
We all lose our tempers now and then.

MAGGIE. I promised to have dinner with Bert and go to a
movie, but we'll come back and play cribbage with you
instead.

WHITESIDE. Fine.

MAGGIE. See you soon, Sherry dear. (*She kisses him lightly
on the forehead and goes on her way*)

(WHITESIDE *looks after her until he hears the doors close.
Then his face lights up again and he bursts happily into
song as he wheels himself into the library*)

WHITESIDE. "I'se des a 'ittle wabbit in the sunshine,
I'se des a 'ittle wabbit in the wain—"

Curtain

ACT TWO

A week later, late afternoon.

The room is now dominated by a large Christmas tree, set in the curve of the staircase, and hung with the customary Christmas ornaments.

SARAH and JOHN are passing in and out of the library, bringing forth huge packages which they are placing under the tree. MAGGIE sits at a little table at one side, going through a pile of correspondence.

JOHN. Well, I guess that's all there are, Miss Cutler. They're all under the tree.

MAGGIE. Thank you, John.

SARAH. My, I never saw anyone get so many Christmas presents. I can hardly wait to see what's in 'em.

JOHN. When'll Mr. Whiteside open them, Miss Cutler?

MAGGIE. Well, John, you see Christmas is Mr. Whiteside's personal property. He invented it and it belongs to him. First thing tomorrow morning, Mr. Whiteside will open each and every present, and there will be the damnedest fuss you ever saw.

SARAH (*bending over the packages*). My, look who he's got presents from! Shirley Temple, William Lyon Phelps, Billy Rose, Ethel Waters, Somerset Maug-ham—I can hardly wait for tonight.

(*The door bell rings.* JOHN *departs for the door*)

SARAH. My, it certainly is wonderful. And Mr. Whiteside's tree is so beautiful, too. Mr. and Mrs. Stanley had to put theirs in their bedroom, you know. They can hardly undress at night.

(*It is* BERT JEFFERSON *who enters*)

BERT. Hello, Maggie. Merry Christmas, Sarah.

SARAH. Merry, Christmas, Mr. Jefferson. (*She and* JOHN *disappear into the dining room*)

BERT (*observing the pile of packages under the tree*). Say, business is good, isn't it? My, what a little quiet blackmail and a weekly radio hour can get you. What did his sponsors give him?

MAGGIE. They gave him a full year's supply of their product, Cream of Mush.

BERT. Well, he'll give it right back to them over the air.

MAGGIE. Wait until you hear tonight's broadcast, old fellow. It's so sticky I haven't been able to get it off my fingers since I copied it.

BERT. I'll bet . . . Look, I'll come clean. Under the influence of God knows what I have just bought you a Christmas present.

MAGGIE (*surprised*). Why, Mr. Jefferson, sir.

BERT. Only I'd like you to see it before I throw away my hard-earned money. Can you run downtown with me and take a look at it?

MAGGIE. Bert, this is very sweet of you. I'm quite touched. What is it? I can't wait.

BERT. A two years' subscription to *Pic, Click, Look,* and *Listen.* . . . Do you think I'm going to tell you? Come down and see.

MAGGIE (*she calls into the library*). Sherry! Sherry, I'm going out for a few minutes. With Horace Greeley. I won't be long. (*She goes into the hallway for her coat and hat*)

BERT (*raising his voice*). Noël, Noël, Mr. W.! How about some cribbage after your broadcast tonight?

(*The* WHITESIDE *wheelchair is rolling into the room*)

WHITESIDE. No, I will not play cribbage with you, Klondike Harry. You have been swindling the be-jesus out of me for two weeks. . . . Where are you off to now, Madame Butterfly?

MAGGIE. I'm being given a Christmas present. Anything you want done downtown?

WHITESIDE. 'Es. B'ing baby a lollipop. . . . What are *you* giving me for Christmas, Jefferson? I have enriched your feeble life beyond your capacity to repay me.

BERT. Yes, that's what I figured, so I'm not giving you anything.

WHITESIDE. I see. Well, I was giving you my old truss, but now I shan't. . . . Maggie, what time are those radio men coming?

MAGGIE. About six-thirty—I'll be here. You've got to cut, Sherry. You're four minutes over. Oh, by the way, there was a wire from Beverly. It's there somewhere. He doesn't know what train he can get out of Chicago, but he'll be here some time this evening.

WHITESIDE. Good! Is he staying overnight?

MAGGIE. No, he has to get right out again. He's sailing Friday on the *Queen Mary*.

BERT. Think I could peek in at the window and get a look at him? Beverly Carlton used to be one of my heroes.

WHITESIDE. Used to be, you ink-stained hack? Beverly Carlton is the greatest single talent in the English theatre today. Take this illiterate numbskull out of my sight, Maggie, and don't bring him back.

BERT. Yes, Mr. Whiteside, sir. I won't come back until Beverly Carlton gets here.

MAGGIE (*as they go on their way*). Where are we going, Bert? I want to know what you've bought me—I'm like a ten-year-old kid.

BERT (*laughing a little*). You know, you look like a ten-year-old kid right now, Maggie, at that.

(*They are out of earshot by this time*)

(WHITESIDE *looks after them intently, listens until the door closes. He considers for a second, then wheels himself over to the telephone)*

WHITESIDE *(on the phone)*. Will you give me the Mansion House, please? . . . No, I *don't* know the number. . . . Hello? Mansion House? . . . Tell me, has a Miss Lorraine Sheldon arrived yet? . . . Yes, that's right— Miss Lorraine Sheldon. From New York. . . . She hasn't, eh? Thank you. *(He hangs up, drums with his fingers on the chair arm, looks at his watch. He slaps his knees impatiently, stretches. Then, vexed at his self-imposed imprisonment, he looks cautiously around the room, peers up the stairs. Then, slowly, he gets out of his chair; standing beside it, he indulges in a few mild calisthenics, looking cautiously around all the while)*

(Then the sound of the library doors being opened sends him scurrying back to his chair. It is MISS PREEN who emerges)

WHITESIDE *(annoyed)*. What do you want, coming in like that? Why don't you knock before you come into a room?

MISS PREEN. But—I wasn't coming in. I was coming out.

WHITESIDE. Miss Preen, you are obviously *in* this room. That is true, isn't it?

MISS PREEN. Yes, it is, but—

WHITESIDE. Therefore you came in. Hereafter, please knock.

(Before MISS PREEN can reply, however, JOHN enters from the dining room)

JOHN *(en route to the front door)*. There are some expressmen here with a crate, Mr. Whiteside. I told them to come around the front.

WHITESIDE. Thank you, John. . . . Don't stand there, Miss Preen. You look like a frozen custard. Go away.

MISS PREEN *(controlling herself as best she can)*. Yes, sir. *(She goes)*

(*At the same time two* EXPRESSMEN, *carrying a crate, enter from the front door*)

JOHN. Bring it right in here. Careful there—don't scrape the wall. Why, it's some kind of animals.

EXPRESSMAN. I'll say it's animals. We had to feed 'em at seven o'clock this morning.

WHITESIDE. Bring it over here, John. Who's it from?

JOHN (*reading from the top of the crate as they set it down*). Admiral Richard E. Byrd. Say!

WHITESIDE (*peering through the slats*). Why, they're penguins. Two—three—four penguins. Hello, my pretties.

EXPRESSMAN. Directions for feeding are right on top. These two slats are open.

JOHN (*reading*). "To be fed only whale blubber, eels and cracked lobster."

EXPRESSMAN. They got Coca-Cola this morning. And *liked* it. (*They go*)

WHITESIDE (*peering through the slats again*). Hello, hello, hello. You know, they make the most entrancing companions, John. Admiral Byrd has one that goes on all his lecture tours. I want these put right in the library with me. Take 'em right in.

JOHN (*picking up the crate*). Yes, sir.

WHITESIDE. Better tell Sarah to order a couple of dozen lobsters. I don't suppose there's any whale blubber in Mesalia.

(*At which point* DR. BRADLEY *obligingly enters from the hall.* MR. WHITESIDE *is equal to the occasion*)

WHITESIDE (*with just the merest glance at the* DOCTOR). Oh, yes, there is.

DR. BRADLEY. The door was open, so I— Good afternoon, Mr. Whiteside. And Merry Christmas.

WHITESIDE. Merry Christmas, Merry Christmas. Do you happen to know if eels are in season, Doctor?

DR. BRADLEY. How's that?

WHITESIDE. Never mind. I was a fool to ask you.

(JOHN *returns from the library, carefully closing the doors*)

JOHN. I opened those two slats a little, Mr. Whiteside—they seem so crowded in there.

WHITESIDE. Thank you, John. (JOHN *goes on his way*) On your way downtown, Doctor, will you send these air mail? Miss Cutler forgot them. (*He hands him a few letters*) Good-bye. Sorry you dropped in just now. I have to do my Yogi exercises. (*He folds his arms, leans back and closes his eyes*)

DR. BRADLEY. But, Mr. Whiteside, it's been a week now. My book, you know—when are we going to start work on the book? (WHITESIDE, *his eyes still closed, places his fingers to his lips, for absolute silence*) I was hoping that today you'd be— (*He stops short as* MISS PREEN *returns from the dining room*) Good afternoon, Miss Preen.

MISS PREEN. Good afternoon, Dr. Bradley. (*She opens the doors to enter the library, then freezes in her tracks. She closes the doors again and turns to the* DOCTOR, *glassy-eyed. She raises a trembling hand to her forehead*) Doctor, perhaps I'm—not well, but—when I opened the doors just now I thought I saw a penguin with a thermometer in its mouth.

WHITESIDE. What's this? Have those penguins got out of their crate?

MISS PREEN. Oh, thank God. I thought perhaps the strain had been too much.

DR. BRADLEY (*incredulous*). Penguins?

WHITESIDE. Yes. Doctor, will you go in and capture them, please, and put them back in the crate? There're four of them.

DR. BRADLEY (*somewhat staggered*). Very well. Do you suppose that later on, Mr. Whiteside, we might—

WHITESIDE. We'll see, we'll see. First catch the penguins. And, Miss Preen, will you amuse them, please, until I come in?

MISS PREEN (*swallowing hard*). Yes, sir.

(*Meanwhile* JOHN *has descended the stairs*)

JOHN. The Christmas tree just fell on Mr. Stanley. He's got a big bump on his forehead.

WHITESIDE (*brightly*). Why, isn't that too bad? . . . Go ahead, Doctor. Go on, Miss Preen.

(RICHARD *pops in from the hallway*)

RICHARD. Hello, Mr. Whiteside.

WHITESIDE. Hello, Dickie, my boy.

DR. BRADLEY (*still lingering*). Mr. Whiteside, will you have some time later?

WHITESIDE (*impatient*). I don't know, Doctor. I'm busy now.

DR. BRADLEY. Well, suppose I wait a little while? I'll—I'll wait a little while. (*He goes into the library*)

WHITESIDE. Dr. Bradley is the greatest living argument for mercy killings. . . . Well, Dickie, would you like a candid camera shot of my left nostril this evening?

RICHARD. I'm sort of stocked up on those. Have you got a minute to look at some new ones I've taken?

WHITESIDE. I certainly have. . . . Why, these are splendid, Richard. There's real artistry in them—they're as good as anything by Margaret Bourke-White. I like all the things you've shown me. This is the essence of photographic journalism.

RICHARD. Say, I didn't know they were as good as that. I just like to take pictures, that's all.

WHITESIDE. Richard, I've been meaning to talk to you about this. You're not just a kid fooling with a camera any more. These are good. This is what you ought to do. You ought to get out of here and do some of the things you were telling me about. Just get on a boat and get off wherever it stops. Galveston, Mexico, Singapore—work your way through and just take pictures—everything.

RICHARD. Say, wouldn't I like to, though! It's what I've

been dreaming of for years. If I could do that I'd be the happiest guy in the world.

WHITESIDE. Well, why can't you do it? If I were your age, I'd do it like a shot.

RICHARD. Well, you know why. Dad.

WHITESIDE. Richard, do you really want to do this more than anything else in the world?

RICHARD. I certainly do.

WHITESIDE. Then do it.

(JUNE *comes quietly in from the dining room. Obviously there is something on her mind*)

JUNE. Hello, Dick. Good afternoon, Mr. Whiteside.

WHITESIDE. Hello, my lovely. . . . So I'm afraid it's up to *you*, Richard.

RICHARD. I guess it is. Well, thank you, Mr. Whiteside. You've been swell and I'll never forget it.

WHITESIDE. Righto, Richard.

RICHARD. June, are you coming upstairs?

JUNE. Ah—in a few minutes, Richard.

RICHARD. Well—knock on my door, will you? I want to talk to you.

JUNE. Yes, I will.

(RICHARD *disappears up the stairs*)

WHITESIDE (*brightly opening his book*). June, my lamb, you were too young to know about the Elwell murder, weren't you? Completely fascinating. I have about five favorite murders, and the Elwell case is one of them. Would you like to hear about it?

JUNE. Well, Mr. Whiteside, I wanted to talk to you. Would you mind, for a few minutes? It's important.

WHITESIDE. Why, certainly, my dear. I take it this is all about your young Lothario at the factory?

JUNE. Yes. I just can't seem to make Father understand. It's like talking to a blank wall. He won't meet him— he won't even talk about it. What are we going to do,

Mr. Whiteside? Sandy and I love each other. I don't
know where to turn.

WHITESIDE. My dear, I'd like to meet this young man. I'd
like to see him for myself.

JUNE. Would you, Mr. Whiteside? Would you meet him?
He's—he's outside now. He's in the kitchen.

WHITESIDE. Good! Bring him in.

JUNE (hesitating). Mr. Whiteside, he's—he's a very sen-
sitive boy. You will be nice to him, won't you?

WHITESIDE. God damn it, June, when will you learn that
I am *always* kind and courteous! Bring this idiot in!

JUNE (calling through the dining room in a low voice).
Sandy. . . . Sandy. . . . (She stands aside as a young
man enters. Twenty-three or -four, keen-looking, neatly
but simply dressed) Here he is, Mr. Whiteside. This is
Sandy.

SANDY. How do you do, sir?

WHITESIDE. How do you do? Young man, I've been hearing a good deal about you from June this past week.
It seems, if I have been correctly informed, that you
two babes in the woods have quietly gone out of your
minds.

JUNE. There's another name for it. It's called love.

WHITESIDE. Well, you've come to the right place. Dr. Sheridan Whiteside, Broken Hearts Mended, Brakes Re-
lined, Hamburgers. Go right ahead.

SANDY. Well, if June has told you anything at all, Mr.
Whiteside, you know the jam we're in. You see, I work
for the union, Mr. Whiteside. I'm an organizer. I've been
organizing the men in Mr. Stanley's factory, and Mr.
Stanley's pretty sore about it.

WHITESIDE. I'll bet.

SANDY. Did June tell you that?

WHITESIDE. Yes, she did.

SANDY. Well, that being the case, Mr. Whiteside, I don't
think I have the right to try to influence June. If she

marries me it means a definite break with her family, and I don't like to bring that about. But Mr. Stanley's so stubborn about it, so arbitrary. You know, this is not something I've done just to spite him. We fell in love with each other. But Mr. Stanley behaves as though it were all a big plot—John L. Lewis sent me here just to marry his daughter.

JUNE. He's tried to fire Sandy twice, out at the factory, but he couldn't on account of the Wagner Act, thank God!

SANDY. Yes, he thinks I wrote that, too.

JUNE. If he'd only let me talk to him. If he'd let Sandy talk to him.

SANDY. Well, we've gone over all that, June. Anyway, this morning I got word I'm needed in Chicago. I may have to go on to Frisco from there. So you see the jam we're in.

JUNE. Sandy's leaving tonight, Mr. Whiteside. He'll probably be gone a year. We've simply got to decide. *Now.*

WHITESIDE. My dear, this is absurdly simple. It's no problem at all. Now, to my jaundiced eye— (*The telephone rings*) Oh-h! . . . Hello. . . . Yes. . . . This is Whiteside. . . . Excuse me—it's a long-distance call. . . . Yes? . . . Yes, I'm on. Who's calling me? (*His tone suddenly becomes one of keen delight*) Oh! Put him on! (*He turns to the young pair*) It's Walt Disney, in Hollywood. (*The phone again*) Hello. . . . Hello. . . . Walt! How's my little dash of genius? . . . Yes, I hoped you would. How'd you know I was here? . . . I see. . . . Yes, I'm listening. Ten seconds more? (*A quick aside to the others*) Mr. Disney calls me every Christmas— (*The phone*) Yes, Walt. . . . Yes, I hear it. It sounds just like static. . . . June! (*He holds the receiver out to* JUNE *for a second; she listens, mystified*) Hello. . . . Thanks, old man, and a very merry Christmas to *you*. . . . Tell me—any news in Hollywood? Who's in Lana Turner's sweater these days? . . . Well,

tell him to get out. . . . Good-bye. (*He hangs up*) Do
you know what that was you listened to? The voice of
Donald Duck.

JUNE. Not really?

WHITESIDE. Mr. Disney calls me every Christmas, no matter where I am. Two years ago I was walking on the
bottom of the ocean in a diving suit with William
Beebe, but he got me. . . . Now, where were we? Oh,
yes. . . . June, I like your young man. I have an un-
erring instinct about people—I've never been wrong.
That's why I wanted to meet him. My feeling is that
you two will be very happy together. Whatever his be-
liefs are, he's entitled to them, and you shouldn't let
anything stand in your way. As I see it, it's no problem
at all. Stripped of its externals, what does it come down
to? Your father. The possibility of making him unhappy.
Is that right?

JUNE. *Very* unhappy.

WHITESIDE. That isn't the point. Suppose your parents *are*
unhappy—it's good for them. Develops their characters.
Look at me. I left home at the age of four and haven't
been back since. They hear me on the radio and that's
enough for them.

SANDY. Then—your advice is to go ahead, Mr. Whiteside?

WHITESIDE. It is. Marry him tonight, June.

JUNE (*almost afraid to make the leap*). You—you mean
that, Mr. Whiteside?

WHITESIDE (*bellowing*). No, I mean you should marry
Hamilton Fish. If I didn't mean it I wouldn't say it.
What do you want me to do—say it all over again? My
own opinion is—

(*The voice of* MR. STANLEY *is heard at the head of the
stairs.* "Come on, Daisy—stop dawdling")

(JUNE *quickly pushes her young man out of the room, as*
MR. *and* MRS. STANLEY *descend the stairs*)

STANLEY (*with deep sarcasm*). Forgive us for trespassing, Mr. Whiteside.

WHITESIDE. Not at all, old fellow—not at all. It's Christmas, you know. Merry Christmas, Merry Christmas.

MRS. STANLEY (*nervously*). Ah—yes. Merry Christmas. . . . Would you like to come along with us, June? We're taking some presents over to the Dexters.

JUNE. No—no, thank you, Mother. I—I have to write some letters. (*She hurries up the stairs*)

STANLEY (*who has been donning his coat*). Come along, Daisy.

(*Turning, he reveals a great patch of court plaster on his head*)

WHITESIDE (*entirely too sweetly*). Why, Mr. Stanley, what happened to your forehead? Did you have an accident?

STANLEY (*just as sweetly*). No, Mr. Whiteside. I'm taking boxing lessons. . . . Come, Daisy.

(*They go*)

(*HARRIET, who has been hovering at the head of the stairs, hurries down as the STANLEYS depart. She is carrying a little Christmas package*)

HARRIET. Dear Mr. Whiteside, I've been trying all day to see you. To give you—*this*.

WHITESIDE. Why, Miss Stanley. A Christmas gift for me?

HARRIET. It's only a trifle, but I wanted you to have it. It's a picture of me as I used to be. It was taken on another Christmas Eve, many years ago. Don't open it till the stroke of midnight, will you? (*The door bell rings. HARRIET looks apprehensively over her shoulder*) Merry Christmas, dear Mr. Whiteside. Merry Christmas.

WHITESIDE. Merry Christmas to you, Miss Stanley, and thank you.

(*She glides out of the room*)

(*In the hallway, as JOHN opens the door, we hear a woman's voice, liquid and melting. "This is the Stanley*

*residence, isn't it?" "Yes, it is." "I've come to see Mr.
Whiteside. Will you tell him Miss Sheldon is here?")*

WHITESIDE. Lorraine! My Blossom Girl!

LORRAINE (*coming into view*). Sherry, my sweet!

(*And quite a view it is.* LORRAINE SHELDON *is known as the
most chic actress on the New York or London stage,
and justly so. She glitters as she walks. She is beautiful,
and even, God save the word, glamorous. . . . Her
rank as one of the Ten Best-Dressed Women of the
World is richly deserved. She is, in short, a siren of no
mean talents, and knows it*)

LORRAINE (*wasting no time*). Oh, darling, look at that poor
sweet tortured face! Let me kiss it! You poor darling,
your eyes have a kind of gallant compassion. How
drawn you are! Sherry, my sweet, I want to cry.

WHITESIDE. All right, all right. You've made a very nice
entrance. Now relax, dear.

LORRAINE. But, Sherry, darling, I've been so worried. And
now seeing you in that chair . . .

WHITESIDE. This chair fits my fanny as nothing else ever
has. I feel better than I have in years, and my only con-
cern is news of the outside world. So take that skunk
off and tell me everything. How are you, my dear?

LORRAINE (*removing a cascade of silver fox from her
shoulders*). Darling, I'm so relieved. You look perfectly
wonderful—I never saw you look better. My dear, do
I look a wreck? I just dashed through New York. Didn't
do a thing about Christmas. Hattie Carnegie and had
my hair done, and got right on the train. And the
Normandie coming back was simply hectic. Fun, you
know, but simply exhausting. Jock Whitney, and Cary
Grant, and Dorothy di Frasso—it was *too* exhausting.
And of course London before that was so magnificent,
my dear—well, I simply never got to bed at all. Darling,
I've so much to tell you I don't know where to start.

WHITESIDE. Well, start with the dirt first, dear—that's what I want to hear.

LORRAINE. Let me see. . . . Well, Sybil Cartwright got thrown right out of Ciro's—it was the night before I sailed. She was wearing one of those new cellophane dresses, and you could absolutely see Trafalgar Square. And, oh, yes— Sir Harry Montrose—the painter, *you* know—is suing his mother for disorderly conduct. It's just shocked *everyone*. Oh, and before I forget Beatrice Lillie gave me a message for you. She says for you to take off twenty-five pounds right away and send them to her by parcel post. She needs them.

WHITESIDE. Nonsense. . . . Now come, dear, what about *you*? What about your love life? I don't believe for one moment that you never got to bed at all, if you'll pardon the expression.

LORRAINE. Sherry dear, you're dreadful.

WHITESIDE. What about that splendid bit of English mutton, Lord Bottomley? Haven't you hooked him yet?

LORRAINE. Sherry, please. Cedric is a very dear friend of mine.

WHITESIDE. Now, Blossom Girl, this is Sherry. Don't try to pull the bed clothes over *my* eyes. Don't tell *me* you wouldn't like to be Lady Bottomley, with a hundred thousand pounds a year and twelve castles. By the way, has he had his teeth fixed yet? Every time I order Roquefort cheese I think of those teeth.

LORRAINE. Sherry, really! . . . Cedric may not be brilliant, but he's rather sweet, poor lamb, and he's very fond of me, and he does represent a kind of English way of living that I like. Surrey, and London for the season—shooting box in Scotland—that lovely old castle in Wales. You were there, Sherry—you know what I mean.

WHITESIDE. Mm. I do indeed.

LORRAINE. Well, really, Sherry, why not? If I can marry
Cedric I don't know why I shouldn't. Shall I tell you
something, Sherry? I think, from something he said just
before I sailed, that he's finally coming around to it. It
wasn't definite, mind you, but—don't be surprised if
I *am* Lady Bottomley before very long.

WHITESIDE. Lady Bottomley! Won't Kansas City be surprised! However, I shall be a flower girl and give the
groom an iron toothpick as a wedding present. Come
ahead, my blossom—let's hear some more of your skul-
duggery.

(*The library doors are quietly opened at this point and
the* DOCTOR's *head appears*)

DR. BRADLEY (*in a heavy whisper*). Mr. Whiteside.

WHITESIDE. What? No, no—not now. I'm busy.

(*The* DOCTOR *disappears*)

LORRAINE. Who's that?

WHITESIDE. He's fixing the plumbing. . . . Now come on,
come on—I want more news.

LORRAINE. But, Sherry, what about this play? After all,
I've come all the way from New York—even on Christmas Eve—I've been so excited ever since your phone
call. Where is it? When can I read it?

WHITESIDE. Well, here's the situation. This young author
—his name is Bert Jefferson—brought me the play with
the understanding that I send it to Kit Cornell. It's a
magnificent part, and God knows I feel disloyal to Kit,
but there you are. Now *I've* done *this* much—the rest
is up to you. He's young and attractive—now, just how
you'll go about persuading him, I'm sure you know more
about that than I do.

LORRAINE. Darling, how can I ever thank you? Does he
know I'm coming—Mr. Jefferson, I mean?

WHITESIDE. No, no. You're just out here visiting me. You'll
meet him, and that's that. Get him to take you to dinner, and work around to the play. Good God, I don't

have to tell you how to do these things. How did you get all those other parts?

LORRAINE. Sherry! . . . Well, I'll go back to the hotel and get into something more attractive. I just dumped my bags and rushed right over here. Darling, you're wonderful. (*Lightly kissing him*)

WHITESIDE. All right—run along and get into your working clothes. Then come right back here and spend Christmas Eve with Sherry and I'll have Mr. Jefferson on tap. By the way, I've got a little surprise for you. Who do you think's paying me a flying visit tonight? None other than your old friend and fellow actor, Beverly Carlton.

LORRAINE (*not too delighted*). Really? Beverly? I thought he was being glamorous again on a tramp steamer.

WHITESIDE. Come, come, dear—mustn't be bitter because he got better notices than you did.

LORRAINE. Don't be silly, Sherry. I never read notices. I simply wouldn't care to act with him again, that's all. He's not staying here, is he? I *hope* not!

WHITESIDE. Temper, temper, temper. No, he's not. . . . Where'd you get that diamond clip, dear? That's a new bit of loot, isn't it?

LORRAINE. Haven't you seen this before? Cedric gave it to me for his mother's birthday. . . . Look, darling, I've got a taxi outside. If I'm going to get back here—

(*At this point the voice of* MAGGIE *is heard in the hallway*)

MAGGIE. Sherry, what do you think? I've just been given the most beautiful . . . (*She stops short and comes to a dead halt as she sees* LORRAINE)

LORRAINE. Oh, hello, Maggie. I knew you must be around somewhere. How are you, my dear?

WHITESIDE. Santa's been at work, my pet. Blossom Girl just dropped in out of the blue and surprised us.

MAGGIE (*quietly*). Hello, Lorraine.

WHITESIDE (*as* JEFFERSON *appears*). Who's that—Bert?

This is Mr. Bert Jefferson, Lorraine. Young newspaper
man. Miss Lorraine Sheldon.

BERT. How ·do you do, Miss Sheldon?

LORRAINE. How do you do? I didn't catch the name—Jefferson?

WHITESIDE (*sweetly*). That's right, Pet.

LORRAINE (*full steam ahead*). Why, Mr. Jefferson, you
don't look like a newspaper man. You don't look like
a newspaper man at all.

BERT. Really? I thought it was written all over me in neon
lights.

LORRAINE. Oh, no, not at all. I should have said you were
—oh, I don't know—an aviator or an explorer or something. They have that same kind of dash about them.
I'm simply enchanted with your town. Mr. Jefferson.
It gives one such a warm, gracious feeling. Tell me—
have you lived here all your life?

BERT. Practically.

WHITESIDE. If you wish to hear the story of his life, Lorraine, kindly do so on your own time. Maggie and I
have work to do. Get out of here, Jefferson. On your
way, Blossom.

LORRAINE. He's the world's rudest man, isn't he? Can I
drop you, Mr. Jefferson? I'm going down to the—Mansion House, I think it's called.

BERT. Thank you, but I've got my car. Suppose I drop
you?

LORRAINE. Oh, would you? That'd be lovely—we'll send
the taxi off. See you in a little while, Sherry. 'Bye, Maggie.

BERT. Good-bye, Miss C. (*He turns to* WHITESIDE) I'm
invited back for dinner, am I not?

WHITESIDE. Yes—yes, you are. At Christmas I always feed
the needy. Now please stop oozing out—*get* out.

LORRAINE. Come on, Mr. Jefferson. I want to hear more

about this charming little town. And I want to know a good deal about you, too.

(*And they are gone*)

(*There is a slight but pregnant pause after they go.* MAGGIE *simply stands looking at* WHITESIDE, *waiting for what may come forth*)

WHITESIDE (*as though nothing had happened*). Now let's see, have you got a copy of that broadcast? How much did you say they wanted out—four minutes?

MAGGIE. That's right—four minutes. . . . She's looking very well, isn't she?

WHITESIDE (*busy with his manuscripts*). What's that? Who?

MAGGIE. The Countess di Pushover. . . . Quite a surprise, wasn't it—her dropping in?

WHITESIDE. Yes—yes, it was. Now come on, Maggie, come on. Get to work.

MAGGIE. Why, she must have gone through New York like a dose of salts. How long's she going to stay?

WHITESIDE (*completely absorbed*). What? Oh, I don't know—a few days . . . (*He reads from his manuscript*) "At this joyous season of the year, when in the hearts of men—" I can't cut that.

MAGGIE. Isn't it curious? There was Lorraine, snug as a bug in somebody's bed on the *Normandie*—

WHITESIDE (*so busy*). "Ere the Yuletide season pass—"

MAGGIE (*quietly taking the manuscript out of his hands*). Now, Sherry dear, we will talk a bit.

WHITESIDE. Now look here, Maggie. Just because a friend of mine happens to come out to spend Christmas with me— (*The door bell rings*) I have a hunch that's Beverly. Maggie, see if it is. Go ahead—run! Run!

(MAGGIE *looks at him—right through him, in fact. Then she goes slowly toward the door*)

(*We hear her voice at the door: "Beverly!" Then, in*

*clipped English tones: "Magpie! A large, moist, inces-
tuous kiss for my Magpie!"*)

WHITESIDE (*roaring*). Come in here, you Piccadilly pen-
pusher, and gaze upon a soul in agony.

(BEVERLY CARLTON *enters, arm in arm with* MAGGIE. *Very
confident, very British, very Beverly Carlton*)

BEVERLY. Don't tell me how you are, Sherry dear. I want
none of the tiresome details. I have only a little time,
so the conversation will be entirely about *me*, and I
shall love it. Shall I tell you how I glittered through the
South Seas like a silver scimitar, or would you rather
hear how I frolicked through Zambesia, raping the
Major General's daughter and finishing a three-act play
at the same time? . . . Magpie dear, you are the moon-
flower of my middle age, and I love you very much. Say
something beautiful to me. Sherry dear, without going
into mountainous waves of self-pity, how are you?

WHITESIDE. I'm fine, you presumptuous Cockney. . . .
Now, how was the trip, wonderful?

BEVERLY. Fabulous. I did a fantastic amount of work. By
the way, did I glimpse that little boudoir butterfly, La
Sheldon, in a motor-car as I came up the driveway?

MAGGIE. You did indeed. She's paying us a Christmas visit.

BEVERLY. Dear girl! They do say she set fire to her mother,
but I don't believe it. . . . Sherry, my evil one, not
only have I written the finest comedy since Molière,
but also the best revue since my last one and an operetta
that frightens me—it's so good. I shall play it for eight
weeks in London and six in New York—that's all. No
matinees. Then I am off to the Grecian Islands. . . .
Magpie, why don't you come along? Why don't you
desert this cannonball of fluff and come with me?

MAGGIE. Beverly dear, be careful. You're catching me at a
good moment.

WHITESIDE (*changing the subject*). Tell me, did you have
a good time in Hollywood? How long were you there?

BEVERLY. Three unbelievable days. I saw everyone from Adrian to Zanuck. They came, poor dears, as to a shrine. I was insufferably charming and ruthlessly firm in refusing seven million dollars for two minutes' work.

WHITESIDE. What about Banjo? Did you see my wonderful Banjo in Hollywood?

BEVERLY. I did. He gave a dinner for me. I arrived, in white tie and tails, to be met at the door by two bewigged flunkies, who quietly proceeded to take my trousers off. I was then ushered, in my lemon silk drawers, into a room full of Norma Shearer, Claudette Colbert, and Aldous Huxley, among others. Dear, sweet, incomparable Banjo.

WHITESIDE. I'll never forget that summer at Antibes, when Banjo put a microphone in Lorraine's mattress, and then played the record the next day at lunch.

BEVERLY. I remember it indeed. Lorraine left Antibes by the next boat.

MAGGIE (half to herself). I wish Banjo were here now.

BEVERLY. What's the matter, Magpie? Is Lorraine being her own sweet sick-making self?

MAGGIE. You wouldn't take her to the Grecian Islands with you, would you, Beverly? Just for me?

WHITESIDE. Now, now. Lorraine is a charming person who has gallantly given up her own Christmas to spend it with me.

BEVERLY. Oh, I knew I had a bit of dirt for us all to nibble on. (He draws a letter out of his pocket)

(Again the library doors are opened and the DOCTOR's head comes through)

DR. BRADLEY. Mr. Whiteside.

WHITESIDE. No, no, not now. Go away.

(The DOCTOR withdraws)

BEVERLY. Have you kidnapped someone, Sherry?

WHITESIDE. Yes, that was Charley Ross . . . Go ahead. Is this something juicy?

BEVERLY. Juicy as a pomegranate. It is the latest report from London on the winter maneuvers of Miss Lorraine Sheldon against the left flank—in fact, all flanks—of Lord Cedric Bottomley. Listen: "Lorraine has just left us in a cloud of Chanel Number Five. Since September, in her relentless pursuit of His Lordship, she has paused only to change girdles and check her oil. She has chased him, panting, from castle to castle, till he finally took refuge, for several week-ends, in the gentlemen's lavatory of the House of Lords. Practically no one is betting on the Derby this year; we are all making book on Lorraine. She is sailing tomorrow on the *Normandie,* but would return on the *Yankee Clipper* if Bottomley so much as belches in her direction." Have you ever met Lord Bottomley, Magpie dear? (*He goes immediately into an impersonation of His Lordship. Very British, very full of teeth, stuttering*) "No v-v-very good shooting today, blast it. Only s-s-six partridges, f-f-four grouse, and the D-D-Duke of Sutherland."

WHITESIDE (*chuckling*). My God, that's Bottomley to the very bottom.

BEVERLY (*still in character*). "R-r-ripping debate in the House today. Old Basil spoke for th-th-three hours. D-d-dropped dead at the end of it. Ripping."

MAGGIE. You're making it up, Beverly. No one sounds like that.

WHITESIDE. It's so good it's uncanny. . . . Damn it, Beverly, why must you race right out of here? I never see enough of you, you ungrateful moppet.

BEVERLY. Sherry darling, I can only tell you that my love for you is so great that I changed trains at Chicago to spend ten minutes with you and wish you a Merry Christmas. Merry Christmas, my lad. My little Magpie. (*A look at his watch*) And now I have just time for one magnificent number, to give you a taste of how brilliant the whole thing is. It's the second number in the revue.

(*He strikes a chord on the piano, but before he can go further the telephone rings*)

WHITESIDE. Oh, damn! Get rid of them, Maggie.

MAGGIE. Hello . . . Oh, hello, Bert . . . Oh! Well, just a minute. . . . Beverly, would you talk to a newspaper man for just two minutes? I kind of promised him.

BEVERLY. Won't have time, Magpie, unless he's under the piano.

MAGGIE. Oh! (*Into the phone*) Wait a minute. (*To* BEVERLY *again*) Would you see him at the station, just for a minute before the train goes? (BEVERLY *nods*) Bert, go to the station and wait for him. He'll be there in a few minutes. . . . 'Bye.

WHITESIDE. The stalls are impatient, Beverly. Let's have this second-rate masterpiece.

BEVERLY (*his fingers rippling over the keys*). It's called: "What Am I to Do?"

> "Oft in the nightfall
> I think I might fall
>   Down from my perilous height;
> Deep in the heart of me,
> Always a part of me,
>   Quivering, shivering light.
> Run, little lady,
> Ere the shady
>   Shafts of time
> Barb you with their winged desire,
> Singe you with their sultry fire.
>   Softly a fluid
>   Druid
>   Meets me,
> Olden
>   and golden
>   the dawn that greets me;

Cherishing,
    Perishing,
Up to the stars
    I climb.

"What am I to do
    Toward ending this madness,
    This sadness,
That's rending me through?
The flowers of yesteryear
    Are haunting me,
    Taunting me,
Darling, for wanting you.
What am I to say
    To warnings of sorrow
    When morning's tomorrow
Greets the dew?
    Will I see the cosmic Ritz
    Shattered and scattered to bits?
What *not* am I to do?"

(*As he swings into the chorus for a second time the door
bell rings, and* JOHN *is glimpsed as he goes to the door*)

(*It is a trio of* RADIO MEN *who appear in the doorway,
their arms filled with equipment for* MR. WHITESIDE'S
broadcast)

WHITESIDE. Oh, come in, Westcott. . . . Beverly, it's su-
    perb. The best thing you've ever written. It'll be played
    by every ragtag orchestra from Salem to Singapore.

BEVERLY. Please! Let *me* say that . . . Ah, the air waves,
    eh? Well, I shan't have to hear you, thank God. I shall
    be on the train.

MAGGIE. Come on, Whiteside, say good-bye. Mr. Westcott,
    he's still four minutes over—you'll have to chisel it out.

WHITESIDE (*as* MAGGIE *starts to wheel him into the li-
    brary*). Stop this nonsense. Beverly, my lamb—

MAGGIE. You can kiss Beverly in London on July twelfth.

(*Then to the technicians*) The microphone set-up is
right there, gentlemen, and you can connect up outside.
John, show them where it is.

WHITESIDE. Maggie, what the hell are you—I will not be
wheeled out of here like a baby who has to have his
diapers changed!

BEVERLY (*calling after the fast-disappearing* WHITESIDE).
Au revoir, Sherry. Merry Christmas. Magpie, come get
a kiss.

MAGGIE (*emerging from the library and closing the doors
behind her*). Beverly, I want one minute. I must have
it. You'll make the train. The station's a minute and a
half from here.

BEVERLY. Why, what's the matter, Magpie?

(*At which the library doors are opened and the* DOCTOR
*emerges, rather apologetically. He is sped on his way
by* MR. WHITESIDE's *roaring voice—"Oh, get out of
here!"*)

DR. BRADLEY. I'm—I'm just waiting in the kitchen until
Mr. Whiteside is— Excuse me. (*He darts out through
the dining room*)

BEVERLY. Who *is* that man?

MAGGIE. Never mind . . . Beverly, I'm in great trouble.

BEVERLY. Why, Magpie dear, what's the matter?

MAGGIE. I've fallen in love. For the first time in my life.
Beverly, I'm in love. I can't tell you about it—there
isn't time. But Sherry is trying to break it up. In his
own fiendish way he's doing everything he can to break
it up.

BEVERLY. Why, the old devil! What's he doing?

MAGGIE. Lorraine. He's brought Lorraine here to smash
it.

BEVERLY. Oh, it's somebody *here*? In this town?

MAGGIE (*nodding*). He's a newspaper man—the one you're
going to see at the station—and he's written a play,
and I know Sherry must be using that as bait. You know

Lorraine—she'll eat him up alive. You've got to help
me, Beverly.

BEVERLY. Of course I will, Magpie. What do you want me
to do?

MAGGIE. I've got to get Lorraine out of here—the farther
away the better—and you can do it for me.

BEVERLY. But how? How can I? I'm leaving.

(*The library doors are opened and* WESTCOTT, *the radio
man, emerges*)

WESTCOTT. Have you a carbon copy of the broadcast, Miss
Cutler?

MAGGIE. It's on that table.

WESTCOTT. Thank you. One of those penguins ate the
original.

(*The voice of* WHITESIDE *is now heard calling from his
room*)

WHITESIDE. Beverly, are you still there?

MAGGIE. No, he's gone, Sherry. (*She lowers her voice*)
Come out here.

(*Maneuvering him into the hall, we see her whisper to
him; his head bobs up and down quickly in assent.
Then he lets out a shriek of laughter*)

BEVERLY. I'd love it. I'd absolutely love it. (MAGGIE *puts
a quick finger to his lips, peers toward the* WHITESIDE
room. But MR. WESTCOTT *has gone in; the doors are
closed*) It's simply enchanting, and bitches Sherry and
Lorraine at the same time. It's pure heaven! I adore it,
and I shall do it up brown. (*He embraces her*)

MAGGIE. Darling, the first baby will be named Beverly.
You're wonderful.

BEVERLY. Of course I am. Come to Chislewick for your
honeymoon and I'll put you up. Good-bye, my lovely.
I adore you.

(*And he is gone*)

(MAGGIE *comes back into the room, highly pleased with*

herself. She even sings a fragment of BEVERLY'S *song.* "What am I to do? Tra-la-la-la-la-la")

(JOHN, *entering from the dining room, breaks the song*)

JOHN. Shall I straighten up the room for the broadcast, Miss Cutler?

MAGGIE. No, John, it isn't television, thank God. They only *hear* that liquid voice.

JOHN. He's really wonderful, isn't he? The things he finds time to do.

MAGGIE. Yes, he certainly sticks his nose into everything, John. (*She goes into the library*)

(JOHN *is putting the room in order when suddenly* JUNE *comes quietly down the stairs. She is dressed for the street and is carrying a suitcase*)

JOHN. Why, Miss June, are you going away?

JUNE. Why—no, John. No. I'm just— Mr. Whiteside is inside, I suppose?

JOHN. Yes, he's getting ready to go on the radio.

JUNE. Oh! Well, look, John—

(*And then* RICHARD *darts down the stairs. A light bag, two cameras slung over his shoulder*)

RICHARD (*to* JUNE, *in a heavy whisper*). Where's Mr. Whiteside? In there?

JUNE. Yes, he is.

RICHARD. Oh! Well, maybe we ought to—

(*The door bell rings.* RICHARD *and* JUNE *exchange looks, then scurry out quickly through the dining room*)

(JOHN *looks after them for a second, puzzled, then goes to the door*)

(*It is* LORRAINE *who comes in, resplendent now in evening dress and wraps, straight from Paris. At the same time* MAGGIE *emerges from the library and* JOHN *goes on his way*)

LORRAINE. Hello, dear. Where's Sherry?

MAGGIE. Inside, working—he's broadcasting very soon.

LORRAINE. Oh, of course—Christmas Eve. What a wonderful man Sheridan Whiteside is! You know, my dear, it must be such an utter joy to be secretary to somebody like Sherry.

MAGGIE. Yes, you meet such interesting people. . . . That's quite a gown, Lorraine. Going anywhere?

LORRAINE. This? Oh, I just threw on anything at all. Aren't you dressing for dinner?

MAGGIE. No, just what meets the eye.

(*She has occasion to carry a few papers across the room at this point.* LORRAINE'S *eye watches her narrowly*)

LORRAINE. Who does your hair, Maggie?

MAGGIE. A little French woman named Maggie Cutler comes in every morning.

LORRAINE. You know, every time I see you I keep thinking your hair could be so lovely. I always want to get my hands on it.

MAGGIE (*quietly*). I've always wanted to get mine on yours, Lorraine.

LORRAINE (*absently*). What, dear? (*One of the radio men drifts into the room, plugs into the control board, drifts out again.* LORRAINE'S *eyes follow him idly. Then she turns to* MAGGIE *again*) By the way, what time does Beverly get here? I'm not over-anxious to meet him.

MAGGIE. He's been and gone, Lorraine.

LORRAINE. Really? Well, I'm very glad. . . . Of course you're great friends, aren't you—you and Beverly?

MAGGIE. Yes, we are. I think he's a wonderful person.

LORRAINE. Oh, I suppose so. But when I finished acting with him I was a perfect wreck. All during that tender love scene that the critics thought was so magnificent he kept dropping peanut shells down my dress. I wouldn't act with him again if I were starving.

MAGGIE (*casually*). Tell me, Lorraine, have you found a new play yet?

LORRAINE (*at once on guard*). No. No, I haven't. There

was a pile of manuscripts waiting in New York for me, but I hurried right out here to Sherry.

MAGGIE. Yes, it was wonderful of you, Lorraine—to drop everything that way and rush to Sherry's wheelchair.

LORRAINE. Well, after all, Maggie dear, what else has one in this world but friends? . . . How long will Sherry be in there, I wonder?

MAGGIE. Not long. . . . Did you know that Mr. Jefferson has written quite a good play? The young man that drove you to the hotel.

LORRAINE. Really? No, I didn't. Isn't that interesting?

MAGGIE. Yes, isn't it?

(*There is a considerable pause. The ladies smile at each other*)

LORRAINE (*evading* MAGGIE'S *eyes*). They've put a polish on my nails I simply loathe. I don't suppose Elizabeth Arden has a branch in this town.

MAGGIE (*busy with her papers*). Not if she has any sense.

LORRAINE. Oh, well, I'll just bear it, but it does depress me. (*She rises, wanders aimlessly for a moment, picks up a book from the table*) Have you read this, Maggie? Everybody was reading it on the boat. I hear you simply can't put it down.

MAGGIE. *I* put it down—right there.

(LORRAINE *casually strikes a note or two on the piano*)
(*The telephone rings*)

MAGGIE (*taking up the receiver a little too casually*). Hello . . . Yes . . . Yes . . . Miss Lorraine Sheldon? Yes she's here . . . There's a trans-Atlantic call coming through for you, Lorraine.

LORRAINE. Trans-Atlantic—for me? Here? Why, what in the world—

MAGGIE (*as she hands over the receiver*). It's London.

LORRAINE. London? . . . Hello. (*Then in a louder tone*) Hello . . . Cedric! Cedric, is this you? . . . Why, Cedric, you darling! Why, what a surprise! How'd you know

I was here? . . . Darling, don't talk so fast and you won't stutter so . . . That's better . . . Yes, now I can hear you . . . Yes, very clearly. It's as though you werⁿ just around the corner. . . . I see . . . What? . . . Darling! Cedric, dearest, would you wait just one moment? (*She turns to* MAGGIE) Maggie, would you mind? It's Lord Bottomley—a *very* personal call. Would you mind?

MAGGIE. Oh, not at all. (*She goes into the dining room; almost does a little waltz step as she goes*)

LORRAINE. Yes, my dearest—now tell me . . . Cedric, please don't stutter so. Don't be nervous. (*She listens for a moment again*) Oh, my darling. Oh, my sweet. You don't know how I've prayed for this, every night on the boat . . . Darling, yes! YES, a thousand times yes! . . . I'll take a plane right out of here and catch the next boat. Oh, my sweet, we're going to be the happiest people in the world. I wish I were there now in your arms, Cedric . . . What? . . . Cedric, don't stutter so . . . Yes, and I love *you*, my darling—oh, so much! . . . Oh, my dear sweet. My darling, my darling. . . . Yes, yes! I will, I will, darling! I'll be thinking of you every moment . . . You've made me the happiest girl in the world . . . Good-bye, good-bye, darling. Good-bye. (*Bursting with her news, she throws open the library doors*) Sherry, Sherry! Do you know what's happened? Cedric just called from London— He's asked me to marry him. Sherry, think of it! At last! I've got to get right out of here and catch the next boat. How far are we from Chicago? I can get a plane from there.

MAGGIE (*emerging, mouse-like, from the dining room*). May I come in?

LORRAINE. Maggie dear, can I get a plane out of here right away? Or I'll even take a train to Chicago and fly from there. I've simply got to get the next boat for England.

When is it—do you know? Is there a newspaper here?

MAGGIE. The *Queen Mary* sails Friday. Why, what's all the excitement, Lorraine? What's happened?

LORRAINE. Maggie, the most wonderful thing in the world has happened. Lord Bottomley has asked me to marry him . . . Oh, Maggie! (*And in her exuberance she throws her arms around her*)

MAGGIE. Really? Well, what do you know?

LORRAINE. Isn't it wonderful? I'm so excited I can hardly think. Maggie dear, you must help me get out of here.

MAGGIE. I'd be delighted to, Lorraine.

LORRAINE. Oh, thank you, thank you. Will you look things up right away?

MAGGIE. Yes, I've a time-table right here. And don't worry, because if there's no train I'll drive you to Toledo and you can catch the plane from there.

LORRAINE. Maggie darling, you're wonderful. . . . Sherry, what's the matter with you? You haven't said a word. You haven't even congratulated me.

WHITESIDE (*who has been sitting through this like a thunder-cloud*). Let me understand this, Lorraine. Am I to gather from your girlish squeals that you are about to toss your career into the ashcan?

LORRAINE. Oh, not at all. Of course I may not be able to play this season, but there'll be other seasons, Sherry.

WHITESIDE. I see. And everything goes into the ashcan with it—Is that right?

LORRAINE. But, Sherry, you couldn't expect me to—

WHITESIDE (*icily*). Don't explain, Lorraine. I understand only too well. And I also understand why Cornell remains the First Actress of our theatre.

MAGGIE (*busy with her time-tables*). Oh, this is wonderful! We're in luck, Lorraine. You can get a plane out of Toledo at ten-three. It takes about an hour to get there. Why, it all works out wonderfully, doesn't it, Sherry?

WHITESIDE (*through his teeth*). Peachy!

LORRAINE (*heading for the phone*). Maggie, what's the number of that hotel I'm at? I've got to get my maid started packing.

MAGGIE. Mesalia three two.

LORRAINE (*into the phone*). Mesalia three two, please . . . Let's see—I sail Friday, five-day boat, that means I ought to be in London Wednesday night. . . . Hello. This is Miss Sheldon. . . . That's right. Connect me with my maid.

MAGGIE (*at the window*). Oh, look, Sherry, it's starting to snow. Isn't that wonderful, Sherry? Oh, I never felt more like Christmas in my life. Don't you, Sherry dear?

WHITESIDE. Shut your nasty little face!

LORRAINE (*on the phone*). Cosette? . . . Now listen carefully, Cosette. Have you got a pencil? . . . We're leaving here tonight by plane and sailing Friday on the *Queen Mary*. Start packing immediately and I'll call for you in about an hour . . . Yes, that's right . . . Now I want you to send these cables for me . . . Ready? . . . The first one goes to Lord and Lady Cunard—you'll find all these addresses in my little book. It's in my dressing case. "Lord and Lady Cunard. My darlings. Returning Friday *Queen Mary*. Cedric and I being married immediately on arrival. Wanted you to be the first to know. Love.—Lorraine." . . . Now send the same message—what? . . . Oh, thank you, Cosette. Thank you very much . . . Send the same message to Lady Astor, Lord Beaverbrook, and my mother in Kansas City . . . Got that? . . . And send a wire to Hattie Carnegie, New York. "Please meet me Sherry-Netherland noon tomorrow with sketches of bridal gown and trousseau.—Lorraine Sheldon." And then send a cable to Monsieur Pierre Cartier, Cartier's, London: "Can you hold in reserve for me the triple string of pearls I picked out in October? Cable me *Queen Mary*.—Lorraine Sheldon." . . . Have you got all that straight, Cosette? . . . That's fine. Now you'll have to rush, my dear—I'll be at the hotel in about an hour, so be ready. . . . Good-bye. (*She hangs up*) Thank goodness for Cosette—I'd die without her. She's the most wonderful maid in the world. . . . Well! Life is just full of surprises, isn't it? Who'd have thought an hour ago that I'd be on my way to London?

MAGGIE. An *hour* ago? No, I certainly wouldn't have thought it an hour ago.

WHITESIDE (*beside himself with temper*). Will you both stop this female drooling? I have a violent headache.

MAGGIE (*all solicitude*). Oh, Sherry! Can I get you something?

LORRAINE. Look here, Sherry, I'm sorry if I've offended you, but after all my life is my own and I'm not going to—

(*She stops as* BERT JEFFERSON *comes in from the outside*)

BERT. Hello, everybody. Say, do you know it's snowing out? Going to have a real old-fashioned Christmas.

WHITESIDE. Why don't you telephone your scoop to the New York *Times*?

MAGGIE. Bert, Miss Sheldon has to catch a plane tonight, from Toledo. Can we drive her over, you and I?

BERT. Why, certainly. Sorry you have to go, Miss Sheldon. No bad news, I hope?

LORRAINE. Oh, on the contrary—very good news. Wonderful news.

MAGGIE. Yes, indeed—calls for a drink, I think. You're not being a very good host, Sherry. How about a bottle of champagne?

BERT. Oh, I can do better than that—let me mix you something. It's a Jefferson Special. Okay, Mr. Whiteside?

WHITESIDE. Yes, yes, yes, yes, yes. Mix anything. Only stop driveling.

BERT (*on his way to the dining room*). Anybody admired my Christmas present yet, Maggie?

MAGGIE. Oh, dear, I forgot. (*She raises her arm, revealing a bracelet*) Look, everybody! From Mr. Jefferson to me.

LORRAINE. Oh, it's charming. Let me see it. Oh! Why, it's inscribed, too. "To Maggie. Long may she wave. Bert." Maggie, it's a lovely Christmas present. Isn't it sweet, Sherry?

WHITESIDE (*glowering*). Ducky!

MAGGIE. I told you it was beautiful, Bert. See?

BERT. Well, shows what you get if you save your coupons.

LORRAINE (*looking from* BERT *to* MAGGIE). Well, what's going on between you two, anyhow? Maggie, are you hiding something from us?

WHITESIDE (*a hand to his head*). Great God, will this drivel never stop? My head is bursting.

BERT. A Jefferson Special will cure anything. . . . By the way, I got a two-minute interview with Beverly Carlton at the station. You were right, Mr. Whiteside— He's quite something.

MAGGIE (*uneasily*). Go ahead, Bert—mix the drinks.

BERT. I was lucky to get even two minutes. He was in a telephone booth most of the time. Couldn't hear what he was saying, but from the faces he was making it looked like a scene from one of his plays.

MAGGIE (*hiding her frenzy*). Bert, mix those drinks, will you?

WHITESIDE (*suddenly galvanized*). Just a minute, if you please, Jefferson. Mr. Carlton was in a telephone booth at the station?

BERT. Certainly was—I thought he'd never come out. Kept talking and making the damnedest faces for about five minutes.

MAGGIE (*tensely*). Bert, for goodness sake, will you—

WHITESIDE (*ever so sweetly*). Bert, my boy, I have an idea

I shall love the Jefferson Special. Make me a double one, will you? My headache has gone with the wind.

BERT. Okay. (*He goes*)

(WHITESIDE, *his eyes gleaming, immediately whirls his wheelchair across the room to the telephone*)

WHITESIDE (*a finger to his lips*). Sssh! Philo Vance is now at work.

LORRAINE. What?

WHITESIDE. Sssh! (*He picks up the telephone. His voice is absolutely musical*) Operator! Has there been a call from England over this telephone within the past half hour? . . . Yes, I'll wait.

LORRAINE. Sherry, what *is* this?

WHITESIDE. What's that? There have been no calls from England for the past three days? Thank you . . . Now, will you repeat that, please? . . . Blossom Girl. (*He beckons to* LORRAINE, *then puts the receiver to her ear*) Hear it, dear? (*Then again to the operator*) Thank you, and a Merry Christmas. (*He hangs up*) Yes, indeed, it seems we're going to have a real old-fashioned Christmas.

LORRAINE (*stunned*). Sherry, what is all this? What's going on? What does this mean?

WHITESIDE. My dear, you have just played the greatest love scene of your career with your old friend, Beverly Carlton.

LORRAINE. Why—why, that's not true. I was talking to Cedric. What do you mean?

WHITESIDE. I mean, my blossom, that that was Beverly you poured out your girlish heart to, not Lord Bottomley. Ah, me, who'd have thought five minutes ago that you would *not* be going to London!

LORRAINE. Sherry, stop it! What is this? I want this explained.

WHITESIDE. Explained? You heard the operator, my dear.

All I can tell you is that Beverly was indulging in one of his famous bits of mimicry, that's all. You've heard him do Lord Bottomley before, haven't you?

LORRAINE (*as it dawns on her*). Yes . . . Yes, of course . . . But—but why would he want to do such a thing! This is one of the most dreadful—oh, my God! Those cables! (*In one bound she is at the telephone*) Give me the hotel—whatever it's called—I want the hotel—I'll pay him off for this if it's the last thing that I— Why, the cad! The absolute unutterable cad! The dirty rotten— Mansion House? Connect me with my maid . . . What? . . . Who the hell do you *think* it is? Miss Sheldon, of course . . . Oh, God! Those cables! If only Cosette hasn't—Cosette! Cosette! Did you send those cables? . . . Oh, God, Oh, God! . . . Now listen, Cosette, I want you to send another cable to every one of those people, and tell them somebody has been using my name, and to disregard anything and everything they hear from me—except this, of course . . . Don't ask questions—do as you're told . . . Don't argue with me, you French bitch—God damn it, do as you're told . . . And unpack—we're not going! (*She hangs up*)

WHITESIDE. Now steady, my blossom. Take it easy.

LORRAINE (*in a white rage*). What do you mean take it easy? Do you realize I'll be the laughingstock of England? Why, I won't dare show my face! I always knew Beverly Carlton was low, but not this low. Why? WHY? It isn't even funny. Why would he do it, that's what I'd like to know. Why would he do it! Why would anyone in the world want to play a silly trick like this? I can't understand it. Do you, Sherry? Do you, Maggie? You both saw him this afternoon. Why would he walk out of here, go right to a phone booth, and try to ship me over to England on a fool's errand! There must have been some reason—there must have. It doesn't make sense otherwise. Why would Beverly Carlton, or anybody else for that matter, want me to— (*She stops as a dim light begins to dawn*) Oh! Oh! (*Her eye, which has been on* MAGGIE, *goes momentarily to the dining room, where* BERT *has disappeared. Then her gaze returns to* MAGGIE *again*) I—I think I begin to—of course! Of course! That's it. Of course that's it. Yes, and that's a very charming bracelet that Mr. Jefferson gave you—isn't it, Maggie dear? Of course. It makes complete sense now. And to think that I nearly—well! Wild horses couldn't get me out of here *now*, Maggie. And if I were you I'd hang onto that bracelet, dear. It'll be something to remember him by!

(*Out of the library comes* MR. WESTCOTT, *his hands full of papers. At the same time the two technicians emerge from the dining room and go to the control board*)

WESTCOTT (*his eyes on his watch*). All right, Mr. Whiteside. Almost time. Here's your new copy. Hook her up, boys. Start testing.

WHITESIDE. How much time?

WESTCOTT (*bringing him a microphone*). Couple of minutes.

(*One of the radio technicians is talking into a microphone, testing:* "One, two, three, four, one, two, three, four. How are we coming in, New York? . . . A, B, C, A, B, C. Mary had a little lamb, Mary had a little lamb")

(MR. *and* MRS. STANLEY, *having delivered their Christmas presents, enter from the hallway and start up the stairs.* MRS. STANLEY *looks hungrily at the radio goings-on, but* MR. STANLEY *delivers a stern* "Come, Daisy," *and she follows him up the stairs*)

(*The voices of the technicians drone on:* "One, two, three, four, one, two, three, four. O.K., New York. Waiting." MR. WESTCOTT *stands with watch in hand*)

(*From the dining room comes* BERT JEFFERSON, *a tray of drinks in hand*)

BERT. Here comes the Jefferson Special . . . Oh! Have we time?

LORRAINE. Oh, I'm sure we have. Mr. Jefferson, I'm not leaving after all. My plans are changed.

BERT. Really? Oh, that's good.

LORRAINE. And I hear you've written a simply marvelous play, Mr. Jefferson. I want you to read it to me—tonight. Will you? We'll go back to the Mansion House right after dinner, and you'll read me your play.

BERT. Why—why, I should say so. I'd be delighted. . . . Maggie, did you hear that? Say, I'll bet *you* did this. You arranged the whole thing. Well, it's the finest Christmas present you could have given me.

(MAGGIE *looks at him for one anguished moment. Then, without a word, she dashes into the hall, grabs her coat and flings herself out of the house*)

(BERT, *bewildered, stands looking after her.* MR. *and* MRS. STANLEY *come pellmell down the stairs. Each clutches a letter, and they are wild-eyed*)

STANLEY. *Mr.* Whiteside! My son has run off on a freighter and my daughter is marrying an anarchist! They say *you* told them to do it!

MRS. STANLEY. My poor June! My poor Richard! This is the most awful—

WESTCOTT. Quiet! Quiet, please! We're going on the air.

STANLEY. How dare you! This is the most outrageous—

WESTCOTT (*raising his voice*). Please! *Please!* Quiet! We're going on the air.

(STANLEY *chokes and looks with fury.* MRS. STANLEY *is softly crying*)

(*In this moment of stillness*, DR. BRADLEY *emerges from the dining room*)

DR. BRADLEY. Oh! I see you're still busy.

STANLEY (*bursting forth*). Mr. Whiteside, you are the—

WESTCOTT (*yelling*). *Quiet!* For God's sake, quiet! QUIET! . . . All right, boys!

(*From the hallway come six* CHOIR BOYS, *dressed in their robes. They take their places by the microphone as the voice of the technician completes the hook-up*)

TECHNICIAN. O.K., New York. (*He raises his arm, waiting to give the signal.* WESTCOTT *is watching him. There is a dead pause of about five seconds.* JOHN *and* SARAH *are on tiptoe in the dining room. Then the arm drops*)

WESTCOTT (*into the microphone*). Good evening, everybody. Cream of Mush brings you Sheridan Whiteside. (*The* LEADER *gestures to the* CHOIR BOYS, *and they raise their lovely voices in "Heilige Nacht." Another gesture from* WESTCOTT, *and* WHITESIDE *begins to speak, with the boys singing as a background*)

WHITESIDE. This is Whiteside speaking. On this eve of eves, when my own heart is overflowing with peace and kindness, I think it is most fitting to tell once again the story of that still and lustrous night, nigh onto two thousand years ago—

(*But suddenly there is an interruption.* MISS PREEN *dashes into the room, clutching her arm and screaming*)

MISS PREEN. A penguin bit me!

(*Cries of "Sssh! Quiet!" from the radio men. The doctor rushes to* MISS PREEN's *side*)

(*But* WHITESIDE *is equal to the occasion. He raises his voice and fights right through*)

WHITESIDE. —when first the star of Bethlehem was glimpsed in a wondrous sky . . .

(*His famous voice goes out over the air to the listening millions as—*

The curtain falls

ACT THREE

Christmas morning.

The bright December sunlight streams in through the window.

But the Christmas calm is quickly broken. From the library comes the roaring voice of MR. WHITESIDE. *"Miss Preen! Miss Preen!"*

MISS PREEN, *who is just coming through the dining room, rushes to open the library doors.*

MISS PREEN (*nervously*). Yes, sir. Yes, sir.

(MR. WHITESIDE, *in a mood, rolls himself into the room*)

WHITESIDE. Where *do* you disappear to all the time, My Lady Nausea?

MISS PREEN (*firmly*). Mr. Whiteside, I can only be in one place at a time.

WHITESIDE. That is very fortunate for this community.

(MISS PREEN *goes indignantly into the library and slams the doors after her*)

(JOHN *emerges from the dining room*)

JOHN. Good morning, Mr. Whiteside. Merry Christmas.

WHITESIDE (*testily*). Merry Christmas, John. Merry Christmas.

JOHN. And Sarah and I want to thank you for the wonderful present.

WHITESIDE. That's quite all right, John.

JOHN. Are you ready for your breakfast, Mr. Whiteside?

WHITESIDE. No, I don't think I want any breakfast. . . . Has Miss Cutler come down yet?

JOHN. No, sir, not yet.

286

WHITESIDE. Is she in her room, do you know?

JOHN. Yes, sir, I think she is. Shall I call her?

WHITESIDE. No, no. That's all, John.

JOHN. Yes, sir.

(MAGGIE *comes down the stairs. She wears a traveling suit, and carries a bag.* WHITESIDE *waits for her to speak*)

MAGGIE. I'm taking the one o'clock train, Sherry. I'm leaving.

WHITESIDE. You're doing nothing of the kind!

MAGGIE. Here are your keys—your driving license. The key to the safe-deposit vault is in the apartment in New York. I'll go in here now and clear things up. (*She opens the library doors*)

WHITESIDE. Just a moment, Mrs. Siddons! Where *were* you until three o'clock this morning? I sat up half the night in this station wagon, worrying about you. You heard me calling to you when you came in. Why didn't you answer me?

MAGGIE. Look, Sherry, it's over, and you've won. I don't want to talk about it.

WHITESIDE. Oh, come, come, come, come, come. What are you trying to do—make me feel like a naughty, naughty boy? Honestly, Maggie, sometimes you can be very annoying.

MAGGIE (*looking at him in wonder*). You know, you're quite wonderful, Sherry, in a way. *You're* annoyed. I wish there was a laugh left in me. Shall I tell you something, Sherry? I think you are a selfish, petty egomaniac who would see his mother burned at the stake if that was the only way he could light his cigarette. I think you'd sacrifice your best friend without a moment's hesitation if he disturbed the sacred routine of your self-centered, paltry little life. I think you are incapable of any human emotion that goes higher up than your stomach, and I was the fool of the world for ever thinking I could trust you.

WHITESIDE (*pretty indignant at this*). Well, as long as I live, I shall never do anyone a good turn again. I won't ask you to apologize, Maggie, but six months from now you will be thanking me instead of berating me.

MAGGIE. In six months, Sherry, I expect to be so far away from you—

(*She is halted by a loud voice from the hallway, as the door bangs. "Hello—hello—hello!" It is* BERT JEFFERSON *who enters, full of Christmas cheer*)

BERT. Merry Christmas, everybody! Merry Christmas! I'm a little high, but I can explain everything. Hi, Maggie! Hi, Mr. Whiteside! Shake hands with a successful playwright. Maggie, why'd you run away last night? Where were you? Miss Sheldon thinks the play is wonderful. I read her the play and she thinks it's wonderful. Isn't that wonderful?

MAGGIE. Yes, that's fine, Bert.

BERT. Isn't that wonderful, Mr. Whiteside?

WHITESIDE. Jefferson, I think you ought to go home, don't you?

BERT. What? No—biggest day of my life. I know I'm a little drunk, but this is a big day. We've been sitting over in Billy's Tavern all night. Never realized it was daylight until it was daylight. . . . Listen, Maggie— Miss Sheldon says the play needs just a little bit of fixing—do it in three weeks. She's going to take me to a little place she's got in Lake Placid—just for three weeks. Going to work on the play together. Isn't it wonderful? Why don't you say something, Maggie?

WHITESIDE. Look, Bert, I suggest you tell us all about this later. Now, why don't you— (*He stops as* DR. BRADLEY *enters from the hallway*)

DR. BRADLEY. Oh, excuse me! Merry Christmas, everybody. Merry Christmas.

BERT. God bless us all, and Tiny Tim.

DR. BRADLEY. Yes. . . . Mr. Whiteside, I thought perhaps if I came very early—

BERT. You know what, Doc? I'm going to Lake Placid for three weeks—isn't that wonderful? Ever hear of Lorraine Sheldon, the famous actress? Well, we're going to Lake Placid for three weeks.

WHITESIDE. Dr. Bradley, would you do me a favor? I think Mr. Jefferson would like some black coffee and a little breakfast. Would you take care of him, please?

DR. BRADLEY (*none too pleased*). Yes, yes, of course.

BERT. Dr. Bradley, I'm going to buy breakfast for *you*—biggest breakfast you ever had.

DR. BRADLEY. Yes, yes. Come along, Jefferson.

BERT. You know what, Doctor? Let's climb down a couple of chimneys. I got a friend doesn't believe in Santa Claus—let's climb down his chimney and frighten the hell out of him. (*He does out with the* DOCTOR)

WHITESIDE (*in a burst of magnanimity*). Now listen to me, Maggie. I am willing to forgive your tawdry outburst and talk about this calmly.

MAGGIE (*now crying openly*). I love him so terribly. Oh, Sherry, Sherry, why did you do it? Why did you do it? (*She goes stumblingly into the library*)

(WHITESIDE, *left alone, looks at his watch; heaves a long sigh. Then* HARRIET *comes down the steps, dressed for the street*)

HARRIET. Merry Christmas, Mr. Whiteside.

WHITESIDE. Oh! . . . Merry Christmas, Miss Stanley.

HARRIET (*nervously*). I'm afraid I shouldn't be seen talking to you, Mr. Whiteside—my brother is terribly angry. I just couldn't resist asking—did you like my Christmas present?

WHITESIDE. I'm very sorry, Miss Stanley—I haven't opened it. I haven't opened any of my presents yet.

HARRIET. Oh, dear. I was so anxious to—it's right here, Mr.

Whiteside. (*She goes to the tree*) Won't you open it now?

WHITESIDE (*as he undoes the string*). I appreciate your thinking of me, Miss Stanley. This is very thoughtful of you. (*He takes out the gift*) Why, it's lovely. I'm very fond of these old photographs. Thank you very much.

HARRIET. I was twenty-two when that was taken. That was my favorite dress. . . . Do you really like it?

WHITESIDE. I do indeed. When I get back to town I shall send *you* a little gift.

HARRIET. Will you? Oh, thank you, Mr. Whiteside. I shall treasure it. . . . Well, I shall be late for church. Good-bye. Good-bye.

WHITESIDE. Good-bye, Miss Stanley.

(*As she goes out the front door,* WHITESIDE'S *eyes return to the gift. He puzzles over it for a second, shakes his head. Mumbles to himself—"What is there about that woman?" Shakes his head again in perplexity*)

(JOHN *comes from the dining room, en route to the second floor with* MRS. STANLEY'S *tray*)

JOHN. Sarah's got a little surprise for you, Mr. Whiteside. She's just taking it out of the oven.

WHITESIDE. Thank you, John.

(JOHN *disappears up the stairs*)

(*Then suddenly there is a great ringing of the door bell. It stops for a second, then picks up violently again— rhythmically, this time. It continues until the door is opened*)

WHITESIDE. Miss Preen! Miss Preen!

(MISS PREEN *comes hurrying from the library*)

MISS PREEN. Yes, sir. Yes, sir.

WHITESIDE. Answer the door, will you? John is upstairs.

(MISS PREEN, *obviously annoyed, hurries to the door*)

(*We hear her voice from the hallway: "Who is it?" An answering male voice: "Polly Adler's?" Then a little shriek from* MISS PREEN, *and in a moment we see the*

*reason why. She is carried into the room in the arms of
a pixie-like gentleman, who is kissing her over and over)*

THE GENTLEMAN CARRYING MISS PREEN. I love you madly—
madly! Did you hear what I said—madly! Kiss me!
Again! Don't be afraid of my passion. Kiss me! I can
feel the hot blood pounding through your varicose veins.

MISS PREEN (*through all this*). Put me down! Put me down,
do you hear! Don't you dare kiss me! Who are you! Put
me down or I'll scream. Mr. Whiteside! Mr. Whiteside!

WHITESIDE. Banjo! Banjo, for God's sake!

BANJO (*quite calmly*). Hello, Whiteside. Will you sign for
this package, please?

WHITESIDE. Banjo, put that woman down. That is my nurse,
you mental delinquent.

BANJO (*putting* MISS PREEN *on her feet*). Come to my room
in half an hour and bring some rye bread. (*And for
good measure he slaps* MISS PREEN *right on the fanny*)

MISS PREEN (*outraged*). Really, Mr. Whiteside! (*She ad-
justs her clothes with a quick jerk or two and marches
into the library*)

BANJO. Whiteside, I'm here to spend Christmas with you.
Give me a kiss! (*He starts to embrace him*)

WHITESIDE. Get away from me, you reform-school fugitive.
How did you get here anyway?

BANJO. Darryl Zanuck loaned me his reindeer. . . . Whiteside, we finished shooting the picture yesterday and I'm
on my way to Nova Scotia. Flew here in twelve hours—
borrowed an airplane from Howard Hughes. Whiteside,
I brought you a wonderful Christmas present. (*He produces a little tissue-wrapped package*) This brassière
was once worn by Hedy Lamarr.

WHITESIDE. Listen, you idiot, how long can you stay?

BANJO. Just long enough to take a bath. I'm on my way to
Nova Scotia. Where's Maggie?

WHITESIDE. Nova Scotia? What are you going to Nova
Scotia for?

BANJO. I'm sick of Hollywood and there's a dame in New York I don't want to see. So I figured I'd go to Nova Scotia and get some good salmon. . . . Where the hell's Maggie? I want to see her. . . . What's the matter with you? Where is she?

WHITESIDE. Banjo, I'm glad you're here. I'm very annoyed at Maggie. Very!

BANJO. What's the matter? . . . (*To his considerable surprise, at this point, he sees* WHITESIDE *get up out of his chair and start to pace up and down the room*) Say, what *is* this? I thought you couldn't walk.

WHITESIDE. Oh, I've been all right for weeks. That isn't the point. I'm furious at Maggie. She's turned on me like a viper. You know how fond I am of her. Well, after all these years she's repaying my affection by behaving like a fishwife.

BANJO. What are you talking about?

WHITESIDE. But I never believed for a moment she was really in love with him.

BANJO. In love with *who*? I just got here—remember.

WHITESIDE. Great God, I'm telling you, you Hollywood nitwit. A young newspaper man here in town.

BANJO (*surprised and pleased*). Maggie finally fell—well, what do you know? What kind of a guy is he?

WHITESIDE. Oh, shut up and listen, will you?

BANJO. Well, go on. What happened?

WHITESIDE. Well. Lorraine Sheldon happened to come out here and visit me.

BANJO. Old Hot-pants—here?

WHITESIDE. Now listen! He'd written a play—this young fellow. You can guess the rest. He's going away with Lorraine this afternoon. To "rewrite." So there you are. Maggie's in there now, crying her eyes out.

BANJO. Gee! . . . (*Thinking it over*) Say, wait a minute. What do you mean Lorraine Sheldon *happened* to come out here? I smell a rat, Sherry—a rat with a beard.

(*And it might be well to add, at this point, that* MR. SHERI-
DAN WHITESIDE *wears a beard*)

WHITESIDE. Well, all right, all right. But I did it for Maggie
—because I thought it was the right thing for her.

BANJO. Oh, sure. You haven't thought of yourself in years.
. . . Gee, poor kid. Can I go in and talk to her?

WHITESIDE. No—no. Leave her alone.

BANJO. Any way I could help, Sherry? Where's this guy
live—this guy she likes? Can we get hold of him?

WHITESIDE. Now, wait a minute, Banjo. We don't want any
phony warrants, or you pretending to be J. Edgar
Hoover. I've been through all that with you before. (*He
paces again*) I got Lorraine out here and I've got to get
her away.

BANJO. It's got to be good, Sherry. Lorraine's no dope. . . .
Now, there must be *something* that would get her out
of here like a bat out of hell. . . . Say! I think I've got
it! That fellow she's so crazy about over in England—
Lord Fanny or whatever it is. Bottomley—that's it!

WHITESIDE (*with a pained expression*). No, Banjo. No.

BANJO. Wait a minute—you don't catch on. We send Lorraine a cablegram from Lord Bottomley—

WHITESIDE. I catch on, Banjo. Lorraine caught on, too. It's
been tried.

BANJO. Oh! . . . I told you she was no dope. . . . (*Seeing* WHITESIDE'S *chair, he sits in it and leans back with
a good deal of pleasure*) Well, you've got a tough proposition on your hands.

WHITESIDE. The trouble is there's so damned little time.
. . . Get out of my chair! (WHITESIDE *gets back into it*)
Lorraine's taking him away with her this afternoon. Oh,
damn, damn, damn. There must be some way out. The
trouble is I've done this job too well. Hell and damna-
tion.

BANJO (*pacing*). Stuck, huh?

WHITESIDE. In the words of one of our greatest lyric poets, you said it.

BANJO. Yeh. . . . Gee, I'm hungry. We'll think of something, Sherry—you watch. We'll get Lorraine out of here if I have to do it one piece at a time.

(SARAH *enters from the dining room bearing a tray on which reposes the culinary surprise that* JOHN *has mentioned. She holds it behind her back*)

SARAH. Merry Christmas, Mr. Whiteside. . . . Excuse me. (*This last to* BANJO) I've got something for you. . . .

(BANJO *blandly lifts the latest delicacy and proceeds to eat it as* SARAH *presents the empty plate to* WHITESIDE)

SARAH (*almost in tears*). But, Mr. Whiteside, it was for you.

WHITESIDE. Never mind, Sarah. He's quite mad.

BANJO. Come, Petrouchka, we will dance in the snow until all St. Petersburg is aflame with jealousy. (*He clutches* SARAH *and waltzes her toward the kitchen, loudly humming the Merry Widow waltz*)

SARAH (*as she is borne away*). Mr. Whiteside! Mr. Whiteside!

WHITESIDE. Just give him some breakfast, Sarah. He's harmless.

(MR. WHITESIDE *barely has a moment in which to collect his thoughts before the library doors are opened and* MISS PREEN *emerges. It is* MISS PREEN *in street clothes this time, and with a suitcase in her hand*)

(*She plants herself squarely in front of* WHITESIDE, *puts down her bag and starts drawing on a pair of gloves*)

WHITESIDE. And just what does this mean?

MISS PREEN. It means, Mr. Whiteside, that I am leaving. My address is on the desk inside; you can send me a check.

WHITESIDE. You realize, Miss Preen, that this is completely unprofessional.

MISS PREEN. I do indeed. I am not only walking out on this

case, Mr. Whiteside—I am leaving the nursing profession. I became a nurse because all my life, ever since I was a little girl, I was filled with the idea of serving a suffering humanity. After one month with you, Mr. Whiteside, I am going to work in a munitions factory. From now on anything that I can do to help exterminate the human race will fill me with the greatest of pleasure. If Florence Nightingale had ever nursed *you*, Mr. Whiteside, she would have married Jack the Ripper instead of founding the Red Cross. Good day. (*And she sails out*)

(*Before* WHITESIDE *has time to digest this little bouquet,* MRS. STANLEY, *in a state of great fluttery excitement, rushes down the stairs*)

MRS. STANLEY. Mr. Stanley is here with June. He's brought June back. Thank goodness, thank goodness. (*We hear her at the door*) June, June, thank God you're back. You're not married, are you?

JUNE (*from the hallway*). No, Mother, I'm not. And please don't be hysterical.

(MRS. STANLEY *comes into view, her arms around a rebellious* JUNE. *Behind them looms* MR. STANLEY, *every inch the stern father*)

MRS. STANLEY. Oh, June, if it had been anyone but that awful boy. You know how your father and I felt. . . . Ernest, thank goodness you stopped it. How did you do it?

STANLEY. Never mind that, Daisy. Just take June upstairs. I have something to say to Mr. Whiteside.

MRS. STANLEY. What about Richard? Is there any news?

STANLEY. It's all right, Daisy—all under control. Just take June upstairs.

JUNE. Father, haven't we had enough melodrama? I don't have to be taken upstairs—I'll go upstairs. . . . Merry Christmas, Mr. Whiteside. It looks bad for John L. Lewis. Come on, Mother—lock me in my room.

MRS. STANLEY. Now, June, you'll feel much better after

you've had a hot bath, I know. Have you had anything
to eat? (*She follows her daughter up the stairs*)

(STANLEY *turns to* MR. WHITESIDE)

STANLEY. I am pleased to inform you, sir, that your plans
for my daughter seem to have gone a trifle awry. She is
not, nor will she ever be, married to that labor agitator
that you so kindly picked out for her. As for my son, he
has been apprehended in Toledo, and will be brought
back home within the hour. Not having your gift for
invective, I cannot tell you what I think of your ob-
noxious interference in my affairs, but I have now arranged that you will interfere no longer. (*He turns toward the hallway*) Come in, gentlemen. (*Two burly*
MEN *come into view and stand in the archway*) Mr.
Whiteside, these gentlemen are deputy sheriffs. They
have a warrant by which I am enabled to put you out
of this house, and I need hardly add that it will be the
greatest moment of my life. Mr. Whiteside— (*He looks
at his watch*) —I am giving you fifteen minutes in which
to pack up and get out. If you are not gone in fifteen
minutes, Mr. Whiteside, these gentlemen will forcibly
eject you. (*He turns to the deputies*) Thank you, gentlemen. Will you wait outside, please? (*The* TWO MEN *file
out*) Fifteen minutes, Mr. Whiteside—and that means
bag, baggage, wheelchair, penguins, octopus and cockroaches. I am now going upstairs to smash our radio, so
that not even accidentally will I ever hear your voice
again.

WHITESIDE. Sure you don't want my autograph, old fellow?

STANLEY. Fifteen minutes, Mr. Whiteside. (*And he goes*)

(BANJO, *still eating, returns from the kitchen*)

BANJO. Well, Whiteside, I didn't get an idea. Any news
from the front?

WHITESIDE. Yes. The enemy is at my rear, and nibbling.

BANJO. Where'd you say Maggie was? In there?

WHITESIDE. It's no use, Banjo. She's taking the one o'clock train out.

BANJO. No kidding? You didn't tell me that. You mean she's quitting you, after all these years? She's really leaving?

WHITESIDE. She is!

BANJO. That means you've only got till one o'clock to do something?

WHITESIDE. No, dear. I have exactly fifteen minutes— (*He looks at his watch*) —ah—fourteen minutes—in which to pull out of my hat the God-damnedest rabbit you have ever seen.

BANJO. What do you mean fifteen minutes?

WHITESIDE. In exactly fifteen minutes Baby's rosy little body is being tossed into the snow. My host has sworn out a warrant. I am being kicked out.

BANJO. What? I never heard of such a thing. What would he do a thing like that for?

WHITESIDE. Never mind, never mind. The point is, I have only fifteen minutes. Banjo dear, the master is growing a little desperate.

BANJO (*paces a moment*). What about laying your cards on the table with Lorraine?

WHITESIDE. Now, Banjo. You know Dream Girl as well as I do. What do *you* think?

BANJO. You're right. . . . Say! If I knew where she was I could get a car and run her over. It wouldn't hurt her much.

WHITESIDE (*wearily*). Banjo, for God's sake. Go in and talk to Maggie for a minute—right in there. I want to think.

BANJO. Could we get a doctor to say Lorraine has small-pox?

WHITESIDE. Please, Banjo. I've got to think.

BANJO (*opening the library doors*). Pardon me, miss, is this the Y.M.C.A.?

(*The doors close*)

(WHITESIDE *is alone again. He leans back, concentrating intensely. He shakes his head as, one after another, he discards a couple of ideas*)

(*We hear the outer door open and close, and from the hallway comes* RICHARD. *Immediately behind him is a stalwart-looking* MAN *with an air of authority*)

THE MAN (*to* RICHARD, *as he indicates* WHITESIDE). Is this your father?

RICHARD. No, you idiot. . . . Hello, Mr. Whiteside. I didn't get very far. Any suggestions?

WHITESIDE. I'm very sorry, Richard—very sorry indeed. I wish I were in position—

STANLEY (*descending the stairs*). Well, you're *not* in position. . . . Thank you very much, officer. Here's a little something for your trouble.

THE MAN. Thank you, sir. Good day. (*He goes*)

STANLEY. Will you go upstairs please, Richard?

(RICHARD *hesitates for a second. Looks at his father, then at* WHITESIDE; *silently goes up the steps*)

(MR. STANLEY *follows him, but pauses on the landing*)

STANLEY. Ten minutes, Mr. Whiteside. (*And he goes*)

(JOHN *enters from the dining room, bringing a glass of orange juice*)

JOHN. Here you are, Mr. Whiteside. Feeling any better?

WHITESIDE. Superb. Any cyanide in this orange juice, John? (*The door bell rings*) Open the door, John. It's probably some mustard gas from an old friend.

JOHN (*en route to the door*). Yes, sir. . . . Say, that crazy fellow made a great hit with Sarah. He wants to give her a screen test.

(*At the outer door we hear* LORRAINE'S *voice*: "Good morning! Is Mr. Whiteside up yet?" JOHN'S *answer*: "Yes, he is, Miss Sheldon—he's right here")

(WHITESIDE *groans as he hears her voice*)

LORRAINE (*entering, in a very smart Christmas morning costume*). Merry Christmas, darling! Merry Christmas!

I've come to have Christmas breakfast with you, my
dear. May I? (*She kisses him*)

WHITESIDE (*nothing matters any more*). Of course, my
sprite. John, a tray for Miss Sheldon—better make it
one-minute eggs.

LORRAINE. Sherry, it's the most perfect Christmas morning
—the snow is absolutely glistening. Too bad you can't
get out.

WHITESIDE. Oh, I'll probably see a bit of it. . . . I hear
you're off for Lake Placid, my blossom. What time are
you going?

LORRAINE. Oh, Sherry, how did you know? Is Bert here?

WHITESIDE. No, he rolled in a little while ago. Worked
rather fast, didn't you, dear?

LORRAINE. Darling, I was just swept off my feet by the play
—it's fantastically good. Sherry, it's the kind of part that
only comes along once in ten years. I'm so grateful to
you, darling. Really, Sherry, sometimes I think that
you're the only friend I have in the world.

WHITESIDE (*dryly*). Thank you, dear. What time did you
say you were leaving—you and Jefferson?

LORRAINE. Oh, I don't know—I think it's four o'clock. You
know, quite apart from anything else, Sherry, Bert is
really a very attractive man. It makes it rather a pleasure, squaring accounts with little Miss Vitriol. In fact,
it's all worked out beautifully. . . . Sherry lamb, I want
to give you the most beautiful Christmas present you've
ever had in your life. Now, what do you want? Anything! I'm so deliriously happy that— (*A bellowing
laugh comes from the library. She stops, lips com-
pressed*) That sounds like Banjo. Is he here?

WHITESIDE. He is, my dear. Just the family circle gathering
at Christmas. (*A look at his watch*) My, how time flies
when you're having fun.

(BANJO *emerges from the library*)

BANJO. Why, hello, Sweetie Pants! How are you?

LORRAINE (*not over-cordial*). Very well, thank you. And you, Banjo?

BANJO. I'm fine, fine. How's the mattress business, Lorraine?

LORRAINE. *Very* funny. It's too bad, Banjo, that your pictures aren't as funny as you seem to think *you* are.

BANJO. You've got me there, mama. Say, you look in the pink, Lorraine. . . . Anything in the wind, Whiteside?

WHITESIDE (*sotte voce*). Not a glimmer.

BANJO. What time does the boat sail?

WHITESIDE. Ten minutes.

LORRAINE. What boat is this?

BANJO. The good ship *Up the Creek.* . . . Oh, well! You feel fine, huh, Lorraine?

LORRAINE. What? Yes, of course I do. . . . Where's that breakfast, Sherry?

(MAGGIE *emerges from the library, a sheaf of papers in her hand. She stops imperceptibly as she sees* LORRAINE)

MAGGIE. I've listed everything except the New Year's Eve broadcast. Wasn't there a schedule on that?

WHITESIDE (*uneasily*). I think it's on the table there, some place.

MAGGIE. Thank you. (*She turns to the papers on the table*)

LORRAINE (*obviously for* MAGGIE's *ears*). New Year's Eve? Oh, Bert and I'll hear it in Lake Placid. You were at my cottage up there once, weren't you, Sherry? It's lovely, isn't it? Away from everything. Just snow and clear, cold nights. (*The door bell rings*) Oh, that's probably Bert. I told him to meet me here. (MAGGIE, *as though she had not heard a word, goes quietly into the library.* LORRAINE *relaxes*) You know, I'm looking forward to Lake Placid. Bert's the kind of man who will do all winter sports beautifully.

BANJO (*gently*). Will he get time?

(*Voices are heard from the hallway.* "Whiteside?" "Yes,

sir." "American Express." JOHN *backs into the room, obviously directing a major operation*)

JOHN. All right—come ahead. Care now—careful—right
in here. It's for you, Mr. Whiteside.

LORRAINE. Why, Sherry, what's this?

(*Into view come two* EXPRESSMEN, *groaning and grunting
under the weight of nothing more or less than an Egyptian mummy case. It seems that* MR. WHITESIDE's *friends
are liable to think of anything*)

EXPRESSMAN. Where do you want this put?

JOHN. Right there.

WHITESIDE. Dear God, if there was one thing I needed
right now it was an Egyptian mummy.

BANJO (*reading from a tag*). "Merry Christmas from the
Khedive of Egypt." What did you send *him?* Grant's
Tomb?

(MR. STANLEY, *drawn by the voices of the* EXPRESSMEN,
*has descended the stairs in time to witness this newest
hue and cry*)

STANLEY (*surveying the scene*). Five minutes, Mr. Whiteside! (*He indicates the mummy case*) Including *that.*
(*And up the stairs again*)

LORRAINE. Why, what was all that about? Who is that
man?

WHITESIDE. He announces the time every few minutes. I
pay him a small sum.

LORRAINE. But what on earth for, Sherry?

WHITESIDE (*violently*). I lost my watch!

(*From the hallway a familiar figure peeps in*)

DR. BRADLEY. Oh, excuse me, Mr. Whiteside. Are you busy?

WHITESIDE (*closing his eyes*). Good God!

DR. BRADLEY (*coming into the room*). I've written a new
chapter on the left kidney. Suppose I— (*He smiles
apologetically at* LORRAINE *and* BANJO) Pardon me.
(*Goes into the library*)

LORRAINE. Is that the plumber again, Sherry? . . . Oh, dear, I wonder where Bert is. . . . Darling, you're not very Christmasy—you're usually bubbling over on Christmas morning. . . . *Who* sent this to you, Sherry —the Khedive of Egypt? You know, I think it's rather beautiful. I must go to Egypt some day—I really must. I know I'd love it. The first time I went to Pompeii I cried all night. All those people—all those lives. Where are they now? Sherry! Don't you ever think about that? I do. Here was a woman—like myself—a woman who once lived and loved, full of the same passions, fears, jealousies, hates. And what remains of any of it now? Just this, and nothing more. (*She opens the case, then, with a sudden impulse, steps into it and folds her arms, mummy-fashion*) A span of four thousand years—a mere atom in the eternity of time—and here am I, another woman living out her life. I want to cry.

(*She closes her eyes, and as she stands there, immobilized, the eyes of* BANJO *and* WHITESIDE *meet. The same idea has leaped into their minds.* BANJO, *rising slowly from the couch, starts to approach the mummy case, casually whistling "Dixie." But just before he reaches it* LORRAINE *steps blandly out*)

LORRAINE. Oh, I mustn't talk this way today. It's Christmas, it's Christmas!

(BANJO *puts on a great act of unconcern*)

WHITESIDE (*rising to the occasion, and dripping pure charm*). Lorraine dear, have you ever played Saint Joan?

LORRAINE. No, I haven't, Sherry. What makes you ask that?

WHITESIDE. There was something about your expression as you stood in that case—there was an absolute halo about you.

LORRAINE. Why, Sherry, how sweet!

WHITESIDE. It transcended any mortal expression I've ever seen. Step into it again, dear.

LORRAINE. Sherry, you're joshing me—aren't you?

WHITESIDE. My dear, I don't make light of these things. I was deeply moved. There was a strange beauty about you, Lorraine—pure Da Vinci. Please do it again.

LORRAINE. Well, I don't know exactly what it was that I did, but I'll— (*She starts to step into the case again, then changes her mind*) Oh, I feel too silly, Sherry.

(BANJO'S *eyes are fixed somewhere on the ceiling, but he is somewhat less innocent than he seems*)

WHITESIDE (*returning to the battle*). Lorraine dear, in that single moment you approached the epitome of your art, and you should not be ashamed of it. You asked me a little while ago what I wanted for a Christmas present. All that I want, Lorraine, is the memory of you in that mummy case.

LORRAINE. Why, darling, I'm—all choked up. (*Crossing her arms, she takes a moment or two to throw herself in the mood, then steps reverently into the case*) "Dust thou art, and dust to dust—"

(*Bang!* BANJO *has closed the case and fastened it.* WHITE- SIDE *leaps out of the chair*)

WHITESIDE. Eureka!

BANJO. There's service for you!

WHITESIDE. Will she be all right in there?

BANJO. Sure—she can breathe easy. I'll let her out as soon as we get on the plane. . . . What are we going to do now? How do we get this out of here?

WHITESIDE. One thing at a time—that's the next step.

BANJO. Think fast, Captain. Think fast.

(*And* MAGGIE *enters from the library, papers in hand.* WHITESIDE *scrambles back into his chair;* BANJO *is again the little innocent*)

MAGGIE. This is everything, Sherry—I'm leaving three car- bons. Is there anything out here? (*She inspects a small basket fastened to his chair*) What's in this basket?

WHITESIDE (*eager to be rid of her*). Nothing at all. Thank you, thank you.

MAGGIE. Shall I file these letters? Do you want this picture?

WHITESIDE. No—throw everything away. Wait—give me the picture. I want the picture.

MAGGIE. The only thing I haven't done is to put all your broadcasts in order. Do you want me to do that?

WHITESIDE (*a flash of recollection has come to him as he takes* HARRIET'S *photograph in his hand, but he contrives to smother his excitement*). What? . . . Ah—do that, will you? Do it right away—it's very important. Right away, Maggie.

MAGGIE. I'll see you before I go, Banjo. (*She goes into the library again, closing the doors*)

WHITESIDE (*watching her out, then jumping up in great excitement*). I've got it!

BANJO. What?

WHITESIDE. I knew I'd seen this face before! I knew it! Now I know how to get this out of here.

BANJO. What face? How?

(*And, at that instant,* MR. STANLEY *comes down the stairs, watch in hand*)

STANLEY (*vastly enjoying himself*). The time is up, Mr. Whiteside. Fifteen minutes.

WHITESIDE. Ah, yes, Mr. Stanley. Fifteen minutes. But just one favor before I go. I would like you to summon those two officers and ask them to help this gentleman down to the airport with this mummy case. Would you be good enough to do that, Mr. Stanley?

STANLEY. I will do nothing of the kind.

WHITESIDE (*ever so sweetly*). Oh, I think you will, Mr. Stanley. Or shall I inform my radio audience, on my next broadcast, that your sister, Harriet Stanley, is none other than the famous Harriet Sedley, who murdered her mother and father with an axe twenty-five years ago in Gloucester, Massachusetts. . . . (*At which* MR. STAN-

LEY *quietly collapses into a chair*) Come, Mr. Stanley, it's a very small favor. Or would you rather have the good folk of Mesalia repeating at your very doorstep that once popular little jingle:

> "Harriet Sedley took an axe
> And gave her mother forty whacks,
> And when the job was nicely done,
> She gave her father forty-one."

Remember, Mr. Stanley, I too am giving up something. It would make a hell of a broadcast. . . . Well?

STANLEY (*licked at last*). Mr. Whiteside, you are the damnedest person I have ever met.

WHITESIDE. I often think so myself, old fellow. . . . Officers, will you come in here, please?

BANJO. Whiteside, you're a great man. (*He places a reverent kiss on the mummy case*)

WHITESIDE (*as the* DEPUTIES *enter*). Come right in, officers. Mr. Stanley would like you to help this gentleman down to the airport with this mummy case. He is sending it to a friend in Nova Scotia.

BANJO. Collect.

WHITESIDE. Right, Mr. Stanley?

STANLEY (*weakly*). Yes. . . . Yes.

WHITESIDE. Thank you, gentlemen—handle it carefully. . . . Banjo, my love, you're wonderful and I may write a book about you.

BANJO. Don't bother—I can't read. (*To* MAGGIE, *as she enters from library*) Good-bye, Maggie—love conquers all, . . . Don't drop that case, boys—it contains an antique. (*And out he goes with the mummy case, to say nothing of* MISS LORRAINE SHELDON)

MAGGIE (*catching on to what has happened*). Sherry! Sherry, was that—?

WHITESIDE. It was indeed. The field is clear and you have my blessing.

MAGGIE. Sherry! Sherry, you old reprobate!

WHITESIDE. Just send me a necktie some time. My hat and coat, Maggie, and also your railroad ticket. I am leaving for New York.

MAGGIE. You're leaving, Sherry?

WHITESIDE. Don't argue, Rat Girl— Do as you're told.

MAGGIE. Yes, Mr. Whiteside. (*She goes happily into the library, just as* BERT *returns*)

BERT. Mr. Whiteside, I want to apologize for—

WHITESIDE. Don't give it a thought, Bert. There's been a slight change of plan. Miss Sheldon is off on a world cruise—I am taking your play to Katharine Cornell. Miss Cutler will explain everything. (MAGGIE *brings* WHITESIDE's *coat, hat, cane*) Oh, thank you, Maggie, my darling.

(*And just then the* DOCTOR *comes out of the library. Still trying*)

DR. BRADLEY. Mr. Whiteside, are you very busy?

WHITESIDE. Ah, yes, Doctor. *Very* busy. But if you ever get to New York, Doctor, try and find me. (*He takes* MAGGIE *in his arms*) Good-bye, my lamb. I love you very much.

MAGGIE. Sherry, you're wonderful.

WHITESIDE. Nonsense. . . . Good-bye, Jefferson. You'll never know the trouble you've caused.

BERT. Good-bye, Mr. Whiteside.

WHITESIDE. Good-bye, Mr. Stanley. I would like to hear, in the near future, that your daughter has married her young man and that your son has been permitted to follow his own bent. OR ELSE. . . . Merry Christmas, everybody! (*And out he strolls*)

(*But the worst is yet to come. There is a loud crash on the porch, followed by an anguished yell*)

(MAGGIE *gives a little shriek and rushes out.* BERT *and the* DOCTOR *rush after her. Down the stairs come* MRS. STANLEY, JUNE *and* RICHARD. *From the dining room* JOHN *and* SARAH *come running,* "What's happened?" "What is it?")

(*And then we see. Into view come* BERT *and the* DOCTOR, *carrying* MR. WHITESIDE *between them. He is screaming his head off*)

WHITESIDE. Miss Preen! Miss Preen! I want Miss Preen back! . . . Mr. Stanley, I am suing you for *three* hundred and fifty thousand dollars!

(MR. STANLEY *throws up his hands in despair.* MRS. STANLEY *simply faints away*)

Curtain